SCHOLAR Study Guide
Advanced Higher Englisn

Authored by:
Literary study: The critical essay
Jan Ainslie (Preston Lodge High School)

Textual analysis
Barbara van der Meulen (LATITUDE Learning & Teaching)

Portfolio and Dissertation
Molly Rae (Bannockburn High School)

Reviewed by:
Iain Valentine (Elgin Academy)

Heriot-Watt University
Edinburgh EH14 4AS, United Kingdom.

First published 2019 by Heriot-Watt University.

This edition published in 2019 by Heriot-Watt University SCHOLAR.

Copyright © 2019 SCHOLAR Forum.

Members of the SCHOLAR Forum may reproduce this publication in whole or in part for educational purposes within their establishment providing that no profit accrues at any stage, Any other use of the materials is governed by the general copyright statement that follows.

All rights reserved. No part of this publication may be reproduced, stored in a retrieval system or transmitted in any form or by any means, without written permission from the publisher.

Heriot-Watt University accepts no responsibility or liability whatsoever with regard to the information contained in this study guide.

Distributed by the SCHOLAR Forum.

SCHOLAR Study Guide Advanced Higher English

Advanced Higher English Course Code: C824 77

ISBN 978-1-911057-71-0

Print Production and Fulfilment in UK by Print Trail www.printtrail.com

Acknowledgements

Thanks are due to the members of Heriot-Watt University's SCHOLAR team who planned and created these materials, and to the many colleagues who reviewed the content.

We would like to acknowledge the assistance of the education authorities, colleges, teachers and students who contributed to the SCHOLAR programme and who evaluated these materials.

Grateful acknowledgement is made for permission to use the following material in the SCHOLAR programme:

The Scottish Qualifications Authority for permission to use Past Papers assessments.

The Scottish Government for financial support.

The content of this Study Guide is aligned to the Scottish Qualifications Authority (SQA) curriculum.

All brand names, product names, logos and related devices are used for identification purposes only and are trademarks, registered trademarks or service marks of their respective holders.

Contents

1 Literary study: the critical essay — 1

1. General principles 3
2. The question 11
3. Planning a literary study essay 19
4. Writing an effective introduction and conclusion 29
5. How to compare 37
6. Using secondary reading 43
7. Exemplar literary essays 49
8. Literary study test 59
9. Acknowledgements 61

2 Textual analysis — 63

1. General principles of textual analysis 65
2. Poetry 69
3. Prose fiction 91
4. Prose non-fiction 109
5. Drama 121
6. Conclusions and consolidation 139
7. Textual analysis test 143
8. Acknowledgements 153

3 Portfolio — 155

1. Introduction 157
2. Discursive writing 167
3. Creative writing 189
4. Annotated exemplars 215
5. Acknowledgements 237

4 Dissertation — 239

1 The process and expectations — 241
2 Comparing texts and developing an argument — 249
3 Annotated exemplars — 259
4 Acknowledgements — 291

Answers to questions and activities — 293

Literary study: The critical essay

1 General principles 3
   1.1 Introduction 4
   1.2 What is the literary study essay? 4
   1.3 What are the skills required for literary study essay success? 5
   1.4 How is the essay assessed? 7
   1.5 What is the difference between a Higher and Advanced Higher literary essay? ... 8
   1.6 Learning points 9

2 The question 11
   2.1 Literary study paper 12
   2.2 Advanced Higher literary study questions 12
   2.3 In the exam 15
   2.4 Learning points 17

3 Planning a literary study essay 19
   3.1 Introduction 20
   3.2 Stage 1: Defining key ideas 20
   3.3 Stage 2: Using key ideas 22
   3.4 Stage 3: Structuring key ideas 25
   3.5 The exam 27
   3.6 Learning points 27

4 Writing an effective introduction and conclusion 29
   4.1 Introductions 30
   4.2 Conclusions 33
   4.3 Learning points 35

5 How to compare 37
   5.1 Introduction 38
   5.2 Putting your proposed comparisons into practice 40
   5.3 Learning points 42

6	**Using secondary reading**	**43**
	6.1 Introduction	44
	6.2 So what should you read?	44
	6.3 How to take notes from your secondary sources	45
	6.4 How to refer to secondary reading in the body of your literary study essay	46
	6.5 Learning points	47
7	**Exemplar literary essays**	**49**
	7.1 Introduction	50
	7.2 Tennessee Williams essay	50
	7.3 Sylvia Plath essay	55
	7.4 Literary essays: Assessment criteria	58
	7.5 Learning points	58
8	**Literary study test**	**59**
9	**Acknowledgements**	**61**

Unit 1 Topic 1

General principles

Contents

   1.1 Introduction 4
   1.2 What is the literary study essay? 4
   1.3 What are the skills required for literary study essay success? 5
       1.3.1 Skill 1: Exploring the main ideas and themes of literary texts 5
       1.3.2 Skill 2: Applying your knowledge and understanding of language to analyse and evaluate 6
       1.3.3 Skill 3: Exploring connections and comparisons between literary texts 6
   1.4 How is the essay assessed? 7
   1.5 What is the difference between a Higher and Advanced Higher literary essay? 8
   1.6 Learning points 9

Learning objective

By the end of this topic you will:

- understand the skills required to complete the essay task in the literary study paper of your final examination;
- understand how the essay is assessed;
- understand the progression from a essay at Higher level to one at Advanced Higher level.

1.1 Introduction

This section is concerned with introducing the skills required to write an essay, which is a key way your ability to critically analyse and evaluate literary texts is tested.

Your ability to critically analyse and evaluate literary texts is tested directly in two areas:

- in the textual analysis part of the literary study external examination;
- in the essay part of the literary study external examination.

1.2 What is the literary study essay?

Writing an essay at Advanced Higher level is a development of two key skills you learned and demonstrated as part of your study of Higher English:

- exploring the main ideas and themes of literary texts;
- applying your knowledge and understanding of language.

In addition to these, a new skill at Advanced Higher is exploring connections and comparisons between literary texts. This means that when you write about your literary texts, you will be discussing connections and comparisons in their key ideas and themes, and how they have been written.

When you write a essay at Advanced Higher, you must deal with at least two texts if you choose to write about drama, two novels or three short stories if you choose to write about prose, and at least three poems if you choose to write about poetry.

These three key skills for writing an essay can be broadly categorised as:

- knowledge and understanding;
- analysis;
- evaluation.

These concepts pervade the Advanced Higher course, and you will have the opportunity to practise them in your study of literature, in your completion of textual analysis and in the planning, preparation and production of your chosen dissertation topic.

You should therefore make learning connections between the skills you are developing in other areas of the course and the specific skill we are focused on here: writing an essay in the literary study paper of your final examination.

TOPIC 1. GENERAL PRINCIPLES 5

1.3 What are the skills required for literary study essay success?

Writing a successful essay demands three key skills:

1. exploring the main ideas and themes of literary texts (knowledge and understanding);
2. applying your knowledge and understanding of language (analysis);
3. exploring connections and comparisons between literary texts (evaluation).

Remember that these skills are interconnected. Any discussion of literary texts involves demonstrating your knowledge and understanding, your ability to analyse, and your ability to evaluate.

1.3.1 Skill 1: Exploring the main ideas and themes of literary texts

This means that you have to demonstrate your knowledge and understanding of the **setting, characters and key events** in your texts, and how these are used to convey the writer's ideas, which in turn connect to his or her **themes**.

Let's look at how this breaks down in practice, using two examples from writers popular at Advanced Higher level: Tennessee Williams and Sylvia Plath.

Tennessee Williams

Stanley Kowalski is a **main character** in Tennessee Williams' play, 'A Streetcar Named Desire'.

Through the key events in the play, and Stanley's interaction with other characters, Williams develops several important ideas about him. He is brash, honest and straightforward in his dealings with other people, often vulgar and 'low-class' in his manners and habits, and has an assumption of entitlement. Stanley believes that hard work and forthrightness will bring rewards of position and relative wealth. He is one of the 'new breed' of American men, not frightened by hard work or hard living.

Williams' ideas about Stanley convey one of the dramatist's themes: that the 'old' America, represented by genteel manners and long-established ways of living, is being crushed underfoot by the new ways, which have no regard for status or tradition.

Sylvia Plath

In Sylvia Plath's poetry about the natural world, she explores through her use of imagery several ideas about nature. She presents it as a hostile environment for humans, where people feel overwhelmed by the magnitude of the natural world, and humankind's supposed superiority is crushed in the face of nature's grandeur, which remains impassive to us.

These ideas are used to convey her **theme** of alienation, and how humans struggle to find meaningful connections and lasting relationships in their lives, which are essentially difficult.

© HERIOT-WATT UNIVERSITY

> **Revise the ideas and themes in your literary texts**
>
> Try this exercise for the texts you have studied.
>
> Take settings, key characters, events, words, images or other techniques and identify the key ideas associated with these aspects of the text. Then make connections between the writer's ideas and his or her themes. Remember, a theme is a concern which affects all our lives, not just the lives of the characters in the text or the persona of a poem. Through their experiences, we learn something about our own experiences. Themes are often concerned with the big experiences in life, such as love, loss, birth, death and the nature of human existence.
>
> So, to successfully demonstrate your knowledge and understanding of your texts' ideas and themes, you need to be able to engage in confident discussion of the writer's ideas and themes and the means by which he or she develops these.

1.3.2 Skill 2: Applying your knowledge and understanding of language to analyse and evaluate

This means that you have to demonstrate your understanding of the writer's **literary techniques** and how the impact of these enhances his or her ideas and themes.

'Literary techniques' breaks down into these more manageable concepts:

- use of language (e.g. word-choice, imagery, sentence structure);
- structural features (e.g. organisation of key events, flashback);
- specific dramatic technique (e.g. stage directions, use of dramatic properties, soliloquy);
- specific poetic technique (e.g. poetic form, rhyme, rhythm);
- features of the narrative (e.g. narrative voice).

Not all of these will be relevant to the discussion of every one of your texts, of course. Remember that essay skill 1 is largely concerned with the *what* (i.e. what happens and why it happens) and essay skill 2 is largely concerned with the *how* (i.e. how specific techniques are used). In practice, however, when you write about literary texts, your discussion of the what and the how are often integrated (i.e. what happens, why it happens and how it is conveyed.)

1.3.3 Skill 3: Exploring connections and comparisons between literary texts

This means that you have to demonstrate your understanding of how characters or the persona of a poem, settings, situations, events and specific techniques are used in similar or different ways in two or more texts to convey the writer's theme(s).

It is likely that for the literary study part of the Advanced Higher course you will study two or more texts by the same author, and these texts will deal with similar universal concerns. However, it may be the case that your teacher has chosen two or more texts by different authors which deal with similar concerns. Either way, you should be in a position to engage with these texts as a body of work, the characters/personas, key events, techniques and setting of which have been used to convey similar ideas and themes.

TOPIC 1. GENERAL PRINCIPLES

The question in your examination will demand that you deal with one concept (either thematic or connected to a specific aspect of the genre, such as character or poetic form) in two or more texts, so you will be directed to make connections and comparisons within a specific focus.

For example, a poetry question might ask:

> With reference to at least three poems by a particular poet, discuss the effectiveness of the poet's use of nature and the natural world in the presentation of significant themes and ideas.

Or, in the prose section:

> Discuss the thematic significance of the presentation of the minor characters in any two novels.

The challenge of writing about two or more texts in the same essay is learning to plan and then execute an effective line of argument, one which allows you to discuss each of your texts in detail at the same time as showing your understanding of the connections between them.

1.4 How is the essay assessed?

The essay is worth 20 marks, and therefore 20% of your final grade. There are four 'pass' bands with marks ranging from 10-20, and two 'fail' bands, with marks ranging from 9-0.

Your essay will be assessed in three broad categories:

- knowledge and understanding;
- analysis;
- evaluation.

Although these are three broad categories, your essay will be judged holistically because the skills which relate to these categories are all interconnected.

In addition, to gain 10 or more marks, your essay must demonstrate 'minimum competence for technical accuracy'. At Advanced Higher level, this means your essay must have 'few errors in the use of structure, style, language and/or literary terminology'.

The detailed marking instructions for all questions in the Advanced Higher English literary study can be located in the Advanced Higher English page on the SQA website (http://bit.ly/1NP9aeB).

Detailed Marking Instructions for all questions — Advanced Higher English Literary Study

	Marks 20—19	Marks 18—16	Marks 15—13	Marks 12-10	Marks 9—6	Marks 5—0
Knowledge and understanding The Literary study demonstrates:	■ comprehensive knowledge and understanding of the texts ■ a full and relevant exploration with sustained consideration of the implications of the question ■ extensive use of textual evidence to support an argument which is clearly focused on the demands of the question	■ secure knowledge and understanding of the texts ■ a relevant exploration which demonstrates secure consideration of the implications of the question ■ extensive use of textual evidence which clearly supports the demands of the question	■ broad knowledge and understanding of the texts ■ a relevant and thoughtful approach to the question ■ use of textual evidence which is relevant to the demands of the question	■ knowledge and understanding of the texts ■ a relevant approach to the question ■ use of textual evidence to address the demands of the question	■ limited knowledge and understanding of the texts ■ a limited approach to the question ■ limited textual evidence to support the demands of the question	■ very little knowledge of the texts ■ very little attempt to answer the question ■ very little textual evidence
Analysis The Literary study demonstrates:	■ relevant analysis of a task-appropriate range of literary techniques and/or features of language which skilfully strengthens the line of argument	■ relevant analysis of a task-appropriate range of literary techniques and/or features of language which strengthens the line of argument	• relevant analysis of a range of literary techniques and features of language which strengthens the line of argument	■ analysis of a range of literary techniques and/or features of language	■ limited analysis of literary techniques and/or features of language	■ very little analysis of literary techniques and/or features of language
Evaluation The Literary study demonstrates:	■ a committed, clear evaluative stance with respect to the texts and the question, and skilfully based on precise evidence discussed within the response.	■ a clearly identifiable evaluative stance with respect to the texts and the question and securely based on evidence discussed within the response	■ a discernible and relevant evaluative stance with respect to the texts and the question and based on evidence discussed within the response.	■ an evaluative stance with respect to the texts and the question but may be based on previously undiscussed evidence or demonstrate some weakness in relevance	■ limited evaluation with respect to the texts and/or lacks relevance to the question and/or evidence	■ very little evidence of evaluation and/or supporting evidence
Technical Accuracy The literary study demonstrates:	• minimum competence for technical accuracy which includes few errors in the use of structure, style, language and/or literary terminology				• significant errors in structure, style, language and/or literary terminology	

Detailed marking instructions for all questions - Advanced Higher English literary study

1.5 What is the difference between a Higher and Advanced Higher literary essay?

It is the third skill 'exploring connections and comparisons between literary texts' which marks the progression between Higher and Advanced Higher. Dealing with at least two texts in one essay, and creating a line of argument which allows for detailed discussion of your chosen texts as well as opportunities to draw meaningful connections and comparisons between them, is a bigger and therefore more demanding task. In Higher, you had 45 minutes to plan and write one essay on one literary text; at Advanced Higher you have 90 minutes to plan and write one essay on two or more texts.

And a word about secondary reading: an important aspect of studying Advanced Higher English is developing literary research skills. Considering critical work about your authors, texts, or concepts associated with them, written by other people, enhances your understanding of texts and can offer helpful 'ways in' to them. The expectation that you will be able to incorporate ideas gained from your secondary reading of critical work relevant to your texts is another significant development from Higher.

You are now ready to look at the topics which follow this introductory overview of the critical essay at Advanced Higher, and to look in detail at each of the skills necessary for success.

1.6 Learning points

Summary

You will now:

- understand the skills required to complete the essay task in the literary study paper of your final examination;
- understand how the essay is assessed;
- understand the progression from an essay at Higher level to one at Advanced Higher level.

Unit 1 Topic 2

The question

Contents

2.1 Literary study paper 12
2.2 Advanced Higher literary study questions 12
    2.2.1 Higher and Advanced Higher critical essay questions 12
    2.2.2 Advanced Higher questions with quotation starters 14
2.3 In the exam 15
2.4 Learning points 17

Learning objective

By the end of this topic you will:

- know the difference between an Advanced Higher literary study essay and a Higher one;
- know the different types of question you might get in the Advanced Higher literary study paper;
- have practised annotating the component parts of an Advanced Higher essay question.

2.1 Literary study paper

In the literary study paper, you will be given a selection of questions specific to each genre and are expected to choose, plan, write and check *one* essay within the time allocation of 90 minutes.

The literary study paper is divided into four genres:

1. poetry;
2. prose fiction;
3. prose non-fiction;
4. drama.

You will have the choice of at least six to seven questions in each genre section.

You cannot write about any of the texts or authors you studied for your dissertation.

2.2 Advanced Higher literary study questions

The essay questions are broader and more open than they are at Higher level.

What does this mean in practice? It means that the questions are less supported; you will be given less direction about how to organise your answer.

2.2.1 Higher and Advanced Higher critical essay questions

Look at the following two examples of Higher critical essay questions.

Critical essay question one

> Choose a play[1] in which a major character's actions influence the emotions of others[2].
>
> Briefly explain[3] how the dramatist presents these actions and emotions[4] and discuss how this contributes to your understanding of the play as a whole[5].
>
> **Notes:**
> [1] This part of the question "keys" you in. It helps you to make a relevant choice of text for the question.
> [2] The focus is a character whose behaviour affects the way other characters feel.
> [3] This part of the question tells you what to *do*.
> [4] Discuss examples of the major character's actions and examples of how other characters' emotions are affected by them.
> [5] This prompts you to connect your discussion of the characters' actions and emotions to the playwright's themes.

TOPIC 2. THE QUESTION 13

Critical essay question two

> Choose a novel or short story[1] which has a satisfying ending[2].
>
> Discuss[3] to what extent the ending[4] provides a successful conclusion[5] to the text as a whole[6].
>
> **Notes:**
>
> [1] This part of the question "keys" you in. It helps you to make a relevant choice of text for the question.
> [2] The focus is the end of the novel or short story.
> [3] This part of the question tells you what to *do*.
> [4] You need to make an evaluative judgement about the ending's effectiveness.
> [5] You need to discuss what happens and what themes are conveyed by the way the novel / short story ends.
> [6] This means you must connect your discussion of the ending to the ideas and theme(s) the writer is exploring throughout the novel / short story. How does the ending tie together the novel / short story's theme?

You can see that first of all, candidates are given support to make a relevant choice of text for the question. They are also directed to deal with *one* literary text in their answer. The second part of the question then helps candidates to organise their answer by suggesting three areas which must be covered. This provides support by suggesting a possible framework.

Now look at these two examples of Advanced Higher essay questions.

Roll over the link text to see annotations referring to each part of the question.

Essay question one

> With reference to at least **three** poems[1], discuss the poetic presentation[2] of the theme of faith or the loss of faith[3].
>
> **Notes:**
>
> [1] You must deal with at least three poems. You do not have to discuss them in equal measure, but each poem must be considered in adequate detail and you must compare the texts
> [2] This means that you must consider *how* the poet conveys his or her ideas: through structure; form; imagery; word choice....
> [3] The focus of your discussion is therefore how the poet's techniques convey one of these themes. You may deal with more than one poet.

© HERIOT-WATT UNIVERSITY

Essay question two

> With close analysis[1] of two novels[2], compare how setting is used[3] to develop a significant theme or themes[4].
>
> **Notes:**
>
> [1] This means an analytical discussion of aspects of setting. This could include a discussion of each novel's location; the time in which the action takes place; the values of this place / time and the characters associated with it; use of symbolism...
> [2] Advanced Higher essay questions might demand comparison of an aspect of at least two texts.
> [3] The focus is setting: **where** and/or **when** the events in the novel take place.
> [4] You must identify an appropriate theme and discuss how aspects of setting convey the writer's theme(s).

You can see that the Advanced Higher question provides less guidance to candidates about how to organise their answer. Candidates are expected to have the knowledge and experience to create an appropriate framework for their ideas which will produce a relevant line of argument in response to the question.

You will also notice that you must deal with at least two texts, and in the case of poetry and short stories, at least three. You are expected to compare your literary texts, and must therefore plan a line of argument and select evidence which gives you opportunities for direct comparison of aspects of your texts.

2.2.2 Advanced Higher questions with quotation starters

Some Advanced Higher questions use a quotation from literary criticism, or a literary text, as the "prompt" for candidates.

Now look at these two examples of Advanced Higher questions with quotation starters.

Roll over the link text to see annotations referring to each part of the question.

TOPIC 2. THE QUESTION

Quotation question one

> "Poetry is the spontaneous overflow[1] of powerful feelings[2]."
>
> With close analysis[3] of at least three poems[4], discuss how far you agree[5] with this quotation.
>
> **Notes:**
>
> [1] Does this suggest something apparently uncontrolled?
> [2] You need to identify what these feelings *are* and what they *relate to*
> [3] You must consider the effect of various poetic techniques (form, structure, imagery, word-choice...) in conveying the "spontaneous overflow of powerful feelings".
> [4] You must always discuss three poems in an essay on poetry.
> [5] **To what extent** do your poems convey "powerful feelings" which appear to "overflow" spontaneously? Of course, you might choose to argue that in your chosen poems the "powerful feelings" are very tightly controlled.

Quotation question two

> 'Money and power[1] - it all comes down to that."
>
> Discuss this quotation[2] with reference to any two novels[3].
>
> **Notes:**
>
> [1] The quotation identifies the *themes* your essay will focus on. It is also possible to consider "money and power" as one inter-related theme.
> [2] You need to discuss *how* the themes of money and power are explored in your novels. You might consider characterisation, setting, symbolism, key incidents/action...
> [3] Advanced Higher essay questions always demand a comparison of an aspect of at least two texts.

Often, the quotation prompt will specify or suggest a theme on which you should focus in your answer, or identify an aspect of the genre which can be discussed with reference to your texts.

2.3 In the exam

When you open the literary study paper and choose your question, you should quickly annotate the question to key you in to what is required. Remember, you will have more questions from which to choose than you had at Higher, and it is likely that several of them will be relevant to your texts.

You need to make good decisions about what the best option is in a relatively short space of time. You must be prepared to think on your feet, and to use what you know about your texts in order to answer the question. The "prepared response" has no place in Advanced Higher!

© HERIOT-WATT UNIVERSITY

Once you've chosen the most appropriate question for you and completed a quick annotation to key you in, you're ready to plan in greater detail. For ideas about how to plan an essay, see the 'Planning a literary study essay' topic in this section.

Annotating questions

This task will help you to practise deconstructing an exam question down to its component parts, so that you are clear about the detail you must cover in your answer.

Below are eight examples of Advanced Higher literary study questions. There are two for each genre. Choose questions relevant to the texts you have studied and try highlighting and annotating them, like the examples earlier in this topic.

Once you have completed your annotation, you can compare it to the suggestions provided in the answers at the end of this topic.

Poetry questions

Q1: With close analysis of at least **three** poems, discuss how the poet(s) reflect on aspects of change.

....

Q2: Analyse the use of one or more poetic form(s) such as: the dramatic monologue; the sonnet; the address; the elegy.
In your answer you should refer to at least **three** poems.

Prose fiction questions

Q3: "The short story form is more than a vehicle for stylistic devices (a collection of miniatures, a vignette, a fragment, a twist in the tale...) and can achieve the presentation of a significant theme."
Discuss how far you agree with this quotation with reference to at least **three** short stories.

....

Q4: Discuss the thematic significance of the presentation of a flawed hero or heroine in any **two** novels.

Prose non-fiction questions

Q5: "It is in the ability to combine the particular with the universal that a writer displays their craft to the fullest extent."
Discuss how successful at least **two** non-fiction texts are in combining "the particular with the universal".

....

Q6: Discuss how at least **two** non-fiction texts present political, social or moral issues in similar or different ways.

Drama questions

Q7: With reference to **two** plays, discuss the effectiveness of the opening scenes in establishing the tone of the action which follows.

....

Q8: With reference to **two** plays, discuss the contribution setting makes to the development of significant theme(s).

2.4 Learning points

Summary

You will now:

- know the difference between an Advanced Higher literary study essay and a Higher one;
- know the different types of question you might get in the Advanced Higher literary study paper;
- have practised annotating the component parts of an Advanced Higher essay question.

Unit 1 Topic 3

Planning a literary study essay

Contents

- 3.1 Introduction 20
- 3.2 Stage 1: Defining key ideas 20
- 3.3 Stage 2: Using key ideas 22
  - 3.3.1 Planning to compare 23
- 3.4 Stage 3: Structuring key ideas 25
- 3.5 The exam 27
- 3.6 Learning points 27

Learning objective

By the end of this topic you will:

- know how to plan a comparative essay.

3.1 Introduction

You have 90 minutes to plan, write and check your essay in the Advanced Higher literary study paper. Planning is very important. Because you are dealing with two or more texts, and a less-supported question than you had at Higher, you must take time to plan your response.

This topic outlines a strategy for planning an effective essay, but it is worth noting that planning well like this is a time-consuming process that you will not have time to do in the exam. The aim is that you complete many plans in preparation for your exam, using the strategy outlined in this topic, which will help you to plan in the exam when you will, by necessity, have to plan much more quickly.

Starting point

The starting point for any essay is the question. Once you've chosen your question, organise your thinking in **three stages**:

1. What is the question asking you to do? What key ideas must you address?
2. What do you know about your chosen texts that will be useful and relevant to address the key ideas of the question?
3. How will you structure your ideas about the texts to create a relevant line of argument that addresses the key ideas of the question and allows you to compare or discuss key aspects of your texts?

In other words, ask yourself: what are the key ideas I must address, what evidence will I use, and how will I organise this evidence?

Let's deal with each stage in turn.

3.2 Stage 1: Defining key ideas

The questions to consider when defining key ideas are:

- What is the question asking you to do? What key ideas must you address?

Your work in the topic on 'The question' should mean that you are now skilled at breaking down a question into its key ideas. If you need more practice at this, you should look at the Advanced Higher English specimen paper which is available online at http://bit.ly/25tS4J2.

TOPIC 3. PLANNING A LITERARY STUDY ESSAY

Annotating a question

Consider the drama question below. Rather than the generic annotations in the topic on 'The question', this annotation is specific to two drama texts: Tennessee Williams' 'A Streetcar Named Desire' and 'Sweet Bird of Youth'.

> "Concealment[1] and discovery[2] are central to any drama."
>
> Discuss the structural[3] and thematic significance[4] of "concealment and discovery" in any two plays.
>
> **Notes:**
>
> [1] **What is being hidden?** In 'Streetcar', Blanche is hiding her past and her alcoholism. In 'Sweet Bird', Chance is hiding from the truth of his past and what he has become. He has no self-knowledge.
> [2] **How is the hidden thing revealed? What is the impact of the revelation and on whom?** In 'Streetcar' - Stanley's relentless pursuit of Blanche and his determination to crush her brings about the revelation of the truth. Impact on Blanche (complete mental breakdown) and on Stella. In 'Sweet Bird' - Chance acquires self-knowledge after Tom Jr. confronts him with the truth and his fanciful plans for success come to nothing.
> [3] **At what point does the revelation of the truth take place? What is significant about this?** In 'Streetcar', inexorable grinding down of Blanche culminates in her rape in Scene 10. In 'Sweet Bird', structured sequence of Act 2, Scene 2 in developing audience's understanding of Chance.
> [4] **What themes are conveyed through the characters' concealment and discovery?** In 'Streetcar', Blanche's concealment of her past conveys Williams' theme of the loss of youth and the illusory worlds we create in order to cope with the reality of that loss. These illusory worlds are often characterised by escape from reality through drug / alcohol addiction and sex. In 'Sweet Bird', Chance's lack of self-knowledge conveys similar themes explored in Streetcar. Both characters are also shown to be defeated by the real world, in all its brutality and violence, represented by Stanley in Streetcar and Boss Finley in Sweet Bird.

By annotating the question, you are beginning the planning process by thinking about the question's key ideas. Already, you will have a number of ideas about what needs to be addressed in order to answer this question.

Stage 1: Defining key ideas

Now choose a question for your texts and complete a text-specific annotation of the question, like the one exemplified above. You could use one you completed for the topic on 'The question' and just add text-specific detail.

© HERIOT-WATT UNIVERSITY

3.3 Stage 2: Using key ideas

The question to consider when using key ideas is:

- What do you know about your chosen texts that will be useful and relevant to address the key ideas of the question?

For this stage, you should write down all the things you know about each text - in this case, ideas about character, key events, setting, dramatic techniques - which are relevant to the question. You can set out these ideas any way that suits you: using the key words of the question as subheadings; in a list; using a spider diagram; or a flowchart.

This is what your ideas for this drama question might look like using a spider diagram:

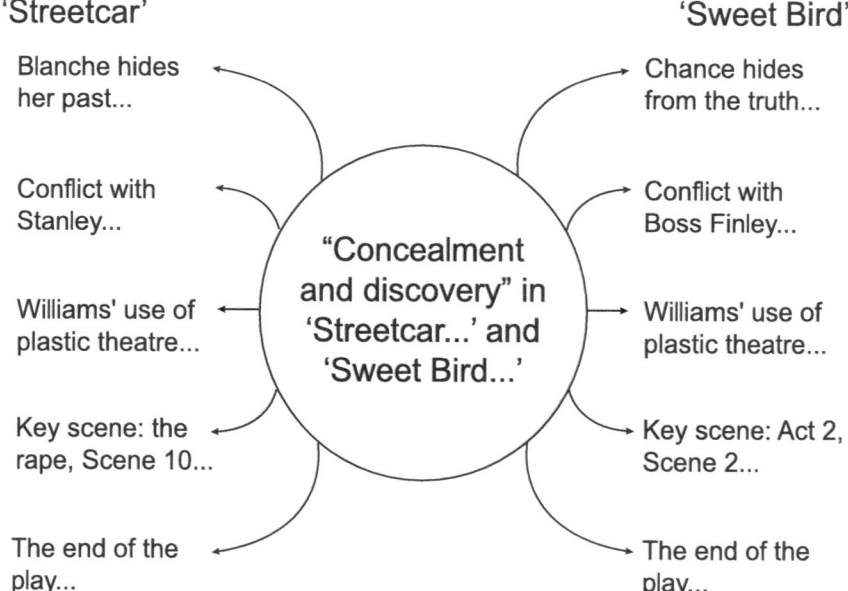

Spider diagram for drama exam question

The truncated notes on the spider diagram above are given in full below.

TOPIC 3. PLANNING A LITERARY STUDY ESSAY

"Concealment and discovery" in 'Streetcar...' and 'Sweet Bird...'

Streetcar:

- Blanche hides her past, when she sought refuge from her loneliness and fear of growing old in relationships with young men. Hides the fragility of her current mental state and her dependence on alcohol as an escape.
- Conflict with Stanley who represents truth and brutal reality.
- Williams' use of plastic theatre - light, music, rape scene backdrop - to convey his themes.
- Key scene: the rape, Scene 10. Culmination of conflict between Stanley and Blanche. Culmination of Williams' theme of truth versus illusion and the brutal nature of the real world. Both of the above correspond with the revelation of the truth about Blanche's past.
- The end of the play: significance of Stella's decision and the card players. Link to Williams' theme.

Sweet Bird:

- Chance hides from the truth of his past and from what he has become. Escapes his reality by his dependence on drugs and sex.
- Conflict with Boss Finley who represents brutal reality.
- Williams' use of plastic theatre - music, backdrops - to convey his themes.
- Key scene: Act 2, Scene 2 where the truth of Chance's pitiful state is revealed through a series of **contrasts**: with his old "friends"; with the reality of the state the Princess is in; and with the unequivocal power held by Boss Finley.
- The end of the play: significance of Chance's decision to stay and the final words of the play. Individual → universal.

Stage 2: Using key ideas

Now write down all the things you know about each of your texts, relevant to your chosen question.

3.3.1 Planning to compare

Now that you have considered your ideas about each text, the next stage is to plan when you will be able to compare aspects of the texts. Remember, this is the main difference between an Advanced Higher essay and an essay you wrote at Higher. You should not think in terms of comparing every single point you make about one text with your other text. Think instead about **choosing two to**

© HERIOT-WATT UNIVERSITY

three main areas of comparison, connected to events in the text, which you can really discuss in detail. Providing an in-depth discussion of two to three key points of comparison is much more effective than trying to deal with too many points in a superficial way.

Using a highlighter pen, highlight points on your spider diagram which stand out as providing opportunities to provide detailed discussion of comparisons between your texts.

Highlighting the spider diagram for the drama question reveals the following key points of comparison:

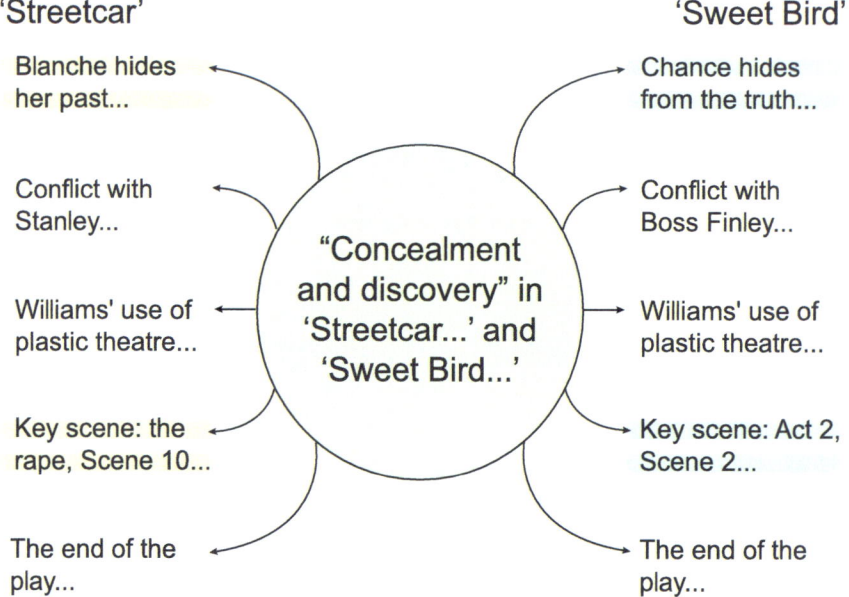

Spider diagram showing points of comparison for drama exam question

There are two areas highlighted in each text on the spider diagram above:

- In 'A Streetcar Named Desire':
    - "Blanche hides her past...";
    - "Key scene: the rape, Scene 10...".
- In 'Sweet Bird of Youth':
    - "Chance hides from the truth...";
    - "Key scene: Act 2, Scene 2...".

Although there are only two key areas highlighted, they are both **significant aspects** of each text.

Key point

Remember, it is more effective to produce a detailed discussion of important areas of comparison, rather than trying to compare everything.

Planning to compare

Now highlight two to three key areas for comparison on your spider diagram of ideas (from Stage 2).

The topic 'Choosing points' gives you more advice about how to compare your texts.

3.4 Stage 3: Structuring key ideas

The question to consider when structuring key ideas is:

- How will you structure your ideas about the texts to create a relevant line of argument that addresses the key ideas of the question and allows you to compare key aspects of your texts?

Now you have all your ideas and you know where you might discuss comparisons between the texts. Your next step is to organise your material. Remember, you should always be thinking about the central aspects of your text - in this case, character, key scenes, setting, dramatic techniques - and how these convey the writer's theme(s).

These aspects should create the overall structure of your essay. Always think of having three sections to your essay, each of which covers one central aspect of the texts. Highlighting your two to three key areas for comparison should give you a natural framework for your essay. If you've highlighted only two key areas of detailed comparison, then your third section might be concerned with aspects of the texts which are individual to each, for example, their endings.

Essay plan for comparing texts

So, using my spider diagram and my highlighted areas for comparison, a plan for my essay on "concealment and discovery" in two plays by Tennessee Williams might look like this:

1. Introduction

2. Section 1: character. Comparative discussion of aspects of Blanche and Chance's characters: their pasts; their lives now; the ways they escape their realities. Focus on idea of concealment, and link to the themes Williams explores through these characters and their experiences.

3. Section 2: key scenes. Comparative discussion of the structural and thematic significance of Scene 10 in 'Streetcar' and Act 2, Scene 2 in 'Sweet Bird', when the truth of the characters' hidden pasts is revealed. Reference to Williams' dramatic techniques (music, lighting, backdrops).

4. Section 3: the significance of each play's ending.

5. Conclusion

© HERIOT-WATT UNIVERSITY

Can you see that by organising your ideas around central aspects of the texts, that you will naturally compare them? Remember, you want to avoid an essay structure which deals with all your ideas about one text, and then all your ideas about the next text. If you use this structure for your essay, it is much more difficult to make meaningful comparisons between the texts.

Comparing short stories

Comparing two plays, novels or non-fiction texts will be easier if you follow this suggested structure. If you are writing about three short stories, however, you can still follow the same structure as the drama exemplar above: organise your material about the texts in terms of their central aspects: character, key events, setting, narrative voice... You do not have to compare all three stories in every section, but make sure that each of the three stories is compared in detail to at least one other story at some stage throughout your essay.

Comparing poems

If you are writing about three poems, you might find it easier - and more effective - to organise your essay in terms of the ideas connected to the question, rather than poetic technique. For example, here is a suggested plan in response to this poetry question:

> With reference to at least three poems by a particular poet, discuss the effectiveness of the poet's use of nature and the natural world in the presentation of significant themes and ideas.

Using three poems by Sylvia Plath to answer this question, you might create the following plan:

1. Introduction
2. Section 1: the overwhelming stature of the natural world
3. Section 2: the hostile nature of the natural world
4. Section 3: the persona's feeling of lack of self-worth in the face of nature's grandeur
5. Conclusion

Can you see how the plan is structured around the poet's ideas about the natural world, and that as you discuss these ideas in the poems, you will naturally discuss the poet's use of technique (word-choice, imagery, symbolism, persona, verse/line structure, etc.)? You do not have to compare all three poems in every section, but make sure that each of the three poems is compared in detail to at least one other poem at some stage throughout your essay.

Key point

Remember, if you are writing about short stories or poems, there is no requirement to give **equal** treatment to all three texts in your essay. It's possible that one of your three texts might not always fit the question as neatly as the other two. For more advice about this, see the topic 'Choosing points'.

3.5 The exam

This topic gives you ideas about how to develop a strategy for planning a comparative literary study essay. Becoming skilled at planning is excellent preparation for your exam, but it is unlikely that in the exam you will have the time to prepare a plan in the way outlined in this topic.

> **Key point**
>
> You should aim to practise planning by creating many detailed plans for different questions. Creating detailed plans also provides great opportunities to revise your texts.

Timing

In the exam, you should aim to spend around 15 minutes planning your essay, and the remaining time writing it, with five minutes or so at the end to have a quick check through of the whole piece.

With roughly an hour and ten minutes to write your essay, it is likely that you might be able to write approximately 1800 words. Remember, this is a detailed comparative essay which should be well-planned and, therefore, well-executed. If your school/centre offers the opportunity to word-process your essays, do not forget the importance of checking your work carefully before you submit it to the invigilator.

3.6 Learning points

> **Summary**
>
> You will now:
>
> - know how to plan a comparative essay.

Unit 1 Topic 4

Writing an effective introduction and conclusion

Contents

4.1 Introductions 30
    4.1.1 Introductions to essays 31
4.2 Conclusions 33
    4.2.1 Conclusions to essays 33
4.3 Learning points 35

Learning objective

By the end of this topic you will have:

- revised how to write an effective introduction;
- revised how to write an effective conclusion;
- practised writing your own introductions and conclusions for a number of different questions.

4.1 Introductions

Writing a successful literary study essay starts with a good introduction. If your introduction is well-organised, demonstrates your understanding of the central ideas in the texts and links these to the focus of the question, then it is likely that the rest of your essay will follow suit.

At its most basic, your introduction should do four things, in this order:

1. state the name of your texts and their author(s);
2. make a statement outlining what each text is about;
3. refer to the key words of the question;
4. make a statement about the key themes of the texts.

In the topic 'Planning a literary study essay', a plan for an essay on "concealment and discovery" in two Tennessee Williams plays was outlined. Following the model above, an introduction to that essay might look like this:

In Tennessee Williams' plays 'A Streetcar Named Desire' and 'Sweet Bird of Youth'[1] he writes about characters who struggle to live in the real world and who seek to escape the harsh reality of these worlds through addiction to drugs and sex. In both plays, the main characters - Blanche Dubois in 'Streetcar' and Chance Wayne in 'Sweet Bird' - try to **conceal the truth** of their past lives - and the nature of their current existences - from others in the play, but ultimately these pasts are **cruelly exposed** by more powerful external forces and each is confronted with the reality of his/her circumstances[2]. Through these characters, Williams explores our attitudes towards lost youth, and the corruption of 'goodness' in the face of a brutal world which threatens to crush us if we are unable to adapt to it[3].

Notes:

[1] This is the name of the texts and their author(s).
[2] This is the statement outlining what each text is about. The key words in the question, 'conceal the truth' and 'cruelly exposed', are highlighted in bold in the above statement.
[3] This is the statement about the key themes of the texts.

You do not need to do anything else in your introduction, but if you choose to do so, you could give a **brief** biography of the author(s) and the social context of their writing. If we did that, the introduction above might look like this:

> In Tennessee Williams' plays 'A Streetcar Named Desire' and 'Sweet Bird of Youth', he writes about characters who struggle to live in the real world and who seek to escape the harsh reality of these worlds through addiction to drugs and sex. Writing in the 1950s, a time of great change in America's social and cultural landscape, Williams' plays are often concerned with characters who struggle to adapt to their new situations because of a fundamental weakness in their personalities.[1] In both plays, the main characters - Blanche Dubois in 'Streetcar' and Chance Wayne in 'Sweet Bird' - try to **conceal the truth** of their past lives - and the nature of their current existences - from others in the play, but ultimately these pasts are **cruelly exposed** by more powerful external forces and each is confronted with the reality of his/her circumstances. Through these characters, Williams explores our attitudes towards lost youth, and the corruption of 'goodness' in the face of a brutal world which threatens to crush us if we are unable to adapt to it.
>
> **Notes:**
>
> [1] A brief biography of Tennessee Williams and the social context in which he wrote these plays.

Remember, whichever approach you choose, keep your introduction concise and relevant to the task: your job is to get onto the main body of your essay as quickly as possible.

Note that you should not use expressions such as "In this essay I will..." or "This essay will explore...". These are not very sophisticated ways of starting an essay because they state the obvious. In fact, you should know from writing essays at Higher level that you are unlikely to use the first person at any stage when writing a literary study essay.

4.1.1 Introductions to essays

Introductions to essays   Go online

The following three questions include essay introductions which are un-highlighted. Highlight the different parts to indicate the following four aspects of the introduction:

- state the name of texts and their author(s);
- make a statement outlining what each text is about;
- refer to the key words of the question;
- make a statement about the key themes of the texts.

Q1: *"Poetry is the spontaneous overflow of powerful feelings."* With close analysis of at least three poems, discuss how far you agree with this quotation.

Introduction

In many of her poems, Sylvia Plath explores the relationship that exists between man and nature. In 'Sleep in the Mojave Desert', we read of the persona and her companion travelling in the bleak wilderness of the Californian desert. 'Two Campers in Cloud Country' again depicts the couple, this time at Rock Lake, whilst in the poems 'Blackberrying' and 'Wuthering Heights', the persona experiences nature alone. These poems, like much of Plath's work, are characterised by their expression of powerful emotions. However, the expression of the persona's feelings is tightly controlled by Plath's precise use of imagery, in particular, as well as other poetic techniques. In all of these poems, Plath suggests that nature is a hostile force and that essentially man is insignificant or impotent, even, in the face of that force.

....

Q2: *"Money and power - it all comes down to that."* Discuss this quotation with reference to any two novels.

Introduction

The novels 'The Great Gatsby' and 'Tender is the Night' by F. Scott Fitzgerald explore the corruption of the so-called jazz-age of America, a time of unprecedented prosperity and corresponding excess. In both novels, the 1920s are portrayed as a time when social and moral values were increasingly tarnished by the relentless pursuit of wealth. The characters' lives are filled with empty pleasures: opulent parties, illicit affairs and indolent days. Gatsby, Daisy and the Divers, Nicole and Dick, illustrate this all-consuming obsession with money and status, and they all illustrate the damage wrought when moral values and basic decency take second place to material acquisition.

....

Q3: *"Effective drama is constructed from more than just dialogue."* Discuss this quotation with reference to any two plays.

Introduction

In Tennessee Williams' plays, 'A Streetcar Named Desire' and 'Sweet Bird of Youth', he writes about characters whose lives have spiraled out of control because they have fundamental flaws in their personalities which they are ultimately unable to overcome. The main characters, Blanche Dubois and Chance Wayne, struggle to live in the real world, and they seek refuge from reality in alcohol, drugs and sex. In both plays, Williams makes significant use of dramatic techniques which go beyond the effective use of dialogue. His use of "plastic theatre" - musical underscoring, costumes, props and other aspects of staging - combines with dialogue to enhance the audience's understanding of characters and his theme of the corruption of "goodness" in the face of a brutal world which threatens to crush us if we are unable to adapt to it.

> **Introduction to essay questions relevant to your literary texts**
>
> Now try writing your own introductions to essay questions relevant to your literary texts. You could use the exemplar questions featured in the topic on 'The question', or essay questions from the Advanced Higher specimen paper. Follow the structure modeled above, and see if you can colour-code each part of your introduction.

4.2 Conclusions

Do not expect to do too much in your conclusion. It is likely that you will be working right up to the time available so your conclusion should be concise and economical. And remember, the golden rule of writing conclusions is never to introduce a new idea!

Your conclusion should do two things:

- return to the main focus of the question, perhaps using its words;
- state for the final time how the writer's theme(s) are conveyed through the aspect identified in the question.

For example, a conclusion to the essay on "concealment and discovery" in two Tennessee Williams plays might read like this:

> In his plays, 'A Streetcar Named Desire' and 'Sweet Bird of Youth', Tennessee Williams creates characters for whom concealment has become a dangerous habit, and the inevitable revelation of their truths ultimately destroys them[1]. Through their experiences, Williams comments on the nature of human existence and how difficult it is to survive in an often hostile world when we are unable to come to terms with who we are, or what we once were [2].
>
> **Notes:**
> [1] Returns to the main focus of the question, using its words.
> [2] States how the writer's theme(s) are conveyed through the aspect identified in the question.

4.2.1 Conclusions to essays

Now try highlighting these three conclusions to essays, using the same colour-coded sections outlined above. The conclusions are in response to the same three essay questions used above.

Conclusions to essays

Go online

The following three questions include essay conclusions which are un-highlighted. Highlight the different parts to indicate the following three aspects of the conclusion:

- return to the main focus of the question;
- use the words of the question (this is not always necessary);
- state for the final time how the writer's theme(s) are conveyed through the aspect identified in the question.

Q4: *"Poetry is the spontaneous overflow of powerful feelings."* With close analysis of at least three poems, discuss how far you agree with this quotation.

Conclusion

In Sylvia Plath's poems about nature, she undoubtedly conveys powerful feelings about humankind's insignificance in the face of nature's overwhelming grandeur. This grandeur, perhaps contrary to our expectations, is often expressed as something hostile and even malevolent: something which can do great damage to us. Plath's poetic technique, however, is very tightly controlled, and rather than feeling particularly spontaneous her poems give the impression of being very precise pieces of art. Through these poems, Plath explores the nature of the human condition and our place in the natural world.

....

Q5: *"Money and power - it all comes down to that."* Discuss this quotation with reference to any two novels.

Conclusion

In F. Scott Fitzgerald's novels, 'The Great Gatsby' and 'Tender is the Night', he explores the connected ideas of money and power through his morally degenerate characters and their empty lives. Through their experiences, Fitzgerald comments on the nature of 1920s America, and the loss of more noble aspirations as a result of the greedy, self-obsessed search for material possessions and social status.

....

Q6: *"Effective drama is constructed from more than just dialogue."* Discuss this quotation with reference to any two plays.

Conclusion

In Tennessee Williams' plays, 'A Streetcar Named Desire' and 'Sweet Bird of Youth', plastic theatre, characterisation and dialogue are all used effectively to comment on the nature of human experience, revealing how individuals who fail to adapt to the truth of their situations will struggle to survive and will, ultimately, be destroyed by the brutal nature of the real world.

TOPIC 4. WRITING AN EFFECTIVE INTRODUCTION AND CONCLUSION 35

Conclusion to essay questions relevant to your literary texts

Now try writing your own conclusions to essay questions relevant to your literary texts. You could use the exemplar questions featured in the topic on 'The question', or essay questions from the Advanced Higher specimen paper. Follow the structure modeled above, and see if you can colour-code each part of your conclusion.

4.3 Learning points

Summary

You will now have:

- revised how to write an effective introduction;
- revised how to write an effective conclusion;
- practised writing your own introductions and conclusions for a number of different questions.

© HERIOT-WATT UNIVERSITY

Unit 1 Topic 5

How to compare

Contents

5.1 Introduction 38
    5.1.1 Planning to compare 38
5.2 Putting your proposed comparisons into practice 40
    5.2.1 Complete the three-step process 42
5.3 Learning points 42

Learning objective

By the end of this topic you will have:

- revised how to choose points of comparison;
- learned how to compare the ideas in your texts;
- learned how to compare the techniques used to convey these ideas.

38 UNIT 1. LITERARY STUDY: THE CRITICAL ESSAY

5.1 Introduction

In the 'Comparison of texts' topic in this section, you learned about how to plan an Advanced Higher essay.

Here's a reminder of the advice given in the 'Comparison of texts' topic about comparing your texts:

> Now that you have considered your ideas about each text, the next stage is to plan when you will be able to compare aspects of the texts. Remember, this is the main difference between an Advanced Higher essay and an essay you wrote at Higher. You should not think in terms of comparing every single point you make about one text with your other text.
>
> Think instead about **choosing two to three main areas of comparison**, connected to events in the text, which you can really discuss in detail. Providing an in-depth discussion of two to three key points of comparison is much more effective than trying to deal with too many points in a superficial way.

One of the exercises you completed was to highlight the ideas which stood out as possible areas where you could have a detailed discussion of comparisons between your texts. Remember that when you compare, you are looking to write about **significant aspects** of the texts.

5.1.1 Planning to compare

Think about comparing your texts using this three-step process:

1. Compare the 'big ideas' of your texts. The 'big ideas' are the themes, so consider what your writer is saying, for example, about the struggle to survive in a hostile world, or the state of a society or culture, or man's relationship with nature.

2. Now think about the means by which your writer conveys these themes. This will be through techniques such as characterisation, setting, aspects of structure, key events or scenes, use of language and dramatic techniques.

3. Now think about which aspects of these techniques are comparable. For example, does your writer present characters who are trying to cope with weaknesses in their personalities, or trying to escape from incidents in their past, or are struggling to reconcile challenging dilemmas in their lives? Or do the settings have similar characteristics which negatively influence the characters' lives or the way a persona feels?

© HERIOT-WATT UNIVERSITY

Comparison of texts for Tennessee Williams' plays

For example, notes on points of comparison for Tennessee Williams' plays, 'A Streetcar Named Desire' and 'Sweet Bird of Youth', following the three-step process, might look like this:

1. The 'big ideas' in 'Streetcar' and 'Sweet Bird':
   - the struggle for survival which characterises human experience;
   - the bleak nature of American culture.
2. The means by which these themes are explored through:
   - characterisation.
   - dramatic techniques and aspects of staging.
   - conflict between protagonists and antagonists.
3. Aspects of these techniques which are comparable:
   - characterisation of Blanche and Chance. Both create fantasy lives rather than face the truth of what they have become; both rely on alcohol and sex to block out the real world and sustain their fantasies; both have arguably been innocent and good, but corrupted by the hostile nature of the world around them;
   - dramatic techniques such as stage direction and aspects of staging such as light and music;
   - conflict with brutal, powerful characters (Stanley and Boss Finley) who represent the real world, which is uncompromising and hostile.

Remember, when you are dealing with two texts, you are expected to deal with each text, and to compare them, in roughly equal measure. But when you are dealing with three texts, if you are writing about poetry or short stories, you do not have to deal with each text in equal measure. Indeed, it might be the case that one of your texts does not fit the question as well as your other choices, and so your discussion of it will be less detailed.

5.2 Putting your proposed comparisons into practice

Here is an example of what part of one of these sections outlined above - the conflict between protagonists and antagonists - might look like.

> **Conflict between protagonists and antagonists**
>
> In both plays, there is significant conflict between the weak protagonists - Blanche and Chance[1] - and their much more powerful antagonists, Stanley and Boss Finley. Through these conflicts, Williams explores the brutal nature of American culture and shows how difficult it is for weaker people to survive in such a hostile environment.
>
> **The uncompromising nature of new American culture**
>
> Stanley Kowalski is Blanche's brother-in-law, and the son of Polish immigrants. As such, he represents the rise of the new America, one which does not rely on family tradition or social status in order to be successful. Stanley is forceful and honest, and he therefore clashes from the very beginning of the play with Blanche, who lives in a world characterised by various illusions which are sustained by lies.[2] From the outset of the play, when he remarks that
>
>> "Some people rarely touch it, but it touches them often"
>
> in response to Blanche's protestations that she doesn't drink, he shows that his forthright nature will not easily bend to Blanche's manipulative will. Williams brings this idea of honesty versus lies to a head when, just before Stanley rapes Blanche, he says to her,
>
>> "I've been onto you from the start! Not once did you pull any wool over this boy's eyes!"
>
> **Conflict with brutal, powerful characters who represent the real world**
>
> There are clear similarities between Stanley's nature and Boss Finley's. Like Stanley's alpha-male status in his friendship group, Boss Finley is a powerful character in St Cloud, who controls people and situations through a combination of fear, blackmail and violence.[3] When Heavenly remarks that he has such an "illusion of power", he replies,
>
>> "I have power, which is not an illusion."
>
> Like Stanley, he resorts to violence when he doesn't get his own way. When Heavenly refuses to speak with her father, Boss Finley is enraged, and the stage direction reads,
>
>> "He would have restrained her forcibly, if an old coloured manservant, Charles, had not, at that moment, come out on the porch."
>
> Stanley, too, resorts to violence when he is provoked: throwing the radio out the window, hitting Stella, and pulling the table cloth and dishes off the table set for Blanche's birthday, proclaiming,
>
>> "Every man is a King! And I am the king around here, so don't forget it!"
>
> Throughout the play, Stanley's music - the vibrant, energetic polka - is used by Williams to underline his life force, and the undeniable power he holds. Similarly, staging is used to reinforce the power that Boss Finley holds, seen perhaps most dramatically after Chance's failed attempts to impress his peers and his first - and only - encounter with Heavenly as she accompanies her father on the rally:
>
>> "As he walks downstage, there suddenly appears on the big TV screen which is the whole back wall of the stage, the image of Boss Finley."

The idea of Boss Finley's giant image looming over Chance is an effective symbol of his absolute authority, and of Chance's ultimate failure to overcome the Boss - and his own past - to reclaim Heavenly.

American values

Both Stanley and Boss Finley are used by Williams to represent American values.[4] Both are morally questionable, bullying, violent men, essentially selfish in their outlook and insensitive to others' needs, and yet they are in the ascendency. As they crush the protagonists, leaving one in the depths of insanity and the other facing metaphorical death, Williams leaves the audience in no doubt that modern American society leaves much to be desired.

Notes:

[1] This section acts as an introduction to the idea of conflict between characters. The idea of 'weak protagonists' in the opening line is a direct link to what the previous section of the essay dealt with: the nature of these flawed characters. Who is involved in the conflict is made clear, and the thematic purpose of the conflict.

[2] One aspect of the source of conflict between Stanley and Blanche is discussed: their opposing forthright and deceitful natures.

[3] This section looks at aspects of Boss Finley's character in comparison to Stanley's. Notice how points about Boss Finley and Stanley are connected by their key characteristics: power and violence.

[4] This is a summing-up section which draws together the purpose of these characters, and their thematic significance.

5.2.1 Complete the three-step process

Now try completing this exercise for your texts. Start by completing the three-step process outlined above.

You could complete the table in the activity below or write your notes in whichever way you prefer.

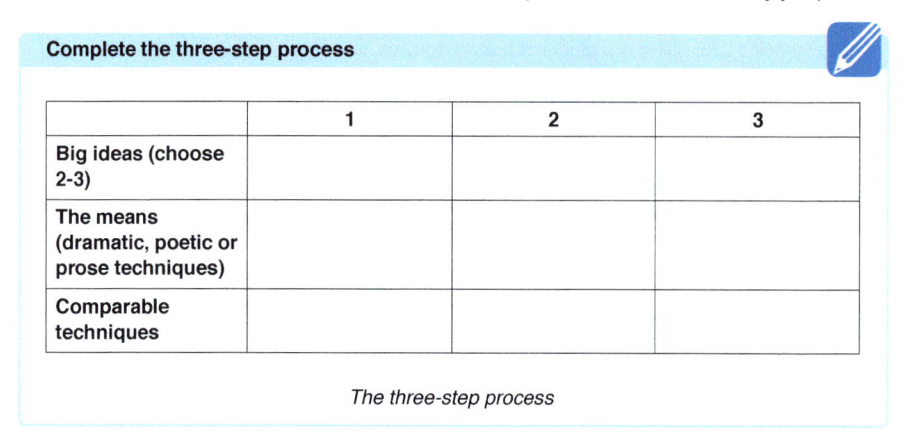

Complete the three-step process

	1	2	3
Big ideas (choose 2-3)			
The means (dramatic, poetic or prose techniques)			
Comparable techniques			

The three-step process

Then write up your sections - these do not need to be tied to any specific question focus (just as the exemplar above isn't in response to a particular question) because what you are doing is practising making comparisons between your texts rather than writing complete essays.

5.3 Learning points

Summary

You will now have:

- revised how to choose points of comparison;
- learned how to compare the ideas in your texts;
- learned how to compare the techniques used to convey these ideas.

Unit 1 Topic 6

Using secondary reading

Contents

6.1 Introduction 44
6.2 So what should you read? 44
6.3 How to take notes from your secondary sources 45
6.4 How to refer to secondary reading in the body of your literary study essay 46
6.5 Learning points 47

Learning objective

By the end of this topic you will:

- know how to incorporate secondary reading into a literary study essay.

6.1 Introduction

Studying Advanced Higher English means that you should have had the opportunity to study a range of texts and authors, and part of this study should have involved you considering secondary writing about your texts.

An important aspect of studying Advanced Higher English is developing literary research skills. Considering critical work about your authors, texts, or concepts associated with them, written by other people, enhances your understanding of texts and can offer helpful 'ways in' to them. The expectation is that you will incorporate ideas gained from your secondary reading of critical work into your dissertation, but referencing secondary sources in the literary study essay is equally useful and can add depth to your work.

6.2 So what should you read?

Good literary criticism can be found in a variety of places, and the source does not need to be in an essay, something we might think of as a traditional academic piece of writing. Easy to access, thoughtful, quality literary criticism can be found in book reviews published by quality newspapers - for example in The Times, The Telegraph and The Guardian, to name a few.

Google Scholar (https://scholar.google.co.uk/) can be a useful online site. Google Scholar provides a simple way to carry out a broad search for scholarly literature. From one place, you can search across many disciplines and sources: articles, theses, books, academic publishers, professional societies, online repositories, universities and other web sites. Some of the sources can be read online, some require a subscription before you can access the material, and some will provide titles of books which you may be able to source from your local library.

If you live near a university offering degrees in the arts, then its library can be accessed by S6 students, as long as you have completed a guest access form and received a temporary pass. Ask your teacher to make contact with the university on your behalf. University libraries provide a wealth of literary criticism and you are usually able to photocopy sections of particular interest without infringing copyright laws. Alternatively, you can spend time in the library browsing resources and taking notes on any relevant articles.

If you are studying a traditional text or author, then the Cambridge Companion (http://bit.ly/29vvd9U) series is a very helpful resource. This series brings together a collection of academic essays on aspects of an author's work, or a particular genre. For example, the 'Cambridge Companion to Tennessee Williams' has fourteen essays covering topics such as Williams' early years as a playwright, critical works on the major plays and Williams' relationship with Broadway critics. There are Cambridge Companion collections on Shakespeare, Ibsen, T.S. Eliot, Arthur Miller, Jane Austen and many more.

Finally, many of you will be familiar with the series York Notes (http://www.yorknotes.com/) and similar guides to literature, and with online sites such as Sparknotes (http://www.sparknotes.com/). These might provide some insight into your chosen text/author, but approach them with caution. They may not provide the level of thinking required for your purposes.

6.3 How to take notes from your secondary sources

A good place to start is by skim reading the article, looking for relevant ideas. Remember, academic pieces of literary criticism are often long and not all of the essay will be relevant to your chosen texts/author. Then, working with a highlighter pen, highlight any helpful and interesting ideas. The next step is the most important: you must show your understanding of what you have read by summarising it in your own words. Write this down beside the highlighted piece of text, if you have space, or write your notes on a separate piece of paper. It is important that you work through other people's ideas and form your own ideas from them, rather than just parroting what someone else has said.

If you're working from a photocopy of the original text, don't forget to write down the exact title of the essay, the name of its author and the book in which it appears, as well as the page number of the quotation/reference (in case you have to find it at a later date).

Remember, unlike in your dissertation, you are not approaching your secondary reading for the literary study from the focus of a specific question. Rather, you are looking to develop your general understanding of characters, key scenes, specific literary techniques and thematic concerns.

Example of how to take notes on a piece of literary criticism

In her essay 'A streetcar running fifty years', Felicia Hardison Londre makes the following point about common aspects of Tennessee Williams' plays: "... the focus on characters who are psychically wounded or otherwise marginalized by mainstream society: characters seeking lost purity, or escape from the ravages of time, or refuge from the harshness of an uncomprehending world, or simply human contact."[1]

Notes: Blanche and Chance fit this profile perfectly. Both are outsiders in the worlds they find themselves in - e.g. Blanche "incongruous to this setting". Both chasing lost innocence, which is particularly associated with their youth. Chance - desperate to be with Heavenly again because she represents his past, before he was corrupted. Blanche - frightened of growing old and no longer being desirable. Stanley doesn't understand Blanche - clash of values; two different ways of life.[2]

Notes:

[1] Quote the source.
[2] Summarise its ideas using your own words.

6.4 How to refer to secondary reading in the body of your literary study essay

It is likely that you will refer to secondary reading in your literary study essay on only two to three occasions. Citing a secondary source and your response to it will add depth to your writing and demonstrate your considered thinking about aspects of the texts, but the primary source - i.e. the texts themselves - will always be the main focus of any literary essay that you write.

Remember that evidence from your texts is what provides the basis for your line of argument; any reference to a secondary source is supporting evidence. One way to incorporate your secondary reading is therefore to use it to support an idea you have about a character, key scene or theme. For example, in a literary essay about Tennessee Williams' plays 'The Glass Menagerie' and 'A Streetcar Named Desire', one idea that might be covered is the comparison between Amanda and Blanche:

Exhibit 1: Example of how to refer to secondary reading in the body of your literary study essay

> *Example of how to refer to secondary reading in the body of your literary study essay*
>
> In both plays, Williams' central female characters cling desperately to the past. They both belong in a more gentle time, when culture and civilised behaviour were valued and they were desired by men operating strictly within the codes of traditional Southern manners. Amanda talks of the day she had, "... seventeen! - gentleman callers!" with whom she talked of "Never anything coarse or common or vulgar". This idea of a cultured past is echoed in Blanche's comment to Mitch that she can't bear a "rude remark or a vulgar action", and in her horrified comment to Stella about Stanley's primitive nature: "You can't have forgotten that much of our bringing up, Stella, that you just suppose that any part of a gentleman's in his nature!"[1]
>
> For both women, however, the past has been reconfigured into a much better time than it really was. **This is an idea explored by** CWE Bigsby in his essay 'Entering the Glass Menagerie'[2]:
>
> "For... Amanda, the past represents her youth, before time worked its dark alchemy. Memory has become myth, a story to be endlessly repeated as a protection against present decline"[3]
>
> **Bigsby identifies** that one way Amanda copes with the bleak reality of her current circumstance is by recreating her past into a time when life was full of possibilities. Her life when she was young has become a 'myth', a fantasy shaped into perfection to block out the harsh realities of what she and her family have become[4]. The fantasy-like nature of this myth is beautifully represented by Williams when Amanda recalls her 'craze' with jonquils in the spring of her debutante year:
> "Jonquils became an absolute obsession... whenever, wherever I saw them, I'd say, 'Stop! Stop! I see jonquils!' I made the young men help me gather the jonquils!"
> The breathless nature of her delivery highlights the idea of the memory of that time having been reshaped into something perfectly romantic and full of hope, emotions which contrast sharply with the bleak reality of her failed marriage, her crippled daughter and her disaffected son, desperate to escape. Williams develops the jonquils metaphor when Amanda fills the apartment with them just before Jim, the much longed for gentleman caller, pays a visit.[5]

> **Notes:**
>
> [1] This paragraph introduces a key idea about the characters: their inability to move on from the past, especially in the face of their disappointing present realities.
> [2] This statement introduces the idea from the secondary source, naming the author and the source. Note the key sentence starter in bold.
> [3] The secondary source is quoted.
> [4] The comment which follows demonstrates understanding of the secondary source's idea. Note the key sentence starter.
> [5] This section develops the idea of Amanda feverishly reinventing her past by referring to another part in the play which demonstrates this.

Can you see how the idea from the secondary source is fully integrated into the candidate's ideas about Blanche and Amanda? The secondary source should always support what you are saying about the text, and therefore you must demonstrate your understanding of it by using it as a springboard for your own discussion.

> **Using secondary reading**
>
> Once you have found some useful ideas from secondary sources, your next step is to practise using them when you write about your texts. You should complete mini sections like the one above. Take an idea about your text, either about a specific character, or key incident, or theme, and consider how you could incorporate an idea from a secondary source. Follow the outline that has been used in the exemplar:
>
> 1. introduce the key idea;
> 2. introduce the secondary source, using the key sentence starter;
> 3. comment on the secondary source to demonstrate your understanding of it;
> 4. develop your point by referring to another part of the text.

6.5 Learning points

> **Summary**
>
> You will now:
>
> - know how to incorporate secondary reading into a literary study essay.

Unit 1 Topic 7

Exemplar literary essays

Contents

7.1 Introduction 50
7.2 Tennessee Williams essay 50
7.3 Sylvia Plath essay 55
7.4 Literary essays: Assessment criteria 58
7.5 Learning points 58

Learning objective

By the end of this topic you will have:

- read two exemplar literary study essays;
- considered how the aspects covered in previous topics are put together in a complete essay.

7.1 Introduction

Considering other Advanced Higher students' work can provide a useful model for how to put together an essay of your own. Two complete essays, written under timed examination conditions in response to unseen questions, are exemplified here. One is on Tennessee Williams, the other on Sylvia Plath.

The first essay, on Tennessee Williams, has been annotated to show its component parts. The second essay, on Sylvia Plath, provides an opportunity for you to annotate the essay's component parts. Picking apart an essay is a very useful task; it helps you to see how an essay is put together which will in turn help you to create your own essay plans and ultimately whole essays. Once you have completed your own annotation of the Sylvia Plath essay, you can then compare it against the one provided for you.

7.2 Tennessee Williams essay

The essay below was written in response to the following exam question:

"Concealment and discovery are central to any drama".

Discuss the structural and thematic significance of concealment and discovery in any two plays.

Tennessee Williams essay

'A Streetcar Named Desire' and 'Sweet Bird of Youth' by Tennessee Williams are two plays which explore concealment and discovery, both thematically and structurally.[1] 'A Streetcar Named Desire', a play set in 1940s New Orleans, features the central character of Blanche DuBois - a somewhat lost woman who goes to stay with her sister, Stella, and her brother-in-law, Stanley Kowalski, after she is fired from her job as an English teacher. In order to escape her troubled past, Blanche drinks excessively, hides from direct light and lies compulsively. Similarly, in 'Sweet Bird of Youth', Chance Wayne, an aspiring, and failing, actor who returns to his home town of St Cloud with washed-up actress, Alexandra Del Lago, in order to reclaim his teenage love, Heavenly Finley, becomes reliant on drugs and alcohol to hide the truth of his past - mainly from himself.[2] In both plays, Tennessee Williams expertly applies a range of literary techniques to emphasise his characters' need to conceal the truth about themselves and, ultimately, their discovery and cruel exposure[3].

Throughout both 'A Streetcar Named Desire' and 'Sweet Bird of Youth', Tennessee Williams successfully uses characterisation to promote the idea of concealment and discovery.[4] From the outset, it is clear to the audience that both of Williams' main characters have complex and difficult pasts[5]. Blanche DuBois, it is revealed, was forced into prostitution following the loss of her childhood home, Belle Reve, and, in order to evade these past hardships, Blanche begins to rely heavily on alcohol to numb her:

"I know you must have some liquor on the place! Where could it be, I wonder? Oh, I spy, I spy!" [She rushes to the closet and removes the bottle; she is shaking all over and panting for breath as she tries to laugh. The bottle nearly slips from her grasp.]

By mentioning that the "bottle nearly slips from her grasp", Williams cleverly highlights how

desperate she is to escape reality and that she has become dependant on the fantasy world provided by her alcoholism. This is shown further through her attempt to laugh as it is suggested that she is trying to downplay how much she really needs a drink and is trying to act as though she is not, in fact, an addict. Blanche's compulsive lying in order to conceal how damaged she truly is, is demonstrated here, too, as the audience is aware that she has already discovered, and drank from, this liquor prior to pretending to uncover it for the first time at this moment. This is significant as it suggests that Blanche cannot admit the truth about her current mental state, even to her sister, Stella: her only remaining family.[6] Comparably, Chance Wayne, who failed in his mission for stardom and, consequently, spent time as a gigolo, cannot face his own reality and finds an escape in drugs, alcohol and sex:
"What did you just take, Chance? You took something out of your pocket and washed it down with liquor."
"Yes, I took a wild dream and - washed it down with another wild dream. Aunt Nonnie, that's my life now..."
Chance's sorry state is emphasised here as the audience can clearly see that he is dependant on drugs and alcohol in order to hide from his past. His relationship with Aunt Nonnie is significant as she is the character who reveals the extent of Chance's fantasies - perhaps most notably, the talent contest entered by Chance and Heavenly that they are originally said to have won. It is soon revealed, however, that this is Chance's embellished version of the story:
"Aunt Nonnie, we didn't win that lousy national contest, we just placed second."
"Chance, you didn't place second. You got honourable mention. Fourth place, except it was just called honourable mention."
"Just honourable mention. But in a national contest, honourable mention means something..."[7]

This creates a contrast[8] with 'A Streetcar Named Desire' as Blanche acknowledges her past but attempts to hide it from others and creates her world of illusion in order to achieve this - and lies to keep this fantasy world intact - whereas, if anything, Chance Wayne is trying to conceal the truth from himself as he longs for fame and fortune and cannot come to terms with the fact that he has not and will not achieve this. His inability to accept the truth of his past and current situation is enforced when he says: "honourable mention means something" as the audience and, indeed, the other characters in the play, can see that Chance's memories of his own past have been greatly exaggerated and he has imagined himself to have been a young man with huge potential in order to cope with the fact that he has achieved nothing.

Williams' characterisation of the antagonists in both plays is important[9]. It is these destructive characters who force the discovery of the protagonists' hidden pasts[10]. In 'A Streetcar Named Desire', Blanche faces conflict with her brother-in-law, Stanley, who tries, and succeeds, to expose her lies and destroy her fantasy world. Likewise, in 'Sweet Bird of Youth', Chance has conflict with Boss Finley, Heavenly's father, who threatens to castrate Chance if he ever returns to St Cloud, which, of course, at the beginning of the play, he does[11]. These characters help to highlight Williams' theme, common to both plays, of illusion versus reality, with Blanche and Chance representing the illusion and Stanley and Boss being the personification of brutal reality.[12]

Scene Ten in 'A Streetcar Named Desire' and Scene Two, Act Two in 'Sweet Bird of Youth' are two structurally important key scenes in both plays when the concealed pasts of the main characters are revealed[13]. In 'A Streetcar Named Desire', Scene Ten is the climax of the conflict between Blanche and Stanley. Here we can see the theme of fantasy versus reality at its strongest as Stanley shatters Blanche's world of illusion by exposing her lies. Williams' use of plastic theatre is especially significant in these scenes as in Scene Ten, when Blanche is raped by Stanley, the use of light adds to the dramatic and threatening tone: "[Lurid reflections appear on the walls around Blanche. The shadows are of a grotesque and menacing form.]"

These distorted figures surrounding Blanche not only help to show her own internal demons but also highlight how Stanley and, equally, reality, is closing in on Blanche and threaten to suffocate her. When Stanley says "we've had this date from the beginning", Williams makes it clear that concealment will inevitably be discovered and brutally exposed. Dominant characters who represent a way of life in the ascendency will inevitably triumph over the weak, those who have failed to adapt to their circumstances[14]. Plastic theatre is used effectively in 'Sweet Bird of Youth' too[15]. Here, Williams uses music in order to explore his theme of dreams versus reality further. In Act Two, Scene Two we see Chance desperately try to pretend that he has made it in the world in front of his old friends but the contrast between him and these friends only makes his fantasy world more evident. In the scene, he sings 'It's a Big Wide Wonderful World' which is incredibly ironic and helps the audience discover Chance's concealed past as he has never mastered the world and gained international fame like he so longed to do. Chance's exaggerated situation is cruelly revealed when the Princess, Alexandra Del Lago, appears in the bar, drunk, and shatters the illusion of glamour that Chance had been boasting about:

"[The Princess looks as if she had thrown on her clothes to escape a building on fire. Her blue-sequined gown is unzipped, or partially zipped, her hair is dishevelled, her eyes have a dazed, drugged brightness]"

The sad reality of Chance's famous movie star is seen by everyone and Chance's fantasy world is discovered. Here, Chance begins to gain self-knowledge and see what he has become but he can never fully grasp his own situation nor save himself from the consequences he faces because he's been romanticising his past for too long. As well as this, in Act Two, Scene Two, Boss Finley's power is made clear through the stage backdrop which displays a huge picture of Boss Finley, looming over Chance's defeated figure, and the audience becomes aware that the only way the play can possibly end is with Chance's destruction[16]. This is clear, too[17], in 'A Streetcar Named Desire':
"[She sinks to her knees. He picks up her inert figure and carries her to the bed. The hot trumpet and drums from the Four Deuces sound loudly.]"

Stanley's rape of Blanche is symbolic of the fantasy world being destroyed by harsh reality. Additionally, the overpowering of the old America by the new America is shown here, with the music of the new America playing while Stanley exposes and destroys his sister-in-law. The sheer power and brutality of Stanley Kowalski is emphasised here by his overpowering of Blanche but, also, Blanche's giving up and inability to fight off Stanley highlights how her constant lies in order to keep up the facade that she is coping with life has exhausted her and, thus, the fantasy world shatters.

Structurally, both of these key scenes act as turning points for the main characters. As their fantasy worlds are cruelly exposed, their ultimate fates are sealed.[18]

The endings of both 'A Streetcar Named Desire' and 'Sweet Bird of Youth' are incredibly significant as both suggest that, after the discovery of the main characters' concealment, life carries on for the other characters[19]. Though Blanche and Chance have effectively been destroyed by their inability to face the truth, and their subsequent exposure and realisation, the other characters in these plays continue to live their lives and survive. Stella's decision to stay with Stanley emphasises this:
"I couldn't believe her story and go on living with Stanley."
The audience is aware that Stella must know the truth about her husband and yet her best chance for survival with her newborn son is to stay with him, thus enforcing Williams' point about how, as humans, we must either adapt, like Stella has been able to, or perish, like Blanche has. Comparably, in 'Sweet Bird of Youth', Chance's decision to stay in St Cloud and face the consequences suggests that he knows he cannot adapt and, therefore, will inevitably be destroyed by Boss Finley and Tom Jnr:
"I don't ask for your pity, but just for your understanding - not even that - no. Just for your recognition of me in you, and the enemy, time, in us all."
Here, it is clear that Chance has accepted his unfortunate fate as he no longer has the energy to fight for himself and, like Blanche, is surrendering to his destruction. Chance has achieved self-knowledge at last, but this time he won't run away from the truth[20]. Williams' theme is clear: the audience can see that time - symbolised for Chance and Blanche by their growing old - is a more powerful force than us, and that unless we can adapt in order to survive, and face the truth about ourselves, it will destroy us[21].

Overall, concealment and discovery are certainly central to two of Tennessee Williams' plays, 'A Streetcar Named Desire' and 'Sweet Bird of Youth'. By exploring his theme of dreams versus reality in both plays, Williams reveals that we must adapt to any changes and learn to survive; something which both his central characters, Blanche DuBois and Chance Wayne, fail to do, and they are ultimately destroyed as a consequence of their weakness. Williams reveals to his audience, through his use of characterisation and other literary techniques, that human experience is complex and that survival can be a struggle, especially when we cannot face the truth of ourselves or our pasts[22].

Notes:
[1] Clear opening statement related to the question.
[2] Statements about the action in each play, with references to the idea of the main characters' concealment.
[3] A concluding statement which comes back to the question.
[4] Section 1 in the argument: how characterisation conveys the idea of concealment and discovery.
[5] The focus is clearly on comparing the main characters.
[6] A discussion of one aspect of Blanche's concealment: her alcoholism.
[7] A discussion of a similar aspect of Chance's character: his escape through sex,

drugs and alcohol.
[8] Link to introduce discussion of a way the characters differ.
[9] The next stage in the argument is clearly signposted. The candidate moves on to consider the role played by other characters.
[10] The use of the words 'discovery' and 'hidden pasts' demonstrate that the candidate is still firmly on-task.
[11] Identification of the role played by the antagonists. Note the use of the word 'Likewise' to signal a comparative point.
[12] Clear statement connecting characters with a central theme in the play.
[13] Section 2 in the argument: the structural importance of key scenes.
[14] Detailed discussion of a key scene in 'Streetcar', covering characterisation, theme and dramatic technique. Clear references to the question tie the candidate's discussion of evidence from the text to the focus of the question.
[15] Connecting statement linking Williams' use of dramatic technique in both plays.
[16] Detailed discussion of the key scene in 'Sweet Bird', covering characterisation, theme and dramatic technique. Clear references to the question tie the candidate's discussion of evidence from the text to the focus of the question.
[17] Linking phrase signalling another point of comparison between the plays.
[18] A summing up statement on this key scenes section, covering the structural significance of the characters' discovery.
[19] Section 3 in the candidate's argument: the endings of the plays.
[20] Discussion of the ends of each play. Note the use of "Though Blanche and Chance...", "Comparably..." and "like Blanche..." to signal the candidate's focus on comparing these characters and their experiences.
[21] Section 3 concludes with a clear statement linking together theme and the question.
[22] A conclusion to the argument, starting with a statement concerning the question, followed by a summary of how the characters in the plays convey Williams' universal concern of the nature of human experience.

7.3 Sylvia Plath essay

The essay below was written in response to the following exam question:

With reference to at least three poems by a particular poet, discuss the effectiveness of the poet's use of nature and the natural world in the presentation of significant themes and ideas.

Exhibit 2: Sylvia Plath essay

Sylvia Plath essay

In the poems, 'Sleep in the Mojave Desert', 'Two Campers in Cloud Country' and 'Blackberrying', Sylvia Plath makes use of the natural world to convey her ideas about the overwhelming stature of nature, the hostility of the natural environment and the persona's feelings of loss of self-worth and identity.

The idea of the over-whelming stature of the natural world is one which is developed throughout 'Two Campers in Cloud Country'. Plath's main concern in this poem is the insignificance of man, compared with the grandeur of the natural world. Although this theme is explored in all three poems, it is of particular significance in 'Two Campers'. We see this from the opening line of the poem, when Plath writes:
"In this country there is neither measure nor balance."

The 'measure' and 'balance' referred to here are presumably those qualities we associate with humans; they are based on human terms and human ways of interpreting the world. If the ways by which humans understand the world - all their 'measure' and 'balance' - have no meaning in the wider context of our natural environment, then humans are, in reality, nothing but a dot on a much vaster landscape. Plath also introduces an important idea developed in many of her poems about nature: the natural world's indifference to man's ways, which man has always assumed are superior.

This theme of the superiority of nature over man is developed when Plath writes about the clouds in Rock Lake, describing them as 'man-shaming'. The sense of superiority which humankind feels about itself is purely self-created and hints at arrogance, but when set against the stature of clouds, mankind's superiority is rendered meaningless. More than this, we are seen to be very much inferior and completely insignificant in comparison to nature. Man would assume that he is superior to a mere cloud in the sky, but Plath shows us that the truth is the reverse: man is nothing compared to the grandeur of nature, whether living or inanimate. We see this again when Plath writes of the clouds:
"No gesture of yours or mine could catch their attention,
No word make them..."

Here we see the basis of human understanding turned on its head. Our 'gestures' and 'words' mean nothing to nature and so we ourselves, and our place in the world, therefore mean nothing too. The combination of this idea and the idea that the "Pilgrims and Indians might not have happened" creates an overall suggestion of the sheer extent of the gap between man and nature. The idea of ineffectual 'gestures' and 'words' combined with the idea of the 'Pilgrims and the Indians' reinforces that nature is very much superior to us. This is because through the reference to the Pilgrims and Indians, Plath shows that generations of whole civilisations have lived in this landscape and left no impression on it. The natural environment is so large and incomparably vaster than humankind that we simply cannot compete with the scale and grandeur of it. It shrugs off our presence and does not pay its respects to us: we mean nothing.

We also see the theme of the overwhelming power of nature in "Sleep in the Mojave Desert". Here Plath uses personification to suggest the power that the natural environment has to distort and control insignificant humankind. We see this when she writes about the 'mad straight road'. In the desert, Plath sees a line of trees along her path, a path which is never ending and which she feels is taunting her. In the same way she used the idea of the pilgrims and Indians in 'Two Campers' to express man's inability to shape or tame nature, in 'Sleep in the Mojave Desert', Plath writes that the landscape gives very little away about its past. She says that, "One can remember men and houses...", suggesting that there is no trace of previous inhabitants. More disturbingly, and different from 'Two Campers', Plath introduces the harshness of the natural world. Plath suggests that the reason for her being only able to 'remember' this civilisation is because it could not be sustained in the harsh environment of the desert. Once again, despite his best efforts, man has been unable to tame nature and claim it for his own.

This idea of nature's hostility towards man is developed in "Blackberrying". In this poem, Plath expresses the idea of the threat of nature, and one of its threats is its overwhelming power over man. We see this conveyed as the persona walks towards the sea, describing the blackberry bushes as 'hooks', as if she is being pulled against her will, hooked into facing a terrible ordeal.

The end of the poem acts to show the threat and danger of the natural world because of its uncontrollable, overwhelming superiority and power over our lives. Here, Plath reaches what she has been anticipating with dread throughout the poem: the sea. She describes the noise of the sea as:
"... a din like silversmiths
Beating and beating at an intractable metal."

The repetition of 'beating' suggests the sea's threatening nature, and the persona's hopelessness of ever being in a position to make a connection with nature. Not only is nature superior to human life, it is also incompatible with it. Nature has no place for humankind and the likening of it to an 'intractable metal' suggests that no amount of human effort can ever change this reality. Nature is simply too powerful, and does not need man's intervention in any way.

We see this idea of the hostility of nature described in all three poems. It is prominent in "Sleep in the Mojave Desert" and 'Blackberrying'. In the first of the two, we get the impression of this idea from the very beginning of the poem. The opening line, "Out here there are no hearthstones", suggests the coldness and lack of comfort towards man. Hearthstones have connotations of warmth and homeliness. The absence of these representative things shows nature's unwillingness to accommodate man and the threat that could result from this. Plath goes on to write:
"It is dry, dry/And the air dangerous".

To suggest that the very air presents danger shows the sheer extent of nature's harshness. The air is, of course, all around, so if it is dangerous then there is no escaping the hostility of nature. It is all around and unavoidable. This idea is echoed in 'Blackberrying' when the persona describes the 'slap' of the wind as she makes her way along the sea path.

We again see the hostility when she writes,
"And the crickets come creeping into our hair
To fiddle the short night away."

The use of the word 'fiddle' here could be interpreted as symbolic of hell and the fiddling duel a person must have with the devil in order to save his or her soul. This suggests a strong conflict between the natural environment and man, comparable to the battle between good and evil or man and the devil. The devil presents a danger and threat to man, and so having nature representative of this figure of the greatest threat draws the same comparison. Just as with the devil, nature is something to be feared and highly wary of, not something that can live harmoniously alongside man.

In a similar way, "Blackberrying" shows a progressive fear of nature and the threat it presents. The word 'blackberries' is repeated in each of the first four lines, which suggests an oppressive, claustrophobic atmosphere in which the persona is stifled. Her path is surrounded by them. She cannot escape them. It is almost as if they are closing in on her. She describes the sea as being, "Somewhere at the end of it". The fact that she cannot see an end emphasises the fear of the situation heightening her claustrophobia and feeling of being trapped.

As well as being caught by the blackberries' hooks, the persona observes that the blackberries insinuate themselves upon her:
"... blue-red juices. These squander on my fingers.
I had not asked for such a blood sisterhood;"

The idea of her blood mixing with the blood-like juice of the berries suggests that the persona feels as if a connection between her and nature has been imposed upon her; a connection which perhaps nature uses to mock her insignificance. The connection is false, allowing nature to show that it does not need her and that she is not welcome. This idea links with the persona's perceived lack of self-worth. Knowing she is insignificant in terms of her stature in the natural world and her inability to tame its wild nature, she feels unworthy of the berries' attention. That she is an outsider in an unfriendly world is reinforced by the symbolic choughs, which caw repeatedly as she makes her way to the sea:
"Theirs is the only voice, protesting, protesting."

Choughs, as a member of the crow family, are traditionally representative of death. They are often used as a metaphor to describe the journey from the physical to the spiritual world, carrying the souls from one to the other. And, for those souls who cannot make it to the spiritual world, the crows cry out. So here it could be said that as the choughs cry out for those who are caught between two worlds, they cry for the persona who is caught between the worlds of nature and humanity, belonging to neither.

We also see a suggestion towards the persona's feeling of self-worthlessness at the end of "Two Campers", but in this poem the suggestion is much less threatening. The persona describes the "old simplicities" as "Lethe", a river in Greek mythology which provokes forgetfulness of the past. It seems that the persona is content to forget the past and live in a world where she is of no significance, and there are no expectations of her. Acceptance of her second-best place in the world brings a liberation and ease.

The natural world in many of Plath's poems is conveyed in a negative light. In these three particular poems, she explores our insignificance in the face of nature's overwhelming grandeur as well as nature's capacity to embody hostility and threat. Her poems about the natural world lead us to contemplate, as the persona does, our place in the world.

Sylvia Plath essay Go online

Q1: Annotate the component parts in the essay above (Exhibit 2). Look for identification of the writer's stages in her argument, references to the question, references to theme, and phrases which signal points of comparison.

Once you have annotated the essay, compare your annotations to those in the answer at the end of this section.

7.4 Literary essays: Assessment criteria

Now that you've annotated this essay, look at the assessment criteria provided by the SQA for assigning a mark to literary essays. What mark would you assign them, and why?

If we look at the criteria for assessing the literary essay, we can see that both essays demonstrate the following features:

- secure understanding of the texts;
- extensive use of textual evidence which clearly supports the demands of the question;
- relevant analysis of a task-appropriate range of literary techniques which strengthens the line of argument;
- a clearly identifiable evaluative stance securely based on evidence discussed within the response.

These characteristics put the essays in the 18-16 range. The Williams essay meets all the criteria comfortably, and is awarded 18 marks. The Plath essay is less secure and is awarded 16.

You will have noticed that there are no secondary sources referenced in these essays. While this does not detract from their overall quality, remember that you can add further depth to your critical analysis by quoting and commenting on secondary sources.

7.5 Learning points

Summary

You will now have:

- read two exemplar literary study essays;
- considered how the aspects covered in previous topics are put together in a complete essay.

Unit 1 Topic 8
Literary study test

60 UNIT 1. LITERARY STUDY: THE CRITICAL ESSAY

Literary study test   Go online

You can see a suggested essay structure in the answers to the following questions. Your teacher can provide you with comments and an indicative mark for your answer.

Q1: Prose Fiction: Question 9 in the 2016 SQA Advanced Higher Literary Study paper

Discuss the role and function of complex central characters in any two novels. *(20 marks)*

....

Q2: Poetry: Question 3 in the 2016 SQA Advanced Higher Literary Study paper

Poetry allows the female voice to be heard and women's experiences to be valued.

With reference to at least three poems by a female poet, discuss the effectiveness of their presentation of women's experiences. *(20 marks)*

....

Q3: Drama: Question 28 in the 2016 SQA Advanced Higher Literary Study paper

Discuss how internal and external conflict is central to the dramatic impact of any two plays. *(20 marks)*

Unit 1 Topic 9

Acknowledgements

- *Tennessee Williams*, A Streetcar Named Desire
- *Tennessee Williams*, Sweet Bird of Youth
- *Sylvia Plath*, Sleep in the Mojave Desert
- *Sylvia Plath*, Two Campers in Cloud Country
- *Sylvia Plath*, Blackberrying
- *Sylvia Plath*, Wuthering Heights
- *F Scott Fitzgerald*, The Great Gatsby
- *F Scott Fitzgerald*, Tender is the Night

Textual analysis

1	General principles of textual analysis	65
	1.1 What is textual analysis?	66
	1.2 Rationale and design	66
	1.3 Choice of texts	66
	1.4 Cumulative approach to tasks	67
	1.5 Exam requirements	67
	1.6 On your marks	68
	1.7 Learning points	68
2	Poetry	69
	2.1 Sound and vision	70
	2.2 Square as a sonnet	70
	2.3 Poems: part one	71
	2.4 Poems: part two	73
	2.5 Poetry: Exam practice	77
	2.6 Writing a critical response	79
	2.7 Video resources	83
	2.8 Annotated poems	84
	2.9 Learning points	90
3	Prose fiction	91
	3.1 Prose fiction	92
	3.2 About time	92
	3.3 Extract one from 'Butcher's Broom'	93
	3.4 Extract two from 'Butcher's Broom'	96
	3.5 Extract three from 'Butcher's Broom'	99
	3.6 Annotated extracts	102
	3.7 Learning points	108
4	Prose non-fiction	109
	4.1 The good news	110
	4.2 Health warnings	110
	4.3 Features (mostly) unique to non-fiction	110
	4.4 Features shared with other genres	111

64 UNIT 2. TEXTUAL ANALYSIS

 4.5 Extract one from 'My Own Story' 112
 4.6 Extract two from 'My Own Story' 113
 4.7 Further work 115
 4.8 Additional information and resources 116
 4.9 Annotated extracts 117
 4.10 Learning points 119

5 Drama **121**
 5.1 Principles of drama 122
 5.2 How this topic will help you 122
 5.3 Learning point: dramatic function 123
 5.4 Learning point: a crash course in Greek tragedy 123
 5.5 Learning point: central conflict 124
 5.6 Extract from drama: Worked example 125
 5.7 Annotated extracts 132
 5.8 Learning points 138

6 Conclusions and consolidation **139**
 6.1 Conclusions 140
 6.2 Checklist: Questions to ask yourself 140
 6.3 Advice: Hold back 140
 6.4 Advice: Annotation, annotation, annotation 141
 6.5 Other resources to help you 141
 6.6 Learning points 141

7 Textual analysis test **143**

8 Acknowledgements **153**

Unit 2 Topic 1

General principles of textual analysis

Contents

1.1 What is textual analysis? 66
1.2 Rationale and design 66
1.3 Choice of texts 66
1.4 Cumulative approach to tasks 67
1.5 Exam requirements 67
1.6 On your marks 68
1.7 Learning points 68

Learning objective

By the end of this topic you will be:

- confident about what textual analysis is;
- aware of how your previous years in English have prepared you for this;
- secure about the demands of the exam.

1.1 What is textual analysis?

By the time you read this you'll already have had five years of learning how to compose a response to a question about a literary text. That's what textual analysis is.

The main differences between the practice in your past and the prospective textual analysis exam is that the response you compose will be on an unseen text and it will have to be more extensive and detailed than at Higher. Everything else you've been taught and all the good habits you bring with you to Advanced Higher English will be of significant value to this, newly compulsory, part of the course.

1.2 Rationale and design

There are four topics representing the four genres you can choose from in your exam:

- poetry;
- prose fiction;
- prose non-fiction;
- drama.

Hence, each topic offers you opportunities to hone your skills in each genre. Most learners will have a genre they're more confident about than others; here, you're encouraged to have a good look at all genres and, hopefully, renew or strengthen your acquaintance with all - including, perhaps, those you weren't too keen on!

Each topic has its own introductory advice about how to tackle the unique challenges brought by each genre. Approaching a non-fiction text is markedly different from tackling poetry, and every attempt has been made to give 'bespoke' pointers for each.

Extracts are accompanied by notes to support your understanding and questions for you to practise. Suggested answers are given for these extracts (more about this in the section 'On your marks' below).

1.3 Choice of texts

Because the over-arching aim here is to offer learners something new as well as build on existing skills and knowledge, an attempt has been made to offer a variety of texts from different periods. The drama text is from a classical Greek tragedy because it lends itself well to the study of dramatic function, conflict and the meaning of tragedy itself. We'll discuss links between it and features of contemporary drama.

The non-fiction text has a contemporary element because of the 2015 film about the movement led by Emmeline Pankhurst; the extracts chosen here aim to draw your attention to the way in which non-fiction is the 'odd one out' in terms of the genres, because so many of its features are unique to non-fiction and it can be easy for any learner to overlook this when writing about it.

You are likely, also, to have heard of either Neil Gunn or of his subject matter in 'Butcher's Broom', a novel about the Highland Clearances, so it is hoped this might generate both interest and a bit of confidence for tackling the prose fiction passages and tasks presented here.

For poetry we start gently with a sonnet and finish, less gently, with a murderous Duke.

1.4 Cumulative approach to tasks

The questions with the extracts are designed to become incrementally more challenging as you work through each topic. Furthermore, the annotated notes with each extract should serve to support your understanding of the extracts and confidence for tackling the questions.

Each topic ends with an exam-type question about an extract more extensive that the previous ones, to give you an idea of what you might get in the exam and allow you to practise this in timed conditions, if you choose to.

1.5 Exam requirements

In one hour and 30 minutes you are essentially required to write a substantial and extensive critical analysis of the text or extract whose question you choose to respond to.

The question belonging to each extract could be either very general, e.g. "Write a critical response to this poem...", essentially giving you carte blanche in terms of which features and techniques you examine, and how; or very specific, for example, the 2013 Drama question:

"Make a detailed analysis of the means by which Michael Frayn [the dramatist] explores the Bohrs' relationship with Heisenberg. In your answer you should pay close attention to:

- dramatic structure;
- dialogue;
- the significance of uncertainty."

As part of your preparation it might be good to consider whether you'd be happier with a very 'open' question (such as the poetry one, above) or indeed more comfortable with a question that offers very specific points, such as the drama one. Throughout the topics here you'll have a chance to practise both.

1.6 On your marks

Your response will be marked out of 20, with three categories being assessed:

- understanding;
- analysis;
- evaluation.

Detailed marking instructions are readily available on the SQA website which, if you aren't already, it is recommended you become familiar with.

A word about the answers given for the tasks in the topics here: for obvious reasons the answers given do not try to represent or emulate a full answer such as the one required from candidates. What is offered in the answers here are many (but not all) of the possible points you could and should make in a response to the relevant questions. Often these are given here in bullet point format for easy of reading.

1.7 Learning points

Summary

You will now be:

- confident about what textual analysis is;
- aware of how your previous years in English have prepared you for this;
- secure about the demands of the exam.

Unit 2 Topic 2

Poetry

Contents
2.1 Sound and vision 70
2.2 Square as a sonnet 70
  2.2.1 Some technical terms for your toolkit 71
2.3 Poems: part one 71
  2.3.1 William Shakespeare 'Sonnet 116' 71
  2.3.2 John Keats 'When I have fears' 72
2.4 Poems: part two 73
  2.4.1 Robert Browning 'The Lost Leader' 73
  2.4.2 Robert Browning 'My Last Duchess' 75
2.5 Poetry: Exam practice 77
2.6 Writing a critical response 79
2.7 Video resources 83
2.8 Annotated poems 84
2.9 Learning points 90

Learning objective

By the end of this topic you will have:

- strengthened your understanding of how form and content work in poetry;
- refreshed your understanding of structural principles in poetry;
- performed a detailed analysis of a dramatic monologue;
- practised identifying and writing about themes in poetry.

2.1 Sound and vision

Reading poetry is as much about how the text looks on paper as about its contents, but this was not always the case: poetry started out as an oral medium, long before the days of print, so it was important for people to be able to remember texts - which is where rhyme comes in. In fact, the more you are able to listen to poetry being performed, the better (see also 'Further resources' in this topic) because it's a great way of strengthening your understanding of a poem.

The other main principle for us here is the way form mirrors content: you're unlikely to find a haiku about a tsunami because there is too much incongruence between the brevity of the former and the overwhelming nature of the latter. That might sound simple, but it's good to remember analysis and evaluation can lie in the 'little things'; poetry doesn't need to be overly complex or esoteric but analysis of poetry does require the reader to make good use of their (figurative) magnifying glass.

2.2 Square as a sonnet

If we are thinking about form and content in poetry there are few better places to start than with the sonnet, so for our 'warm-up' we will do a bit of work on this form. The compact, efficient, precise sonnet does not always play by one set of rules, but it remains instantly recognisable whether it takes the form of the Italian or the English sonnet. Simply put, the Italian-style sonnet comprises an octave and a sestet (8 + 6) with a volta (a break, or 'turn') in between, while the English (or Shakespearean) sonnet is structured by 3 quatrains and a couplet (4 + 4 + 4 + 2). Each type of sonnet has its own rhyme scheme holding their 14 lines together and generally does appear square in shape because the iambic pentameter allows for little variation in line length. There is an assumption that you are familiar with this form and these terms.

(Fun to know: in 1862 the poet George Meredith wrote a series of 50 sonnets of 16 (!) lines each, called 'Modern Love', on the subject of the collapse of a marriage. One critic referred to the sequence as "a grave moral mistake" - although whether this was because the sonnets had 16 lines or whether it was to do with the subject matter is unknown.)

The poet Dante Rossetti called the sonnet "a moment's monument" and this is where the close link with form and content emerges: if the sonnet's main themes tend to be celebrations of immortality, love, loss, time or eternity - i.e. capturing, forever, a person or emotion - what better form to do this in than a poem that resembles a photograph in the way it captures a moment?

The sonnet's relatively strict rules can teach us a lot about linguistic techniques such as inversion (the changing of word order), rhyme scheme and, especially, metre - all of which stand you in good stead for an analysis of any other type of poem.

Although you won't be presented with an individual sonnet on your exam, it is not inconceivable that a series of sonnets or other shorter poems might be used. The point of the exercises with the sonnets is to engage with rhyme, rhythm, sound and word order - important structural principles for all poetry.

2.2.1 Some technical terms for your toolkit

- *octave*: eight lines in a poem with its own rhyme scheme;
- *sestet*: six lines in a poem with its own rhyme scheme;
- *quatrain*: four lines in a poem with its own rhyme scheme;
- *volta*: the break or 'turn' two stanzas in a poem that marks a change in direction or feeling;
- *couplet*: two lines of poetry; in an English-style sonnet, these are the final two lines;
- *iamb*: a metric foot (unit) comprising one unstressed and one stressed syllable (as in the words 'without' and 'before');
- *enjambment*: the 'running over' of a sentence in poetry from one line to the next, so that the reader doesn't stop at the end of the line but continues until punctuation makes you stop. The use of enjambment is very common and affects many things: meaning or understanding, rhythm and sound.

2.3 Poems: part one

The following two poems are sonnets. For our purposes there is an assumption that you will be familiar with the first sonnet from Shakespeare, so we will not dwell on its message or its 'meaning' but use it as a 'warm-up' for some structural principles.

2.3.1 William Shakespeare 'Sonnet 116'

The following poem by William Shakespeare, 'Sonnet 116', was published in 1609.

Exhibit 3: William Shakespeare 'Sonnet 116'

Let me not to the marriage of true minds
Admit impediments. Love is not love
Which alters when it alteration finds,
Or bends with the remover to remove:
O no! it is an ever-fixed mark,
That looks on tempests, and is never shaken;
It is the star to every wandering bark,
Whose worth's unknown, although his height be taken.
Love's not Time's fool, though rosy lips and cheeks
Within his bending sickle's compass come;
Love alters not with his brief hours and weeks,
But bears it out even to the edge of doom.
If this be error and upon me proved,
I never writ, nor no man ever loved.

Read the above poem as often as you need until your understanding is comfortable: write down any points you think are interesting and any questions you have. When you're ready, complete the following questions.

> **Notions of change and permanence**
>
> **Q1:** Given the main themes of everlasting love and the idea that true love is not subject to outside threats, highlight the terms in this poem associated with the notions of change and, conversely, permanence.

> **Change the word order**
>
> **Q2:** Change the word order of the first quatrain, retaining both the meaning and the exact words.
>
> Let me not to the marriage of true minds
> Admit impediments. Love is not love
> Which alters when it alteration finds,
> Or bends with the remover to remove:
>
> Note: the idea is to see how vital word order is to structure and rhyme. If you read the lines with changed word-order out loud a few times you'll probably discover it's tricky to 'find' the iambic pentameter - especially in line two - even though the same words have been retained.

2.3.2 John Keats 'When I have fears'

What follows is a sonnet modelled on Shakespeare's type - Keats was an admirer - but, as you will see, with some very significant differences. In some ways this sonnet is far more challenging to study. Keats died at the age of 25 and this poem, written when he was 21, seems to express his fears of premature death.

Note that there is a tricky bit of inversion in lines two and three: "Before piles of printed books contain the sum of all my works (the full ripen'd grain) like full grain-stores".

The following poem by John Keats, 'When I have fears', was published in 1848.

Exhibit 4: John Keats 'When I have fears'

When I have fears that I may cease to be
Before my pen has glean'd my teeming brain,
Before high-piled books, in charact'ry,
Hold like rich garners the full ripen'd grain;
When I behold, upon the night's starr'd face,
Huge cloudy symbols of a high romance,
And think that I may never live to trace
Their shadows with the magic hand of chance;
And when I feel, fair creature of an hour!
That I shall never look upon thee more,
Never have relish in the faery power
Of unreflecting love; - then on the shore
Of the wide world I stand alone, and think,
Till Love and Fame to nothingness do sink.

TOPIC 2. POETRY

Read the poem as often as you need until your understanding is comfortable: write down any points you think are interesting and any questions you have. When you're ready, work through the annotated poem Exhibit 9 - in the 'Annotated poems' section at the end of this topic - and questions.

> **John Keats 'When I have fears'**
>
> **Q3:** "Even more so than in Sonnet 116 there are explicit references to writing and the creative process here - in fact, the artist's pain at not being able to leave behind a body of work is a central concern."
> Highlight the terms and images in the poem that support this statement.
> ....
>
> **Q4:** With these 14 lines we can see clearly that Keats has structured this sonnet into quatrains and a couplet, in accordance with the Shakespearean tradition.
> Identify all of the structural principles employed by Keats in this poem and comment on their appropriateness or effectiveness.

> **Two sonnets**
>
> **Q5:** Make a detailed analysis of the contrasting ways in which both sonnets (Exhibit 3 and Exhibit 4) address the theme of time and its effects. You can arrange your response in bullet points or in any way you like.

2.4 Poems: part two

We mentioned sound at the start of this topic and it features prominently in our next two poems, both by Robert Browning and chosen to link with the learning points of the sonnets while extending our understanding beyond these.

2.4.1 Robert Browning 'The Lost Leader'

What follows here is a poem about a poet - William Wordsworth - of whom Browning had been a great admirer. The past perfect tense is significant here given the poem is Browning's response to what he saw as Wordsworth's abandonment of their erstwhile shared liberal politics and the latter's switch to more conservative, establishment values. Browning felt Wordsworth had 'sold out', which becomes apparent in the opening line.

The piece is highly structured, comprising two stanzas of 16 lines each and with a strict end-rhyme scheme of ABAB - though you will note the extensive use of alliteration, assonance and exclamation that also contribute sound to this noisy, angry poem.

The following poem by Robert Browning, 'The Lost Leader', was published in 1845.

© HERIOT-WATT UNIVERSITY

Exhibit 5: Robert Browning 'The Lost Leader'

Just for a handful of silver he left us,
Just for a riband to stick in his coat-
Found the one gift of which fortune bereft us,
Lost all the others she lets us devote;
They, with the gold to give, doled him out silver,
So much was theirs who so little allowed:
How all our copper had gone for his service!
Rags-were they purple, his heart had been proud!
We that had loved him so, followed him, honoured him,
Lived in his mild and magnificent eye,
Learned his great language, caught his clear accents,
Made him our pattern to live and to die!
Shakespeare was of us, Milton was for us,
Burns, Shelley, were with us-they watch from their graves!
He alone breaks from the van and the freemen
-He alone sinks to the rear and the slaves!

We shall march prospering -not thro' his presence;
Songs may inspirit us-not from his lyre;
Deeds will be done-while he boasts his quiescence,
Still bidding crouch whom the rest bade aspire:
Blot out his name, then, record one lost soul more,
One task more declined, one more footpath untrod,
One more devils'-triumph and sorrow for angels,
One wrong more to man, one more insult to God!
Life's night begins: let him never come back to us!
There would be doubt, hesitation and pain,
Forced praise on our part-the glimmer of twilight,
Never glad confident morning again!
Best fight on well, for we taught him-strike gallantly,
Menace our heart ere we master his own;
Then let him receive the new knowledge and wait us,
Pardoned in heaven, the first by the throne!

Read the poem as often as you need until your understanding is comfortable: write down any points you think are interesting and any questions you have. When you're ready, work through the annotated poems Exhibit 10 - in the 'Annotated poems section at the end of this topic - and questions.

Robert Browning 'The Lost Leader'

Q6: In a detailed analysis of 'The Lost Leader' (Exhibit 10), discuss how structure and sound contribute to the tone of this poem.

2.4.2 Robert Browning 'My Last Duchess'

The impact and success of the dramatic monologue depends on the quality of the 'voice' the poet gives to his or her imaginary speaker. This genre allows the poet to flex some poetic muscle and have quite a bit of fun in the process. After all, creating an imaginary speaker allows poets some distance between themselves and the world imagined and inhabited by their character. However, Browning's speaker here is thought to be based on the real-life, 16th century Italian Duke, Alfonso II.

In this poem, the Duke is chatting with an agent employed by a Count to arrange the marriage of the Count's daughter. Our speaker, the Duke, is a candidate for this match, and is showing the agent around his house before dinner. The iambic pentameter and rhyming couplet are back, but - crucially - it's enjambment and punctuation we rely on for its rhythm, our understanding and, ultimately, its devastating impact.

The following poem by Robert Browning, 'My Last Duchess', was published in 1842.

Exhibit 6: Robert Browning 'My Last Duchess'

That's my last Duchess painted on the wall,
Looking as if she were alive. I call
That piece a wonder, now; Fra Pandolf's hands
Worked busily a day, and there she stands.
Will't please you sit and look at her? I said
"Fra Pandolf" by design, for never read
Strangers like you that pictured countenance,
The depth and passion of its earnest glance,
But to myself they turned (since none puts by
The curtain I have drawn for you, but I)
And seemed as they would ask me, if they durst,
How such a glance came there; so, not the first
Are you to turn and ask thus. Sir, 'twas not
Her husband's presence only, called that spot
Of joy into the Duchess' cheek; perhaps
Fra Pandolf chanced to say, "Her mantle laps
Over my lady's wrist too much," or "Paint
Must never hope to reproduce the faint
Half-flush that dies along her throat." Such stuff
Was courtesy, she thought, and cause enough
For calling up that spot of joy. She had
A heart—how shall I say?—too soon made glad,
Too easily impressed; she liked whate'er
She looked on, and her looks went everywhere.
Sir, 'twas all one! My favour at her breast,
The dropping of the daylight in the West,
The bough of cherries some officious fool
Broke in the orchard for her, the white mule
She rode with round the terrace —all and each
Would draw from her alike the approving speech,
Or blush, at least. She thanked men—good! but thanked
Somehow—I know not how—as if she ranked
My gift of a nine-hundred-years-old name

With anybody's gift. Who'd stoop to blame
This sort of trifling? Even had you skill
In speech—which I have not—to make your will
Quite clear to such an one, and say, "Just this
Or that in you disgusts me; here you miss,
Or there exceed the mark"—and if she let
Herself be lessoned so, nor plainly set
Her wits to yours, forsooth, and made excuse-
E'en then would be some stooping; and I choose
Never to stoop. Oh, sir, she smiled, no doubt,
Whene'er I passed her; but who passed without
Much the same smile? This grew; I gave commands;
Then all smiles stopped together. There she stands
As if alive. Will't please you rise? We'll meet
The company below, then. I repeat,
The Count your master's known munificence
Is ample warrant that no just pretense
Of mine for dowry will be disallowed;
Though his fair daughter's self, as I avowed
At starting, is my object. Nay, we'll go
Together down, sir. Notice Neptune, though,
Taming a sea-horse, thought a rarity,
Which Claus of Innsbruck cast in bronze for me!

Read the poem as often as you need until your understanding is comfortable: write down any points you think are interesting and any questions you have. When you're ready, work through the annotated poem (Exhibit 11) - in the 'Annotated poems section at the end of this topic - and question.

Robert Browning 'My Last Duchess'

Q7: In a detailed analysis of 'My Last Duchess' (Exhibit 11), discuss how Browning builds up the drama, the horror that unfolds, as he relates the story of his last Duchess.

Other resources for studying 'My Last Duchess':

- Margaret Atwood's short story My Last Duchess in her collection Moral Disorder is about two students arguing about the various interpretations of the poem.
- YouTube alone has a wealth of readings, performances, lectures and other material to enhance your learning and understanding of My Last Duchess.

2.5 Poetry: Exam practice

What follows now is a poem of the sort of length you can expect on the exam, followed by an exam-type question for practice. Remember: when you are asked to make a "detailed analysis" you are taking a magnifying glass and commenting on everything you notice within the poem, in terms of the question being asked.

The following poem by Walt Whitman, 'This Compost', was published in 1900.

Exhibit 7: 'This Compost' by Walt Whitman

1

Something startles me where I thought I was safest;
I withdraw from the still woods I loved;
I will not go now on the pastures to walk;
I will not strip the clothes from my body to meet my lover the sea;
I will not touch my flesh to the earth, as to other flesh, to renew me.

O how can it be that the ground does not sicken?

How can you be alive, you growths of spring?
How can you furnish health, you blood of herbs, roots, orchards, grain?
Are they not continually putting distemper'd corpses within you?

Is not every continent work'd over and over with sour dead?

Where have you disposed of their carcasses?
Those drunkards and gluttons of so many generations;
Where have you drawn off all the foul liquid and meat?
I do not see any of it upon you to-day—or perhaps I am deceiv'd;
I will run a furrow with my plough—I will press my spade through the sod, and turn it up underneath;
I am sure I shall expose some of the foul meat.

2

Behold this compost! behold it well!

Perhaps every mite has once form'd part of a sick person—Yet behold!
The grass of spring covers the prairies,

The bean bursts noiselessly through the mould in the garden,
The delicate spear of the onion pierces upward,
The apple-buds cluster together on the apple-branches,
The resurrection of the wheat appears with pale visage out of its graves,
The tinge awakes over the willow-tree and the mulberry-tree,
The he-birds carol mornings and evenings, while the she-birds sit on their nests,
The young of poultry break through the hatch'd eggs,
The new-born of animals appear—the calf is dropt from the cow, the colt from the mare,
Out of its little hill faithfully rise the potato's dark green leaves,
Out of its hill rises the yellow maize-stalk—the lilacs bloom in the door-yards;

The summer growth is innocent and disdainful above all those strata of sour dead.

What chemistry!
That the winds are really not infectious,
That this is no cheat, this transparent green-wash of the sea, which is so amorous after me,
That it is safe to allow it to lick my naked body all over with its tongues,
That it will not endanger me with the fevers that have deposited themselves in it,
That all is clean forever and forever.
That the cool drink from the well tastes so good,
That blackberries are so flavorous and juicy,
That the fruits of the apple-orchard, and of the orange-orchard—that melons, grapes, peaches, plums, will none of them poison me,
That when I recline on the grass I do not catch any disease,
Though probably every spear of grass rises out of what was once a catching disease.

3

Now I am terrified at the Earth! it is that calm and patient,
It grows such sweet things out of such corruptions,
It turns harmless and stainless on its axis, with such endless successions of diseas'd corpses,
It distils such exquisite winds out of such infused fetor,
It renews with such unwitting looks, its prodigal, annual, sumptuous crops,
It gives such divine materials to men, and accepts such leavings from them at last.

Poetry: Exam practice

Q8: Make a detailed study of the ways in which Walt Whitman presents the central concern of this poem. You may consider:

- structure
- sound
- any other feature you consider significant.

2.6 Writing a critical response

Poem one: William Blake 'The Tyger'

Write a critical response to this poem.

Poem one: William Blake 'The Tyger'

Tyger! Tyger! burning bright
In the forests of the night,
What immortal hand or eye
Could frame thy fearful symmetry?

In what distant deeps or skies
Burnt the fire of thine eyes?
On what wings dare he aspire?
What the hand dare seize the fire?

And what shoulder, and what art,
Could twist the sinews of thy heart?
And when thy heart began to beat,
What dread hand? and what dread feet?

What the hammer? what the chain?
In what furnace was thy brain?
What the anvil? what dread grasp
Dare its deadly terrors clasp?

When the stars threw down their spears,
And water'd heaven with their tears,
Did he smile his work to see?
Did he who made the Lamb make thee?

Tyger! Tyger! burning bright
In the forests of the night,
what immortal hand or eye,
Dare frame thy fearful symmetry?

Poem two: Robert Burns 'To A Mouse, On Turning Her Up in Her Nest With The Plough'

Write a critical response to this poem.

Poem two: Robert Burns 'To A Mouse, On Turning Her Up in Her Nest With The Plough'

I
Wee, sleekit, cowrin, tim'rous beastie,
Oh, what a panic's in thy breastie!
Thou need na start awa sae hasty,
Wi' bickering brattle!
I was be laith to rin an' chase thee,
Wi' murd'ring pattle!

II
I'm truly sorry man's dominion
Has broken Nature's social union,
An' justifies that ill opinion
Which makes thee startle
At me, thy poor, earth-born companion
An' fellow-mortal!

III
I doubt na, whyles, but thou may thieve;
What then? poor beastie, thou maun live!
A daimen-icker in a thrave
'S a sma' request;
I'll get a blessin wi' the lave,
And never miss't!

IV
Thy wee-bit housie, too, in ruin!
Its silly wa's the win's are strewin!
An' naething, now, to big a new ane,
O' foggage green!
An' bleak December's winds ensuin,
Baith snell an' keen!

V
Thou saw the fields laid bare an' waste,
An' weary winter comin fast,
An' cozie here, beneath the blast,
Thou thought to dwell,
Till crash! the cruel coulter past
Out thro' thy cell.

VI
That wee bit heap o' leaves an stibble,
Has cost thee mony a weary nibble!
Now thou's turn'd out, for a' thy trouble,

TOPIC 2. POETRY

But house or hald,
To thole the winter's sleety dribble,
An' cranreuch cauld!

VII
But, Mousie, thou art no thy lane,
In proving foresight may be vain:
The best-laid schemes o' mice an' men
Gang aft a-gley,
An' lea'e us nought but grief an' pain,
For promis'd joy!

VIII
Still thou art blest, compared wi' me!
The present only toucheth thee:
But och! I backward cast my e'e,
On prospects drear!
An' forward, tho' I cannot see,
I guess an' fear!

Poem three: Ella Wheeler Wilcox 'Inevitable'

Write a critical response to this poem.

Poem three: Ella Wheeler Wilcox 'Inevitable'

To-day I was so weary and I lay
In that delicious state of semi-waking,
When baby, sitting with his nurse at play,
Cried loud for "mamma," all his toys forsaking.

I was so weary and I needed rest,
And signed to nurse to bear him from the room.
Then, sudden, rose and caught him to my breast,
And kissed the grieving mouth and cheeks of bloom.

For swift as lightning came the thought to me,
With pulsing heart-throes and a mist of tears,
Of days inevitable, that are to be,
If my fair darling grows to manhood's years;

Days when he will not call for "mamma," when
The world with many a pleasure and bright joy,
Shall tempt him forth into the haunts of men
And I shall lose the first place with my boy;

When other homes and loves shall give delight,
When younger smiles and voices will seem best.
And so I held him to my heart to-night,
Forgetting all my need of peace and rest.

Poem four: William Knox 'Mortality'

Write a critical response to this poem.

Poem four: William Knox 'Mortality'

O why should the spirit of mortal be proud?
Like a fast-flitting meteor, a fast-flying cloud,
A flash of the lightning, a break of the wave,
He passes from life to his rest in the grave.

The leaves of the oak and the willow shall fade,
Be scattered around, and together be laid;
And the young and the old, and the low and the high,
Shall moulder to dust, and together shall lie.

The child that a mother attended and loved,
The mother that infant's affection that proved;
The husband that mother and infant that blessed,
Each, all, are away to their dwelling of rest.

The maid on whose cheek, on whose brow, in whose eye,
Shone beauty and pleasure,—her triumphs are by;
And the memory of those that beloved her and praised
Are alike from the minds of the living erased.

The hand of the king that the scepter hath borne,
The brow of the priest that the miter hath worn,
The eye of the sage, and the heart of the brave,
Are hidden and lost in the depths of the grave.

The peasant whose lot was to sow and to reap,
The herdsman who climbed with his goats to the steep,
The beggar that wandered in search of his bread,
Have faded away like the grass that we tread.

The saint that enjoyed the communion of heaven,
The sinner that dared to remain unforgiven,
The wise and the foolish, the guilty and just,
Have quietly mingled their bones in the dust.

So the multitude goes, like the flower and the weed
That wither away to let others succeed;
So the multitude comes, even those we behold,
To repeat every tale that hath often been told.

For we are the same that our fathers have been;
We see the same sights that our fathers have seen,—
We drink the same stream, and we feel the same sun,
And we run the same course that our fathers have run.

The thoughts we are thinking, our fathers would think;
From the death we are shrinking, they too would shrink;

To the life we are clinging to, they too would cling;
But it speeds from the earth like a bird on the wing.

They loved, but the story we cannot unfold;
They scorned, but the heart of the haughty is cold;
They grieved, but no wail from their slumber may come;
They enjoyed, but the voice of their gladness is dumb.

They died, ay! they died! and we things that are now,
Who walk on the turf that lies over their brow,
Who make in their dwellings a transient abode,
Meet the changes they met on their pilgrimage road.

Yea! hope and despondence, and pleasure and pain,
Are mingled together like sunshine and rain;
And the smile and the tear, and the song and the dirge,
Still follow each other, like surge upon surge.

'Tis the wink of an eye, 'tis the draught of a breath,
From the blossom of health to the paleness of death,
From the gilded saloon to the bier and the shroud,—
O why should the spirit of mortal be proud?

2.7 Video resources

Video sharing website YouTube has a wealth of clips in which sonnets are performed or just read aloud. The more you hear poetry the greater your understanding will be.

An excellent, recent, example is actor Juliet Stevenson's reading of Sonnet 116 where, as you would expect from a skilled actor, pronunciation, intonation and pace greatly aid the listener's understanding. In particular, notice the extended pause at the end of line 12, just before the final couplet, to heighten the impact of these last two lines:

- Juliet Stevenson reads Shakespeare's Sonnet 116 (https://youtu.be/cKyuzXwSolA).

2.8 Annotated poems

William Shakespeare 'Sonnet 116' - annotated

Exhibit 8: William Shakespeare 'Sonnet 116' - annotated
The following poem by William Shakespeare, 'Sonnet 116', was published in 1609.

Let me not to the marriage of true minds
Admit impediments. Love is not love
Which alters when it alteration finds,
Or bends with the remover to remove:
O no! it is an ever-fixed mark,[1]
That looks on tempests, and is never shaken[2];
It is the star to every wandering bark,
Whose worth's unknown, although his height be taken.
Love's not Time's fool, though rosy lips and cheeks
Within his bending sickle's compass come;
Love alters not[3] with his brief hours and weeks,
But bears it out[4] even to the edge of doom.
If this be error and upon me proved,
I never writ[5], nor no man ever loved.

Notes:

[1] Terms associated with the notions of change and permanence.
[2] Term associated with the notion of permanence.
[3] Term associated with the notion of permanence.
[4] Term associated with the notion of permanence.
[5] It is common in the sonnet to have an explicit reference to art or writing or the creative process - a self-conscious element on the part of the poet given that the sonnet was intended to immortalize a person or an idea.

John Keats 'When I have fears' - annotated

Exhibit 9: John Keats 'When I have fears' - annotated

The following poem by John Keats, 'When I have fears', was published in 1848.

When I have fears that I may cease to be
Before my pen has glean'd[1] my teeming[2] brain,
Before high-piled books, in charact'ry[3],
Hold like rich garners[4] the full ripen'd grain;
When I behold, upon the night's starr'd face,
Huge cloudy symbols of a high romance[5],
And think that I may never live to trace
Their shadows with the magic hand of chance;
And when I feel, fair creature of an hour[6]!
That I shall never look upon thee more,
Never have relish in the faery power
Of unreflecting love; - then[7] on the shore
Of the wide world I stand alone, and think,
Till Love and Fame to nothingness do sink.[8]

Notes:

[1] "Glean'd" = to collect patiently or laboriously from
[2] "Teeming" = overflowing/abundant
[3] "Charact'ry" = printing or handwriting
[4] "Garners" = grain store
[5] "High romance" = elevated thoughts or feelings
[6] Expression of the relatively short life we all have.
[7] The third quatrain appears to have been short-changed: its fourth line is really only half a line, the other half having been 'borrowed' by the couplet. Possibly reflects the poet's belief that love is short-lived. "Then" indicates the beginning of the resolution of his fears.
[8] Possible resolution of his fears of death and being forgotten: "I stand alone and think until these huge feelings about love and fame disappear into nothingness", i.e. gaining perspective by taking some calm reflection time rather than being led by emotions.

Robert Browning 'The Lost Leader' - annotated

Exhibit 10: Robert Browning 'The Lost Leader' - annotated
The following poem by Robert Browning, 'The Lost Leader', was published in 1845.

Just for a handful of silver[1] he left us,
Just for a riband to stick in his coat[2]-
Found the one gift of which fortune bereft us,
Lost all the others she[3] lets us devote;
They, with the gold to give, doled him out silver,
So much was theirs who so little allowed:
How all our copper[4] had gone for his service!
Rags-were they purple[5], his heart had been proud!
We that had loved him so, followed him, honoured him,
Lived in his mild and magnificent eye,
Learned his great language, caught his clear accents,
Made him our pattern to live and to die![6]
Shakespeare was of us, Milton was for us,
Burns, Shelley, were with us-they watch from their graves!
He alone breaks from the van[7] and the freemen
-He alone sinks to the rear and the slaves[8]!

We shall march prospering[9] -not thro' his presence;
Songs may inspirit us-not from his lyre[10];
Deeds will be done-while he boasts his quiescence[11],
Still bidding crouch whom the rest bade aspire:
Blot out his name, then, record one lost soul more,
One task more declined, one more footpath untrod,
One more devils'-triumph and sorrow for angels,
One wrong more to man, one more insult to God![12]
Life's night begins: let him never come back to us!
There would be doubt, hesitation and pain,
Forced praise on our part-the glimmer of twilight,
Never glad confident morning again!
Best fight on well, for we taught him-strike gallantly,[13]
Menace our heart ere we master his own;
Then let him receive the new knowledge and wait us,
Pardoned in heaven, the first by the throne!

Notes:

[1] Wordsworth accepted a grant by the government in his later years.
[2] Ribbon. Wordsworth was made Poet Laureate.
[3] Lady Fortune (as mentioned in line 3).
[4] "Gold... silver...copper": diminishing value.

[5] A colour associated with royalty and power.
[6] Strong words; cumulative effect (loved, followed, honoured) enhanced by assonance and repetition of 'him'; 'loved...lived...learned...', 'mild...magnificent': lots of alliteration; rhyme in 'language', 'accents' and 'pattern; finishing with exclamation mark. Also: use of "We" and then "language...accents...pattern..." all references to their shared occupation as poets. "Pattern" links with the craft of poetry as well as the notion of an example, a model to aspire to.
[7] The vanguard, which is the front - the position of a trailblazer, a leader for change; its literal meaning is the front of a military formation, connotations of which continue in the next stanza with 'march' and 'fight' and 'strike gallantly' later on.
[8] It is suggested that, the bitter irony, for Browning, in Wordsworth joining the establishment, is that he goes from leader to 'slave' in that he joins the masses that look up to establishment figures.
[9] Second stanza addresses what Browning's future intentions are.
[10] A harp-like instrument.
[11] Being still/dormant/inactive.
[12] Insistent repetition of 'one more' sounds like a chant on a protest march ("we shall march prospering").
[13] Further military references giving the impression of an army of poets opposed to Wordsworth's change.

© HERIOT-WATT UNIVERSITY

Robert Browning 'My Last Duchess' - annotated

Exhibit 11: Robert Browning 'My Last Duchess' - annotated
The following poem by Robert Browning, 'My Last Duchess', was published in 1842.

That's my last[1] Duchess painted on the wall,
Looking as if she were alive. I call
That piece a wonder, now; Fra Pandolf[2]'s hands
Worked busily a day, and there she stands.
Will't please you sit and look at her? I said
"Fra Pandolf" by design, for never read
Strangers like you that pictured countenance,
The depth and passion of its earnest glance,
But to myself they turned (since none puts by
The curtain I have drawn for you, but I)
And seemed as they would ask me, if they durst,
How such a glance came there; so, not the first
Are you to turn and ask thus[3]. Sir, 'twas not[4]
Her husband's presence only, called that spot
Of joy into the Duchess' cheek; perhaps
Fra Pandolf chanced to say, "Her mantle laps
Over my lady's wrist too much," or "Paint
Must never hope to reproduce the faint
Half-flush that dies along her throat." Such stuff
Was courtesy, she thought, and cause enough
For calling up that spot of joy. She had
A heart—how shall I say?—too soon made glad,
Too easily impressed; she liked whate'er
She looked on, and her looks went everywhere.
Sir, 'twas all one! My favour at her breast,
The dropping of the daylight in the West,
The bough of cherries some officious fool
Broke in the orchard for her, the white mule
She rode with round the terrace[5] -all and each
Would draw from her alike the approving speech,
Or blush, at least. She thanked men - good! but thanked
Somehow - I know not how - as if she ranked
My gift of a nine-hundred-years-old name
With anybody's gift. Who'd stoop to blame
This sort of trifling? Even had you skill
In speech—which I have not—to make your will
Quite clear to such an one, and say, "Just this
Or that in you disgusts me; here you miss,
Or there exceed the mark"—and if she let
Herself be lessoned so, nor plainly set

Her wits to yours, forsooth, and made excuse-
E'en then would be some stooping; and I choose
Never to stoop[6]. Oh, sir, she smiled, no doubt,
Whene'er I passed her; but who passed without
Much the same smile? This grew; I gave commands;
Then all smiles stopped together. There she stands
As if alive[7]. Will't please you rise? We'll meet
The company below, then. I repeat,
The Count your master's known munificence[8]
Is ample warrant that no just pretense
Of mine for dowry will be disallowed;
Though his fair daughter's self, as I avowed
At starting, is my object[9]. Nay, we'll go
Together down, sir. Notice Neptune, though,
Taming a sea-horse[10], thought a rarity,
Which Claus of Innsbruck cast in bronze for me!

Notes:

[1] The significance of this term becomes clear only in the reading of the poem.
[2] The poem is set in an Italian context so this (imaginary) artist's name is 'brother Pandalf'
[3] Tricky syntax: "Because every stranger who sees the painting, without fail, turns to me and asks about the quality of her expression, so you are not the first".
[4] These lines (up to ...As if alive") tell the story of the fate that befell the hapless Duchess. The lines before and after it function as introductory discourse and/or polite small talk where we only 'hear' the Duke's speech to what must be an increasingly alarmed agent.
[5] A list of things his wife delighted in - but, to the Duke's annoyance, she delighted in each of these equally and he wanted his gifts to be ranked much higher than those of others.
[6] The Duke makes clear that even for him to have sat down with his wife to explain to her what it was about her behaviour that annoyed him so, was beneath him.
[7] The end of his narrative echoes line two in this poem.
[8] great generosity
[9] "Though, as I have said from the start, it's his daughter I want".
[10] A throw-away comment on the surface - but we know there's no such thing in poetry. Notice the reference to 'taming' a wild animal - "thought a rarity" - following the Duke's apparent wishes to have had a 'tame' wife.

© HERIOT-WATT UNIVERSITY

2.9 Learning points

Summary

You will now have:

- strengthened your understanding of how form and content work in poetry;
- refreshed your understanding of structural principles in poetry;
- performed a detailed analysis of a dramatic monologue;
- practised identifying and writing about themes in poetry.

Unit 2 Topic 3

Prose fiction

Contents

3.1 Prose fiction 92
3.2 About time 92
3.3 Extract one from 'Butcher's Broom' 93
3.4 Extract two from 'Butcher's Broom' 96
3.5 Extract three from 'Butcher's Broom' 99
3.6 Annotated extracts 102
3.7 Learning points 108

Learning objective

By the end of this topic you will better understand:

- the novelist's use of
    - pace;
    - time;
    - narration;
- how pace, time and narration affect the reader's experience.

3.1 Prose fiction

As you know, prose fiction is extended writing and offers considerable freedom for both reader and writer.

For the purposes of textual analysis at Advanced Higher, prose fiction can be distinguished by two forms: the short story and the novel. The exam will present you with either of these: the 2013 exam offered an entire short story for analysis, so this is something you could expect, whereas other exams have had an extended passage from a novel. The short story has in common with drama that the action, central concern or problem to be resolved is introduced quickly because of the obvious time constraints of these forms. It can be very satisfying to be presented with an entire short story in the exam because you get the 'full picture' and will be able to comment on every aspect of it without relying on introductory summaries by the exam authors setting the context. In this section we will focus on the novel, particularly on aspects of pace, time, and narration.

3.2 About time

What makes prose fiction, in novel form, unique among the genres is how it can afford to treat time - the reader's time and its own time. Whereas playwrights, poets and journalists need to be mindful of the limitations of, respectively, their audience, their form and their publication, novelists have fewer restrictions to worry about.

In England, the Victorian novelists had a particularly good time of it in this regard: having become a popular form with a captive middle-class audience with time on their hands, 19th century novels tended to be very lengthy. Think of Dickens' tomes and the big novels by the Brontë sisters, Thomas Hardy, George Eliot (Mary Ann Evans) and others. The action, or the plot, in a novel can take a considerable time to get going; can take several twists and turns; can comprise various layers, additions and complexities. Plots can span generations of characters' lives and decades - even centuries - across time. Novelists can take ages to describe something or lead up to something - which can be taxing for the reader, depending on the quality of the writing and other factors.

Let's test these points by studying the opening pages of Neil M. Gunn's novel Butcher's Broom. Published in 1934, it is a vast tale about several characters' lives in a remote part of the Scottish Highlands around the time of the infamous Clearances in the 19th century - when ordinary people who worked the land were 'cleared' (forcibly evicted, often violently) from their homes and land to make room for the more profitable sheep.

3.3 Extract one from 'Butcher's Broom'

This extract is from the opening pages of Neil M. Gunn's novel 'Butcher's Broom', in which the reader is immediately introduced to the main character, Mairi, an old woman and a highly-respected healer in her remote Highland community.

Exhibit 12: *Extract one from 'Butcher's Broom'*

The old woman stood on the Darras, the doorway, between the bright sea and the dark hills; and when at last she turned from the sea and lifted her burden to her back, the door closed behind her. But the vacant glitter remained in her eyes and they held their stare until the valley began to pour slowly into them its dark comfort. For a long time she was like one who had turned into her own house and found it empty, and walked in a silence that was a hearkening to presences withdrawn beyond the walls and fading away.

Every now and then there was a glint in this vagueness, for she had been born by the sea, and sea-water readily curls over and breaks on the shore of the mind. Looked at from a great distance childhood is little more than the breaking of small bright waves on a beach. And whatever of pain and coldness there may have been, the brightness keeps a certain wild strangeness, a restless fly-away, that the hills do not know and never quite conquer.

The sea had been in a good mood that morning, had had that pleasant scent that is the breath of fine weather. A person could always tell what the weather is to be by smelling the sea. There is the grey dark smell, cold inside the nostrils, ominous; the damp raw smell, husky to the throat, unsettled; the keen dry lifting tang of wind; but when good weather has newly come, how the sea brims and sways and breathes its sweet fragrance on the air! This morning, too, there had been the extra exhilaration of autumn, that indescribable quickening that the skin takes in a shiver.

All of that sea she now carried in her basket as she went back among the companionable hills. For in addition to fish, she had many kinds of weed and shell. The clear pink dulse , gathered not off other sea-plants but off the rocks, was one of her most useful specifics. Eaten raw, it had a cleansing effect; boiled, with a pinch of butter added to the infusion, it acted as a tonic, bracing the flesh, making it supple, and drawing taut the muscles of the stomach. It could be preserved, too, by drying. A man working in a field could put a dry blade or two in his mouth and chew away at them. At first they were tasteless as gristle, but in a very short time they yielded back their juices, which began to run about the gums and fill the whole mouth with a richness that had to be frequently swallowed. When the dried dulse was ground into a powder and taken fasting, it sickened and expelled worms. Other ailments, like the stone and colic, yielded to it.

Linarich, slake, and sea-tangle had also their many uses; though she had not much of each with her now, for slake was mostly needed in the spring, when, after the rigour of winter, the cattle were weak and costive. Linarich, perhaps, was more useful at any time. It helped to soothe and heal the skin after a blister plaster. In the case of sciatica, for example, the ancient custom was to cut spirewort into small pieces, pack them in a limpet shell, and fasten the shell to the thigh-bone in order to raise a big blister, from which the watery matter could be drained away. After the third draining, a linarich plaster dried and healed the wound.

It was in her nature not to return home without such gifts. She had spent two days with a relative by marriage whose husband had been suffering from a mysterious fever and could not sweat. They had sent for her, for Dark Mairi of the Shore. She had a reputation for healing among the people of that land. She was a small woman, roundly built, deep-chested and straight, yet she did not give an impression of bodily strength so much as of something delicate and hardy that persists evenly. Her skin was pale and little wrinkled; her eyes dark, and of a jewelled smallness. But perhaps the suggestion of persistence, of abidingness, that was the silent note struck by her person, was

94   UNIT 2. TEXTUAL ANALYSIS

sustained most distinctly by the cheek-bones that did not obtrude in round knobs but ran straight back towards her ears, each in a visible ridge. These ridges drew the skin taut and gave the frontal expression a curious flattened steadiness. Her hair was black and coarse-grained, with grey strands showing here and there in a good light. It was drawn firmly back from her forehead, tautening the skin at the temples, as the cheek-bones tautened it down the sides of her face. Her head was raised in a watchfulness that was sometimes direct and glimmering and sometimes staring-blind.

This 'blindness' in her expression had often the air of unintelligence, and when she smiled it could be seen as a sort of weakness running thinly all over her face. To move her out of her unthinking self seemed to expose her, to show that apart from what she was unthinkingly she was very little. One might as well have exposed a stone by causing it to smile or a piece of a mountain. Indeed, in her steady unthinking darkness, she might have walked out of a mountain and might walk into it again, leaving no sign.

The sick man had looked at her with expectation. She asked him questions quietly. She smiled her small weak smile. She put her hand on his forehead. Her hand was very cold. Her smile did not touch her eyes at all. She was not concerned. She would soon put him all right. Oh yes. She did not even say what was wrong with him. And the doubt that had clouded the man's eyes faded out, not into eagerness or impatience, but into an almost stupid peace. She prepared her drink and gave it to him. It was hot and harsh to the throat as oily sea-water. 'It's strong,' he said. 'Strong enough,' she answered and packed the extra clothes around him. 'Strong,' he muttered, and his body shuddered as under a convulsion and settled down into the bed, fatally accepting what was coming to it. When it relaxed from its next shudder there was a crawling warmth under the skin. The warmth grew; it became a glowing live heat. Soon his whole body was a white dry furnace. He was being consumed, burnt up. Out of that heat the storm burst. The drops ran into runnels. These runnels tickled his face and his chest, and made his eyes water. 'God, 'I'm sweating!' he gasped. 'Sweat you,' said she. When she saw his hair steaming, she turned away and began asking his wife the news of the place. The two women sat down and told each other all they knew of everybody, so that their neighbours in their lives and their actions were brought clearly before them. In this way the wife became happy and greatly moved towards Dark Mairi, to whom she unburdened herself, enjoying now what had been her saddest moments. In the morning the man was quite spent, but his eyes and his mind were clear and steady. 'I'm weak as a fly,' he jested. 'You'll be strong as a horse,' she replied. Whereupon the strength of the horse began to trickle into him. 'God's blessing with you,' he said. 'And with yourself,' she answered, looking at him a moment then turning away.

Read the extract carefully, twice, and make sure you understand it. When you're ready, read the annotated extract - Exhibit 14 in the 'Annotated extracts' section at the end of this topic - and complete the following questions.

© HERIOT-WATT UNIVERSITY

Extract one from 'Butcher's Broom'

Q1: The slow pace of the narrative

In the above extract, some words and phrases contribute to the slow pace of the narrative from the very start. Highlight the words and phrases which show features of the text used to contribute to the leisurely pace.

....

Q2: The importance of nature and the natural world

The importance of nature and the natural world is another major feature of this extract and Gunn goes to considerable lengths to present this. Highlight where and how in the text Gunn shows the reader the importance and closeness of characters' relationship with the natural world.

96 UNIT 2. TEXTUAL ANALYSIS

3.4   Extract two from 'Butcher's Broom'

Extract two offers some relief from lengthy descriptions and introduces to the reader new characters, dialogue, improvisation and humour. This is equally 'descriptive' - just with fewer adjectives: the exchanges tell us a lot about the people, the place and the culture, the way they spend their time and the value they place on linguistic dexterity and wit.

This scene takes place slightly later in the opening chapter when the action moves to a house in the community where a ceilidh is taking place. Two youngsters, who live with Dark Mairi but are not her children, have gone there - one of them with permission (Elie, a teenager) and one without (Davie, Mairi's young grandson).

Exhibit 13: Extract two from 'Butcher's Broom'

In a land of tall men, old Angus was small, with a white cropped beard, a quiet humour, and twinkling eyes. He was very knacky with his hands , built cages out of thin birch withies, and bred singing linnets in his barn. He was always willing to try a new thing, and in the spring had bought oats from the coast in the belief that the ground must get tired of the same old seed. And the new seed would have done very well had it not been for the stronger crop of yellow flowers that grew up with the corn, to the amusement (and perhaps not a little to the satisfaction) of some of his neighbours. Nor was it of any use for Angus to suggest now that the flower seeds must have been introduced to the ground after he had sown the oats. The picture of the old man solemnly flailing sheaves of withered flowers made good fun. The colour of the bread, it was maintained, would at least tally with the linnets' wings. It might even turn the linnets into canaries! Angus had long hankered after canaries. What about a barnful of them! One young man there, with a cripple foot, was goaded into improvising:

'When Angus Ossian Finn Mac Cumhal
is turned into a fairy,
he'll eat a bit of his own yellow bread
and whistle like a canary.'

Which hit off Angus's knowledge of the ancient poetry and of the fairies well enough. But Angus answered the poet at once:

'When Murdoch son of Murdoch
has grown old and hairy,
alas if he should find
he never made a tune
so well as a canary.'

Whereat everyone cheered the old man. In fact this improvising was one of their great amusements, and some nights at the ceilidh they hit a lucky vein. One or two of the girls were very good at it. Occasionally a couple of lines were struck out that instantly delighted and then haunted the mind. 'That's you on your back, Murdoch!' called Seonaid, the dark girl, boldly. As enemies, they never gave quarter. Murdoch murmured innocently:

'If I am on my back
and Angus is a fairy,
how kind of you to come
and offer your canary.'

There was an explosion of laughter, for Murdoch's satire was nearly always two-edged. He had ruddy cheeks, dark eyes, and a quick attractive smile. With a spot of colour, the girl changed the rhythm:

© HERIOT-WATT UNIVERSITY

'If you were a whole barnful of canaries,
if you were a whole green mound of fairies,
I would sell the lot for Angus's empty cage with a crow in it.'

But the great game among the children was riddles, and one boy piped up, 'How could an empty cage have a crow in it?'

'When you are older, Iain my young calf,' said Seonaid, 'you may find that you too may not be in it though you are there.'

'Let me explain it to you, Iain,' said Angus, gripping the boy by the shoulder. 'Some day, like Murdoch there, you may be anxious to draw the attention of a fine girl, like Seonaid, but she, not caring, will look at the place on which you will be standing as though it were empty.'

'I should like to see her try it!' said Iain.

'What would you do to her?'

I'd hit her one on the nose.'

Murdoch laughed.

'There is meat and drink in its laugh, as the fox said when he ran away with the bagpipes,' misquoted Seonaid.

Then the war of proverbs started. They came hurtling from all corners, sometimes inaptly, but with Murdoch and Seonaid carrying on the main combat. The company obviously delighted in this, more than in the verse-making, which sometimes had an air of artificiality or strain, except in the case of Murdoch, who nearly always said something that stuck, often with a double meaning, particularly on the subject of women.

When Seonaid had Murdoch floundering for an apt reply, Elie heard Davie's excited voice putting the words in his mouth, 'I am too accustomed to a wood to be frightened of a canary.'

'Is it my friend Davie who's sending fuel to the wood? ' cried Angus. But Davie had ducked down out of sight.

'It's invisible you ·should be, you rascal!' cried Elie.

'I am like MacKay's cat-still in the flesh!' came Davie's voice.

Seonaid smiled, and the boldness of her glance melted into a rare attractiveness.

'The wren may be small, but it will make a noise', she said.

'Your hour, Davie,' said Murdoch,' is pursuing you.'

'Now, now,' said Angus, 'Fingal never fought a fight without offering terms.'

'Fingal's door is always free to the needy,' said Murdoch, without glancing at Seonaid, who remarked mildly, 'The heaviest ear of corn bends its head the lowest.'

'That's your head between the door and the door- post,' laughed one man at Murdoch, whose colour had risen. It's never difficult to guess the egg from your cackle,' Murdoch answered him shortly. But the man did not take it amiss for he saw that Murdoch, for all his laughing mouth, was beginning to be nettled. Seonaid seemed to have the power that in the long run cramped his wits. At the least opportunity they got fighting like this. Indeed the very sight of him raised her hackle. And there were times when he could clearly have throttled her.

Anna, the woman of the house and daughter-in-law to old Angus, was tall and broad and comely, with smooth dark hair and pleasant manners. She sat with her hands in her lap, smiling, saying to herself that in a moment she would stop this and call the girls to the waulking of the cloth, and yet delaying because of the gaiety. She liked this sound and fun in her home; she liked old Angus, whom she treated as one of her sons, of whom she had three, the second being Colin, who avoided Elie's eyes as pointedly as Elie avoided his. Anna now watched the fun climb to the point where Murdoch, desperately pressed, defended himself with the saying, 'The dung-heap is mother to the meal chest'.

Read the extract carefully, twice, and make sure you understand it. When you're ready, read the annotated extract - Exhibit 15 in the 'Annotated extracts' section at the end of this topic - and complete the following questions.

Extract two from 'Butcher's Broom'

Q3: A sympathetic view

Highlight other examples in this extract where Gunn offers readers a sympathetic view of any character(s) and their exchanges/activities in this scene.

....

Q4: The importance of tradition

Identify other words and phrases in the extract that refer to this tradition and comment on how these terms help your understanding of the importance of this tradition.

....

Q5: The pace of the narrative

Identify further indications throughout the extract that contribute to the pace of the narrative and comment on the author's reasons for doing this.

3.5 Extract three from 'Butcher's Broom'

Read this longer extract from the same novel and consider the exam-type question at the end of it. Note that Riasgan is the name of the Sutherland hamlet where the novel is set.

There are no further annotations or notes given; use your learning from the previous passages and tasks to form your response.

Social and working lives of the Riasgan people

Using this extract, make a detailed study of the means used by Neil M. Gunn to present aspects of the social and working lives of the Riasgan people.

Extract three from 'Butcher's Broom'

With its harvest gathered and its meat salted, the Riasgan got through the early winter with a strong pulse. Each season of the year had its occupation and interest, and though none might compare in delight with the long summer evenings and freedom of the shieling life, yet there was a lot to be said for the early winter.

Food and fuel were stored in their first plenty; outside labour to a large extent was suspended, stock had been sold for cash and young unhoused beasts strayed over all the holdings at will; nothing could be injured; nothing destroyed; interest in life was contemplative or joyous or malicious; the dark nights called for the ceilidh and fun and songs, for intrigue and love-thoughts, for surprising outbursts of passion or oddities of behaviour, for the visits of 'characters' like the packman with gossip and story and fascinating merchandise in his pack. The packman indeed brought them the latest styles, the best romance, the most scandalous biography, and the catchiest verse of the season. And in the full flow of that, Angus's classics were given a rest. Women carded and spun, the weaver wove, the tailor visited houses and made clothes, youths swung flails and old men winnowed. Even Gilleasbuig grew fluent in his prayers, for God had been mindful of his stock, and he urged God to bring sinners to repentance, to set up His rule on earth, and so put an early and final stop to the Devil and his ways.

With all this there went leisure and a leaning to inclination. The women were the more persistent and fruitful workers, and found the males frequently in their way. Many of the tasks about house they would not let a man perform - even if he had wanted to, which, of course, he did not. In this matter of work there was so strong a custom that if a man did a woman's work, where a woman was fit to do it, the feeling of shamed surprise would be felt stronger by the woman than by the man. The system worked very well, for the man in his sphere and the woman in hers were each equally governing and indispensable. Thus the difference between a man and a woman was emphasised and each carried clear before the other the characteristics and mystery of the male and female sex. Men were not knowing with regard to their women. They left them their realm and could thus on occasion meet them like strangers and even make a verse or a song about them. In life's major dealings, like cattle droving, marketing, hunting, and war, women would have felt helpless without their men. Yet more than their usefulness, men were to them their final ornament, and their secret pride in them, when worthy, was complete.

During this early winter season too, what with the new barley, so readily turned into malt, the menfolk had conspiracies of their own. Many of them would be away for days on end, and old Angus had the reputation of bringing the liquor from the pot in the distilling bothy sooner and cleaner than anyone else. His whisky, they said, had a flavour all its own. So well liked was he by the men that some of the women thought a man of his years should have more sense, forgetting that he was only very little over sixty. The men also went hunting the hill for deer and the river for salmon; and so ancient had been their gaming rights, that no new laws or restrictions in favour of landlord or lessee could ever convict them in their own minds of poaching. And if poaching it must be called, then so much the greater the zest in its pursuit.

So that, altogether, this season that followed the in-gathering of the grain and potatoes, with its Harvest Homes and Hallowe'ens culminating in the great New Year festival which continued for the better part of a fortnight, had its own attractions. But once the new year had settled in, a thin quickening, like the movement in a healthy but lean stomach, could be felt in man and beast. The testing time lay immediately ahead, when it was within the providence of Nature to be cruel or kind. It was at this time that the talk got going of conscription for war.

There was a thin covering of snow on the ground when Davie approached the house of Angus Sutherland. Kirsteen cried to him that she was making a great big snow man, but Davie, instead of going to help, stood looking at her out of his dark eyes. Her method of carrying handfuls of snow and patting them into position was adjudged by him to be a real lassie's way of making a snow man. Her living glance caught his disapproval, and, returning a cold dislike, she enquired, 'What are you going to my house for?' 'Not you,' said Davie, and drifted round to the barn where he could hear the clip of the flails. As he hesitated before the door, he heard footsteps, and, turning, saw the young daughter approaching with snow in her right fist and wrath on her face. 'You cheeky thing! she observed and threw the snow, which, not being properly packed into a ball, broke into ineffective fragments. Davie laughed and went into the barn.

Colin was flailing sheaves of oats which contained a great number of those withered flower stalks over which Angus had been twitted. His body swayed with a powerful rhythm, and so fine was his judgment that the tip of the loose arm of the flail clipped an overhead couple at every swing, for the curving roof was low set to the walls. This clipping sound was the mark of the expert, for it did not seem to interfere with the final thresh of the stick, yet gave the exquisite satisfaction of doing things to a hair's breadth. Davie liked the sound. Colin liked it himself, and when he had threshed the grain-and flower seeds-from the sheaf, his whirling flail contrived to whisk the straw towards his eldest brother, young Angus (Angus og), who gathered and tied it into bundles or windlings.

'How's life, Davie?' called Colin as he laid out another sheaf. Colin's chest looked broad and full of power. Above that chest his features appeared small, but finely made and hardy. Davie liked him at that moment - his compact strength, his clean assurance. Even his cheerfulness had a hard fighting glint. Colin often appeared to have this brisk cheerfulness before his brother, Angus og, who was half a head taller, slow in action like his father, Hector, and had an odd sideways glance from his eyes that appeared to sum a man up craftily when he wasn't looking. Davie respected Angus og, half fearing his reserve. His dark hair had something of brown in it that was absent from Colin's. Colin derived from his grandfather, Angus, as Kirsteen, her fair hair shot with gold, recalled to Anna her own mother. Hector, Angus og, and the youngest son, who was in Morayshire learning to be a mason, were much of a piece physically.

As Colin drew Davie into conversation, he made loud careless jokes that seemed like an instinctive barrier raised against or challenging Angus og. His eyes were clear and bright, his arms and shoulders supple as the flail, his waist drawn to a round pillar above his flexing hips. 'Canary seed!' he scoffed cheerfully. 'What they're going to do with this, Black Donald alone knows!' Happening to turn his head, Davie met the eyes of Angus og;

And when he left the barn, Kirsteen challenged his right of entry to her house. He was having a hard day of it! Nor could he rightly snowball a female on her own doorstep. It must be this talk of the army! She looked sharp and vindictive as a weasel. He actually did not know what to do and was standing with a sheepish expression when Anna appeared at the door and scolded her daughter for lack of manners and hospitality. 'He - he - ' began Kirsteen wildly, then, to Davie's amazement, burst into tears.

Anna invited him in and he found his old friend Angus by the fire. 'What havoc is this you're doing amongst the women, Davie?' He was very busy boring small holes with a red-hot wire in a sheepskin spread taut over the frame of a riddle, and Davie knew by his keen interest and extra good humour that he was inventing something. He was asked his opinion of the holes, and if he could guess the riddle. 'They may laugh at you and me, Davie, but we'll show them a trick or two! Put that in the fire again.' When the little black holes were all over the skin and Anna had complained finally about the smell, they got up and went to the barn. Colin welcomed them satirically, but Angus, paying no attention to him, laid the riddle on the floor and with cupped hands lifted the oats and flower seeds into it; then carefully he carried the riddle towards the door, where he began a circular motion that set the seeds sliding over the skin. From underneath came a small rain of the round flower seeds only: the oats remained in the riddle. 'You see how it's done, Davie: the holes are just big enough to let through the seeds but too little to let through the oats. Simple, isn't it?'

Colin was delighted with this; so was Davie; and so was old Angus. The pile of seeds grew. 'Lord, it's great, that!' cried Colin. He laughed, as at some animal performing a ridiculous trick. Even Angus og, leaning on a. birch handle, smiled. 'No one under- stood,' said old Angus, riddling away, 'why I grew these flowers in the corn. But now you know, Davie: I was wanting the seeds for my linnets.' At that Davie himself became noisy with mirth. ' I knew! ' he cried challengingly at Colin. Colin, with a quick lurch, couped him in the straw.

It was a moment of divine ease when life bubbles up clear at the source. The joy of creation, first creation, when what is made is not of use so much as of wonder, and attracts ripples of laughter around its sheer surprise. All Angus's inventions gathered something of that about them. Their usefulness was a divine joke. And to be in the midst of the joke, and welcomed there, was to experience for irresponsible minutes a state of perfect freedom, in which the instinct to play catches its ow crystal circles and flings them like lassos to snare and double up.

3.6 Annotated extracts

Extract one from 'Butcher's Broom' - annotated

Exhibit 14: Extract one from 'Butcher's Broom' - annotated

The following text is an annotated extract from Neil M. Gunn's 'Butcher's Broom', published in 1934.

> The old woman stood on the Darras, the doorway, between the bright sea and the dark hills; and when at last she turned from the sea and lifted her burden to her back, the door closed behind her. But the vacant glitter remained in her eyes and they held their stare until the valley began to pour slowly into them its dark comfort. For a long time she was like one who had turned into her own house and found it empty, and walked in a silence that was a hearkening to presences withdrawn beyond the walls and fading away.
>
> Every now and then there was a glint in this vagueness, for she had been born by the sea, and sea-water readily curls over and breaks on the shore of the mind. Looked at from a great distance childhood is little more than the breaking of small bright waves on a beach.[1] And whatever of pain and coldness there may have been, the brightness keeps a certain wild strangeness, a restless fly-away, that the hills do not know and never quite conquer.
>
> The sea had been in a good mood that morning[2], had had that pleasant scent that is the breath of fine weather. A person could always tell what the weather is to be by smelling the sea. There is the grey dark smell, cold inside the nostrils, ominous; the damp raw smell, husky to the throat, unsettled; the keen dry lifting tang of wind; but when good weather has newly come, how the sea brims and sways and breathes its sweet fragrance on the air! This morning, too, there had been the extra exhilaration of autumn, that indescribable quickening that the skin takes in a shiver.
>
> All of that sea she now carried in her basket as she went back among the companionable hills. For in addition to fish, she had many kinds of weed and shell. The clear pink dulse[3], gathered not off other sea-plants but off the rocks, was one of her most useful specifics. Eaten raw, it had a cleansing effect; boiled, with a pinch of butter added to the infusion, it acted as a tonic, bracing the flesh, making it supple, and drawing taut the muscles of the stomach. It could be preserved, too, by drying. A man working in a field could put a dry blade or two in his mouth and chew away at them. At first they were tasteless as gristle, but in a very short time they yielded back their juices, which began to run about the gums and fill the whole mouth with a richness that had to be frequently swallowed. When the dried dulse was ground into a powder and taken fasting, it sickened and expelled worms. Other ailments, like the stone and colic, yielded to it. [4]
>
> Linarich, slake, and sea-tangle had also their many uses; though she had not much of each with her now, for slake was mostly needed in the spring, when, after the rigour of winter, the cattle were weak and costive. Linarich, perhaps, was more useful at any time. It helped to soothe and heal the skin after a blister plaster. In the case of sciatica, for example, the ancient custom was to cut spirewort into small pieces, pack them in a limpet shell, and fasten the shell to the thigh-bone in order to raise a big blister, from which the

watery matter could be drained away. After the third draining, a linarich plaster dried and healed the wound.[5]

It was in her nature not to return home without such gifts. She had spent two days with a relative by marriage whose husband had been suffering from a mysterious fever and could not sweat. They had sent for her, for Dark Mairi of the Shore[6]. She had a reputation for healing among the people of that land. She was a small woman, roundly built, deep-chested and straight, yet she did not give an impression of bodily strength so much as of something delicate and hardy that persists evenly. Her skin was pale and little wrinkled; her eyes dark, and of a jewelled smallness. But perhaps the suggestion of persistence, of abidingness, that was the silent note struck by her person, was sustained most distinctly by the cheek-bones that did not obtrude in round knobs but ran straight back towards her ears, each in a visible ridge. These ridges drew the skin taut and gave the frontal expression a curious flattened steadiness. Her hair was black and coarse-grained, with grey strands showing here and there in a good light. It was drawn firmly back from her forehead, tautening the skin at the temples, as the cheek-bones tautened it down the sides of her face. Her head was raised in a watchfulness that was sometimes direct and glimmering and sometimes staring-blind.[7]

This 'blindness' in her expression had often the air of unintelligence, and when she smiled it could be seen as a sort of weakness running thinly all over her face. To move her out of her unthinking self seemed to expose her, to show that apart from what she was unthinkingly she was very little. One might as well have exposed a stone by causing it to smile or a piece of a mountain. Indeed, in her steady unthinking darkness, she might have walked out of a mountain and might walk into it again, leaving no sign.[8]

The sick man had looked at her with expectation. She asked him questions quietly. She smiled her small weak smile. She put her hand on his forehead. Her hand was very cold. Her smile did not touch her eyes at all. She was not concerned. She would soon put him all right. Oh yes.[9] She did not even say what was wrong with him. And the doubt that had clouded the man's eyes faded out, not into eagerness or impatience, but into an almost stupid peace. She prepared her drink and gave it to him. It was hot and harsh to the throat as oily sea-water. 'It's strong,' he said. 'Strong enough,' she answered and packed the extra clothes around him. 'Strong,' he muttered, and his body shuddered as under a convulsion and settled down into the bed, fatally accepting what was coming to it. When it relaxed from its next shudder there was a crawling warmth under the skin. The warmth grew; it became a glowing live heat.[10] Soon his whole body was a white dry furnace. He was being consumed, burnt up. Out of that heat the storm burst. The drops ran into runnels. These runnels tickled his face and his chest, and made his eyes water. 'God,' 'I'm sweating!' he gasped. 'Sweat you,'[11] said she. When she saw his hair steaming, she turned away and began asking his wife the news of the place. The two women sat down and told each other all they knew of everybody, so that their neighbours in their lives and their actions were brought clearly before them.[12] In this way the wife became happy and greatly moved towards Dark Mairi, to whom she unburdened herself, enjoying now what had been her saddest moments. In the morning the man was quite spent, but his eyes and his mind were clear and steady. 'I'm weak as a fly,' he jested. 'You'll be strong as a horse,' she replied. Whereupon the strength of the horse began to trickle into him.[13] 'God's blessing with you,' he said. 'And with yourself,' she answered, looking at him a moment then turning away.

Notes:

[1] Metaphor that immediately connects with nature.
[2] Personification that extends the connection with the natural world.
[3] A type of seaweed
[4] This shows the intimate relationship with nature that people had; so close in fact that people's very lives depended on their and each other's knowledge of plants and other organisms for food, healing, etc. This kind of long description can be tough to read, but is the nature of prose fiction, particularly older works that were longer than many novels tend to be now.
[5] This shows the intimate relationship with nature that people had; so close in fact that people's very lives depended on their and each other's knowledge of plants and other organisms for food, healing, etc. This kind of long description can be tough to read, but is the nature of prose fiction, particularly older works that were longer than many novels tend to be now.
[6] Her name: enigmatic but also typical, as surnames were unknown at the time. People had 'bynames' which come from a very complex system, so for our purposes we will say Mairi's 'byname' was of a descriptive sort and related to her particular skills.
[7] The character is described in as much detail as the setting, and the author is not in any rush. Nor is the character. Important to note her 'quietness' her stillness, her slowness (of movement) reflected in the way Gunn describes her. These people lived by the seasons and the tides; not by clocks and timetables.
[8] As with her name, there seems to be an air of mystery surrounding Dark Mairi, as if she is a ghost or spirit who 'leaves no sign' of her presence.
[9] Short sentences, suggesting now that Mairi is at work her movements are efficient, expert, business-like, calm.
[10] Continues the possibility that he's been given something to die peacefully "stupid peace"; "strong enough"; "fatally accepting".
[11] Sounds like a command or a spell, even. Possibly the syntax is derived from the Gaelic.
[12] An almost comical contrast from the tense drama the reader has just witnessed: women sitting down for a gossip now that the man's fever has broken to the point his hair is "steaming".
[13] Another spell, command, or prediction? Mairi's will is done.

Extract two from 'Butcher's Broom' - annotated

Exhibit 15: Extract two from 'Butcher's Broom' - annotated

The following text is an annotated extract from Neil M. Gunn's 'Butcher's Broom', published in 1934.

In a land of tall men, old Angus was small, with a white cropped beard, a quiet humour, and twinkling eyes. He was very knacky with his hands[1], built cages out of thin birch withies, and bred singing linnets in his barn. He was always willing to try a new thing, and in the spring had bought oats from the coast in the belief that the ground must get tired of the same old seed. And the new seed would have done very well had it not been for the stronger crop of yellow flowers that grew up with the corn, to the amusement (and perhaps not a little to the satisfaction) of some of his neighbours. Nor was it of any use for Angus to suggest now that the flower seeds must have been introduced to the ground after he had sown the oats. The picture of the old man solemnly flailing sheaves of withered flowers made good fun. The colour of the bread, it was maintained, would at least tally with the linnets' wings. It might even turn the linnets into canaries! Angus had long hankered after canaries. What about a barnful of them! One young man there, with a cripple foot, was goaded into improvising[2]:

'When Angus Ossian Finn Mac Cumhal
is turned into a fairy,
he'll eat a bit of his own yellow bread
and whistle like a canary.'

Which hit off Angus's knowledge of the ancient poetry and of the fairies well enough. But Angus answered the poet at once[3]:

'When Murdoch son of Murdoch
has grown old and hairy,
alas if he should find
he never made a tune
so well as a canary.'

Whereat everyone cheered the old man. In fact this improvising was one of their great amusements, and some nights at the ceilidh they hit a lucky vein. One or two of the girls were very good at it. Occasionally a couple of lines were struck out that instantly delighted and then haunted the mind. 'That's you on your back, Murdoch!' called Seonaid, the dark girl, boldly. As enemies, they never gave quarter. Murdoch murmured innocently:

'If I am on my back
and Angus is a fairy,
how kind of you to come
and offer your canary.'

There was an explosion of laughter, for Murdoch's satire was nearly always two-edged. He had ruddy cheeks, dark eyes, and a quick attractive smile. With a spot of colour, the girl changed the rhythm:

'If you were a whole barnful of canaries,
if you were a whole green mound of fairies,
I would sell the lot for Angus's empty cage with a crow in it.'

But the great game among the children was riddles, and one boy piped up, 'How could an empty cage have a crow in it?'

'When you are older, Iain my young calf,' said Seonaid, 'you may find that you too may not be in it though you are there.'

'Let me explain it to you, Iain,' said Angus, gripping the boy by the shoulder. 'Some day, like Murdoch there, you may be anxious to draw the attention of a fine girl, like Seonaid, but she, not caring, will look at the place on which you will be standing as though it were empty.'

'I should like to see her try it!' said Iain.

'What would you do to her?'

I'd hit her one on the nose.'

Murdoch laughed.

'There is meat and drink in its laugh, as the fox said when he ran away with the bagpipes,' misquoted Seonaid.

Then the war of proverbs started. They came hurtling from all corners, sometimes inaptly, but with Murdoch and Seonaid carrying on the main combat. The company obviously delighted in this, more than in the verse-making, which sometimes had an air of artificiality or strain, except in the case of Murdoch, who nearly always said something that stuck, often with a double meaning, particularly on the subject of women.

When Seonaid had Murdoch floundering for an apt reply, Elie heard Davie's excited voice putting the words in his mouth, 'I am too accustomed to a wood to be frightened of a canary.'

'Is it my friend Davie who's sending fuel to the wood? ' cried Angus. But Davie had ducked down out of sight.

'It's invisible you ·should be, you rascal!' cried Elie.

'I am like MacKay's cat-still in the flesh!' came Davie's voice.

Seonaid smiled, and the boldness of her glance melted into a rare attractiveness.

'The wren may be small, but it will make a noise', she said.

'Your hour, Davie,' said Murdoch,' is pursuing you.'

'Now, now,' said Angus, 'Fingal never fought a fight without offering terms.'

'Fingal's door is always free to the needy,' said Murdoch, without glancing at Seonaid, who remarked mildly, 'The heaviest ear of corn bends its head the lowest.'

'That's your head between the door and the door- post,' laughed one man at Murdoch, whose colour had risen. It's never difficult to guess the egg from your cackle,' Murdoch answered him shortly. But the man did not take it amiss for he saw that Murdoch, for all his laughing mouth, was beginning to be nettled. Seonaid seemed to have the power that in the long run cramped his wits. At the least opportunity they got fighting like this. Indeed the very sight of him raised her hackle. And there were times when he could clearly have throttled her.

Anna, the woman of the house and daughter-in-law to old Angus, was tall and broad and comely, with smooth dark hair and pleasant manners. She sat with her hands in her lap, smiling, saying to herself that in a moment she would stop this and call the girls to the waulking of the cloth[4], and yet delaying because of the gaiety. She liked this sound and fun in her home; she liked old Angus, whom she treated as one of her sons, of whom she had three, the second being Colin, who avoided Elie's eyes as pointedly as Elie avoided his. Anna now watched the fun climb to the point where Murdoch, desperately pressed, defended himself with the saying, 'The dung-heap is mother to the meal chest'.

Notes:

[1] We can argue that Gunn has chosen an editorial omniscient narration in this novel, meaning the narrator is all-seeing, aware of characters' feelings, and - crucially - shapes the readers' opinion of the characters by commenting on them and their actions.

[2] This is the first mention of the spontaneous verse-making that's such an important part of the traditional ceilidh.

[3] In contrast with the previous passage, this one is less leisurely and has more action, speech and pace. This line seems to indicate the start of the increased tempo of the narrative.

[4] Home-made tweed (still made today) is 'waulked' or beaten/pounded against a table or slab to make it softer and tighter. This was done by groups of women during the course of an entire day, accompanied by singing songs to keep the beat or rhythm (these were 'waulking songs').

3.7 Learning points

Summary

By the end of this topic you will better understand:

- the novelist's use of
    - pace;
    - time;
    - narration;
- how pace, time and narration affect the reader's experience.

Unit 2 Topic 4

Prose non-fiction

Contents

4.1	The good news	110
4.2	Health warnings	110
4.3	Features (mostly) unique to non-fiction	110
4.4	Features shared with other genres	111
4.5	Extract one from 'My Own Story'	112
4.6	Extract two from 'My Own Story'	113
4.7	Further work	115
4.8	Additional information and resources	116
4.9	Annotated extracts	117
4.10	Learning points	119

Learning objective

By the end of this topic you will have:

- strengthened your understanding of the features specific to non-fiction;
- increased your confidence in engaging with non-fiction texts.

4.1 The good news

If you were fortunate enough to have enjoyed and to have felt confident about Reading for Understanding, Analysis and Evaluation at National 5 and Higher, you are likely to want to have a good stab at the prose non-fiction option in the Textual Analysis exam. There is a huge variety of topics possible and it will be particularly interesting if you like 'real-life' texts; factual content; reading about people's lives; history; modern studies; politics. Non-fiction texts generally expect a degree of know-how on the part of the reader, both in terms of language-use and general knowledge. If all of this sounds good to you, you'll be in good hands.

As with the other genres within Textual Analysis, you'll be expected to give a "detailed analysis" of the text in front of you. The non-fiction option is likely to present you with an interesting, complex and challenging passage of some length and will make demands of you in ways that other genres do not. The aim of this section is to help students recognise some of the challenges this can pose.

4.2 Health warnings

The tricky thing about non-fiction is that students can become overly focused on what they know to be features and techniques unique to non-fiction while forgetting that many of the features of prose, poetry and drama also appear in non-fiction. It would be a poor non-fiction piece whose author didn't employ aspects of imagery, structure, tone and various lexical devices as aptly as the more obvious conventions of non-fiction. Hence, a student expected to produce a detailed analysis of a piece of journalism will need to be very aware that the journalist's portrayal of factual events, inclusion of statistics and addition of anecdote will very likely be accompanied by elements of setting, dialogue and symbolism.

The linguistic challenge can be heightened by the use of jargon so that you might only want to choose the non-fiction option if you're either comfortable with the topic or if there isn't much jargon in the text. Make your choice of which genre to go for after checking all four and by all means choose non-fiction if the topic interests you. However, if the first few paragraphs of the text do not draw your attention or the language baffles you, it might be wise to choose another option.

4.3 Features (mostly) unique to non-fiction

Features (mostly) unique to non-fiction:

- opinion (or: subjectivity);
- facts (or: objectivity);
- statistics;
- historical events and people;
- personal memories (events);
- anecdotes;
- hyperbole;

- jargon;
- footnotes or endnotes;
- emotive content and emotive language;
- personal/intimate detail and/or feelings;
- instruction;
- explanation;
- reflection;
- confession;
- first person narrative.

The 'Further Work' section later in this topic has tasks that invite you to actively engage with these features.

4.4 Features shared with other genres

Features shared with other genres:

- Structural devices: repetition, sentence lengths, punctuation, episodic devices such as flashbacks;
- All aspects of imagery: simile, metaphor, personification;
- Dialogue;
- Setting;
- Symbolism;
- Aspects of tone: formal, confessional, colloquial, didactic, patronising, informative.

In memoirs, depending on the author and the life events presented, the tone can be informal or colloquial or confessional. However, as we see in the passages presented in this section, the tone in memoirs can, equally, be formal and informative given the nature of the author, the era of publication and - importantly for the passages here - the gravity of the subject and events presented.

The colloquial tone can be marked by: a 'chatty' style; straightforward vocabulary; the use of abbreviations; the use of slang and jargon - for example, words and expressions used in a particular city or (sub) culture. You can imagine that an autobiography by Snoop Dogg will have very different linguistic properties than the political memoirs of Margaret Thatcher.

A confessional tone is used when highly personal or sensitive content is being shared, as in letters and diaries. It doesn't have to mean anything is being 'confessed' but the effect is that a 'closeness' or 'bond' is created between the writer and the reader.

Didactic and patronising tones occur when the author has something to prove or points to score, is upset about an issue or responding to another author in a disagreeable way. Think of letters in newspapers, for example (including the comments sections underneath on-line articles), social media posts, blogs or, indeed, more traditional texts in which a patronising person is being portrayed (see also: characterisation). The didactic tone is less disagreeable but occurs when an author takes the 'moral high ground' or takes a 'know-it-all' stance.

Aspects of characterisation

The fun with characterisation in non-fiction is that it's real people (past or present) being characterised. The author's portrayal of a person's voice, physique, dress and mannerism is as vital to a reader's appreciation of 'real' people as it to that of fictional characters. In addition, and unique to non-fiction, the reader can get the author's opinion of the person being characterised - sometimes with explosive consequences: think of famous people's memoirs characterising other (famous) people in less-than-flattering terms. But, as with characterisation in other genres, the effect can also be humorous and engaging and, in the hands of a skilled-enough author, can take on elements of tragi-comedy, or farce. The term 'stranger than fiction' really does apply to many a non-fiction episode or real-life event. One of the best (recent) examples of this can be found in Jackie Kay's memoir, Red Dust Road, with a conversation (and a 'character') so unique that only a reading by the author herself will do justice to it (see: Additional Information/resources below)

4.5 Extract one from 'My Own Story'

This is the opening passage from Emmeline Pankhurst's memoir My Own Story, published in 1914. Pankhurst is famous for having spent her life leading the movement for women's suffrage (the right to vote in political elections) in England in the late 19th and early 20th centuries. She died in 1928, shortly after women were granted suffrage.

Exhibit 16: Extract one from 'My Own Story'

Those men and women are fortunate who are born at a time when a great struggle for human freedom is in progress. It is an added good fortune to have parents who take a personal part in the great movements of their time. I am glad and thankful that this was my case.

One of my earliest recollections is of a great bazaar which was held in my native city of Manchester, the object of the bazaar being to raise money to relieve the poverty of the newly emancipated negro slaves in the United States. My mother took an active part in this effort, and I, as, a small child, was entrusted with a lucky bag by means of which I helped to collect money.

Young as I was - I could not have been older than five years - I knew perfectly well the meaning of the words slavery and emancipation. From infancy I had been accustomed to hear pro and con discussions of slavery and the American Civil War. Although the British government finally decided not to recognise the Confederacy, public opinion in England was sharply divided on the questions both of slavery and of secession. Broadly speaking, the propertied classes were pro-slavery, but there were many exceptions to the rule. Most of those who formed the circle of our family friends were opposed to slavery, and my father, Robert Goulden, was always a most ardent abolitionist. He was prominent enough in the movement to be appointed on a committee to meet and welcome Henry-Ward Beecher when he arrived in England for a lecture tour. Mrs Harriet Beecher Stowe's novel, 'Uncle Tom's Cabin', was so great a favourite with my mother that she used it continually as a source of bedtime stories for our fascinated ears. These stories, told almost fifty years ago, are as fresh in my mind today as events detailed in the morning's papers. Indeed they are more vivid, because they made a much deeper impression on my consciousness.

TOPIC 4. PROSE NON-FICTION

Read the extract carefully, twice, and make sure you understand it: write down any points you think are interesting and any questions you have. When you're ready, read the annotated extract - Exhibit 18 in the 'Annotated extracts' section at the end of this topic - and complete the following questions.

Extract one from 'My Own Story'

Q1: In what ways, and how effectively, does Pankhurst merge details of her personal history with events from world history?

4.6 Extract two from 'My Own Story'

This extract, from later on in the same text, has other things to teach us. Vocabulary is hardly an issue here, but what is striking is Pankhurst's address to her audience: her understanding that some of them are American and that these readers may not be familiar with some of the specifics of English history and legislation. This overt acknowledgement of an audience is unique to non-fiction and is very worth noting. Linguistically, be aware of the sometimes long, fluent sentences and don't be too put off by all the historical figures' names.

Exhibit 17: Extract two from 'My Own Story'

For the benefit of American readers I shall explain something of the operation of our English Poor Law. The duty of the law is to administer an act of Queen Elizabeth, one of the greatest reforms effected by that wise and humane monarch. When Elizabeth came to the throne she found England, the Merrie England of contemporary poets, in a state of appalling poverty. Hordes of people were literally starving to death, in wretched hovels, in the street, and at the very gates of the palace. The cause of all this misery was the religious reformation under Henry VIII, and the secession from Rome of the English Church. King Henry, it is known, seized all the Church lands, the abbeys and the convents, and gave them as rewards to those nobles and favourites who had supported his policies. But in taking over the Church property the Protestant nobles by no means assumed the Church's ancient responsibilities of lodging wayfarers, giving alms, nursing the sick, educating youths, and caring for the young and the superannuated. When the monks and the nuns were turned out of their convents these duties devolved on no one. The result, after the brief reign of Edward VI and the bloody one of Queen Mary, was the social anarchy inherited by Elizabeth.

This great queen and great woman, perceiving that the responsibility for the poor and the helpless rightfully rests on the community, caused an act to be passed creating in the parishes public bodies to deal with local conditions of poverty. The Board of Poor Law Guardians disburses for the poor the money coming from the Poor Rates (taxes), and some additional moneys allowed by the local government board, the president of which is a cabinet minister. Mr John Burns is the present incumbent of the office. The Board of Guardians has control of the institution we call the workhouse. You have, I believe, almshouses [sic], or poorhouses, but they are not quite so extensive as our workhouses, which are all kinds of institutions in one. We had, in my workhouse, a hospital with nine hundred beds, a school with several hundred children, a farm, and many workshops.

When I came into office I found that the law in our district, Chorlton, was being very harshly administered. The old board had been made up of the kind of men who are known as rate savers. They were guardians, not of the poor but of the rates, and, as I soon discovered, not very astute guardians even of money. For instance, although the inmates were being very poorly fed, a frightful waste of food was apparent. Each inmate was given each day a certain weight of food, and bread formed so much of the ration that hardly anyone consumed all of his portion. In the farm department pigs were kept on purpose to consume this surplus of bread, and as pigs do not thrive on a solid diet of stale bread the animals fetched in the market a much lower price than properly fed farm pigs. I suggested that, instead of giving a solid weight of bread in one lump, the loaf be cut in slices and buttered with margarine, each person being allowed all that he cared to eat.

Read the extract carefully, twice, and make sure you understand it: write down any points you think are interesting and any questions you have. When you're ready, read the annotated extract - Exhibit 19 in the 'Annotated extracts' section at the end of this topic - and complete the following questions.

Extract two from 'My Own Story'

Q2: Nature and scale of poverty

In a detailed analysis of the extract, discuss in what ways, and how effectively, Pankhurst explains to her readers the nature and scale of the "state of appalling poverty" that initiated the Poor Law.

4.7 Further work

Techniques and features typically found in prose non-fiction - 'My Own Story'

Returning to the above section 'Features (mostly) unique to non-fiction' with the list of techniques and features typically found in prose non-fiction, try some of the following exercises.

The following four techniques and features are typically found in prose non-fiction:

- personal feelings and opinion;
- personal memories;
- historical events and people;
- explanation.

For example, for 'personal feelings and opinion' you would highlight where Pankhurst is being subjective, e.g. her fondness for Queen Elizabeth, her sympathy for the boy in Uncle Tom's Cabin. It would be equally valuable to highlight features and techniques normally found in fiction, drama or poetry where you see this in the passages.

Q3: Identify where the four techniques and features listed above can be found in extract one from 'My Own Story' (see Exhibit 16 in the 'Annotated extracts' section at the end of this topic).

....

Q4: Identify where the four techniques and features listed above can be found in extract two from 'My Own Story' (see Exhibit 17 in the 'Annotated extracts' section at the end of this topic).

....

Q5: Identify where the four techniques and features listed above can be found in another prose non-fiction extract of your choosing, either on paper or electronically, remembering the golden rule that it must be about something that interests you.

Techniques and features typically found in prose non-fiction - choose a text

Find another text, either on paper or online, about any of the topics or themes introduced by the Pankhurst passages (if they interest you) and give it the 'TA treatment', i.e. study it with an eye to writing a detailed analysis of the text's features and techniques, as shown throughout this section and tasks.

© HERIOT-WATT UNIVERSITY

4.8 Additional information and resources

Video clip from 'Red Dust Road'   Go online

To gain an appreciation of how skilled writers can use characterisation to great humorous effect even in dire situations, watch this short video clip:

- Jackie Kay reading from her 2012 memoir, Red Dust Road (https://youtu.be/6572Kv-O5w0)

Advisory note for teachers: this clip contains language unsuitable for younger learners. Please review the clip prior to asking students to watch it, particularly in spaces where younger learners might be present.

The scene she reads takes place in a hotel room in Nigeria, where she has travelled to find her birth father and whom she has now just met for the first time. His name is Jonathan and he is a devout, over-zealous, Christian minister who has just spent several hours 'praying away' the 'sin' that is his daughter (Kay). The author has endured this ordeal politely but has been drinking white wine throughout.

Notice, in particular, how the author impersonates Jonathan's voice, speech and (facial) expression to bring this 'character' to life.

4.9 Annotated extracts

Extract one from 'My Own Story' - annotated

Exhibit 18: Extract one from 'My Own Story' - annotated

The following text is an annotated extract from Emmeline Pankhurst's memoir 'My Own Story', published in 1914.

> Those men and women are fortunate who are born at a time when a great struggle for human freedom is in progress. It is an added good fortune to have parents who take a personal part in the great movements of their time. I am glad and thankful that this was my case.
>
> One of my earliest recollections[1] is of a great bazaar which was held in my native city of Manchester, the object of the bazaar being to raise money to relieve the poverty of the newly emancipated negro slaves in the United States[2]. My mother took an active part in this effort, and I, as, a small child, was entrusted with a lucky bag by means of which I helped to collect money.
>
> Young as I was - I could not have been older than five years - I knew perfectly well the meaning of the words slavery and emancipation. From infancy I had been accustomed to hear pro and con discussions of slavery and the American Civil War. Although the British government finally decided not to recognise the Confederacy[3], public opinion in England was sharply divided on the questions both of slavery and of secession. Broadly speaking, the propertied classes were pro-slavery, but there were many exceptions to the rule. Most of those who formed the circle of our family friends were opposed to slavery, and my father, Robert Goulden, was always a most ardent abolitionist. He was prominent enough in the movement to be appointed on a committee to meet and welcome Henry-Ward Beecher when he arrived in England for a lecture tour. Mrs Harriet Beecher Stowe's novel, 'Uncle Tom's Cabin'[4], was so great a favourite with my mother that she used it continually as a source of bedtime stories for our fascinated ears. These stories, told almost fifty years ago, are as fresh in my mind today as events detailed in the morning's papers. Indeed they are more vivid, because they made a much deeper impression on my consciousness.
>
> **Notes:**
>
> [1] Recollection/memory: one powerful feature unique to non-fiction.
> [2] Appropriate and effective for this famous suffrage activist to begin her memoir by introducing the theme of the emancipation of American slaves.
> [3] The term used for the Confederate States of America, a number of southern states who seceded (separated from) from the United States in 1861.
> [4] American novel published in 1852 and a landmark in terms of sales and its anti-slavery influence.

Extract two from 'My Own Story' - annotated

Exhibit 19: Extract two from 'My Own Story' - annotated

The following text is an annotated extract from Emmeline Pankhurst's memoir 'My Own Story', published in 1914.

For the benefit of American readers[1] I shall explain something of the operation of our English Poor Law. The duty of the law is to administer an act of Queen Elizabeth[2], one of the greatest reforms effected by that wise and humane monarch. When Elizabeth came to the throne she found England, the Merrie England of contemporary poets, in a state of appalling poverty. Hordes of people were literally starving to death, in wretched hovels, in the street, and at the very gates of the palace. The cause of all this misery was the religious reformation under Henry VIII, and the secession from Rome of the English Church. King Henry, it is known, seized all the Church lands, the abbeys and the convents, and gave them as rewards to those nobles and favourites who had supported his policies[3]. But in taking over the Church property the Protestant nobles by no means assumed the Church's ancient responsibilities of lodging wayfarers, giving alms, nursing the sick, educating youths, and caring for the young and the superannuated[4]. When the monks and the nuns were turned out of their convents these duties devolved on no one. The result, after the brief reign of Edward VI and the bloody one of Queen Mary, was the social anarchy inherited by Elizabeth.

This great queen and great woman, perceiving that the responsibility for the poor and the helpless rightfully rests on the community, caused an act to be passed creating in the parishes public bodies to deal with local conditions of poverty. The Board of Poor Law Guardians disburses for the poor the money coming from the Poor Rates (taxes), and some additional moneys allowed by the local government board, the president of which is a cabinet minister. Mr John Burns is the present incumbent of the office. The Board of Guardians has control of the institution we call the workhouse. You have, I believe, almshouses [sic], or poorhouses[5], but they are not quite so extensive as our workhouses, which are all kinds of institutions in one. We had, in my workhouse, a hospital with nine hundred beds, a school with several hundred children, a farm, and many workshops[6].

When I came into office[7] I found that the law in our district, Chorlton, was being very harshly administered. The old board had been made up of the kind of men who are known as rate savers. They were guardians, not of the poor but of the rates, and, as I soon discovered, not very astute guardians even of money. For instance, although the inmates were being very poorly fed, a frightful waste of food was apparent. Each inmate was given each day a certain weight of food, and bread formed so much of the ration that hardly anyone consumed all of his portion. In the farm department pigs were kept on purpose to consume this surplus of bread, and as pigs do not thrive on a solid diet of stale bread the animals fetched in the market a much lower price than properly fed farm pigs. I suggested that, instead of giving a solid weight of bread in one lump, the loaf be cut in slices and buttered with margarine, each person being allowed all that he cared to eat.

Notes:

[1] Direct address to potential audience unfamiliar with certain English laws.
[2] Queen of England from 1558 - 1603.
[3] This is known as the Dissolution of the Monasteries, a major event in English history.
[4] Those people too old to work.
[5] Another direct address to American readers, this time drawing a comparison between what she is explaining and a similar facility in American society, to help clarify.
[6] The scale of this workhouse suggests it's the size of a small town.
[7] Pankhurst had newly been elected onto the Board of Poor Law Guardians, by a very large majority, in her native city of Manchester.

4.10 Learning points

Summary

By the end of this topic you will have:

- strengthened your understanding of the features specific to non-fiction;
- increased your confidence in engaging with non-fiction texts.

Unit 2 Topic 5

Drama

Contents

5.1 Principles of drama	122
5.2 How this topic will help you	122
5.3 Learning point: dramatic function	123
5.4 Learning point: a crash course in Greek tragedy	123
5.5 Learning point: central conflict	124
5.6 Extract from drama: Worked example	125
5.6.1 Features of language	131
5.6.2 Choose an extract	132
5.7 Annotated extracts	132
5.8 Learning points	138

Learning objective

By the end of this topic you will better understand the development of:

- dramatic function;
- the language in drama;
- the central conflict in drama.

122   UNIT 2. TEXTUAL ANALYSIS

5.1   Principles of drama

Textual analysis of a dramatic work requires you to recognise and discuss in considerable detail techniques and features specific to plays. You'll have learned how important it is, in any critical response to literature, to show you can distinguish between the different genres by identifying and commenting on the distinct features for each. Hence, when discussing a poem, you'll want to be explicit about discussing rhyme, rhythm and stanzas to show that you are writing about a poem. For plays, you'll be trying to be explicit about including terms like stage directions, staging, audience dialogue and conflict, so particular to the study of drama.

To enhance and extend these habits, the learning points in this section comprise three principles specific to drama :

- dramatic function;
- tragedy;
- central conflict.

The aim of the extract and tasks here is to help us recognise them, understand them and be able to write about them confidently and in detail.

5.2   How this topic will help you

As you will find in the specimen exam papers on SQA's website, the textual analysis questions for all four genres tend to be along the lines of:

- Make a detailed analysis of... [the extract given]; or
- How effectively does the writer portray the theme of... / develop your understanding of...

For either of these questions you will be asked to discuss aspects of language use, structure, genre conventions, theme(s), etc.

For example, the 2013 exam question for Drama asks:

> Make a detailed analysis of the means by which Michael Frayn [the playwright] explores the Bohrs' relationship with Heisenberg. In your answer you should play close attention to
>
> a) Dramatic structure
>
> b) Dialogue
>
> c) The significance of uncertainty [one of the main themes].

We need to be clear about what **detailed analysis** is and this topic, Drama, will help you do that. At Advanced Higher level you're encouraged to take your thinking up a level, and the study of this section invites you to do this. Undertaking detailed analysis is a bit like using a microscope to study features, techniques and their effects that can be easy to miss. And while it is expected that many of the concepts and tasks here will be familiar to a student of Advanced Higher English, it is also hoped that some of it might be new or can act as a good 'refresher' in your learning.

© HERIOT-WATT UNIVERSITY

5.3 Learning point: dramatic function

We tend to learn that 'characters' in a play or other imaginative works represent 'people'. Let's take this further and start thinking of them not just as 'people' but more as representations of ideas or concepts. Thus, Macbeth is not just an ambitious and ultimately ruthless character/person: he represents the *idea* of ambition; the *idea* of ruthlessness. He stands as a warning against the dangers of wanting too much; of listening to others too much; of losing everything because of excessive pride (more on that later). Macbeth's dramatic function, then - his 'job', really - is to show the kind of weakness humans are capable of and the devastation such weakness can bring about.

Behind every warmongering Macbeth we hope to find an antidote, a character who offers the 'voice of reason' in an attempt to mitigate some of the havoc being wreaked. Take Banquo, for example: here, too, we may regard the character as a 'person', but his dramatic function is to represent the *ideas* of integrity, honesty and fairness. His character remains steadfastly good, as Macbeth used to be before he got carried away with his ambitions. Banquo, then, represents these virtues, and his contributions try to maintain some balance in the play (another dramatic function). The notion of 'reason' (or reasonable-ness) is as human a trait as ruthlessness - only it tends to claim fewer victims.

Objects and aspects of staging also have dramatic functions: to stay with Macbeth, his dagger's dramatic function is to *represent* Macbeth's decision to kill; to *represent* his descent into madness - so: representing the beginning of the end. But taken on the literal level it is, of course, the actual, physical dagger with which he kills King Duncan, marking a key structural moment in the play.

5.4 Learning point: a crash course in Greek tragedy

Sophocles

Sophocles was one of a number of prolific playwrights in 5th Century BC in Athens, Greece, and became one of the great tragedians of his day. A major platform for writers to showcase new plays in those days was the spring festival in Athens, attended by tens of thousands of Athenians in vast, open-air theatres. Before any work was even accepted for performance at this festival, however, it had to have been selected by a special committee (a bit like a talent show, but with more gravity). Playwrights had to submit several works for this competition, including three tragedies, often, but not always, submitted as a trilogy.

Whilst 'Antigone' (which we will study here) is one of what is known as 'the Theban plays' (Thebes being a city not far from Athens) along with 'King Oedipus' and 'Oedipus at Colonus', and while these three plays are connected in many ways, they do not form a trilogy because they were written many years apart and are not published in the order they were written.

Tragedy

The true meaning of tragedy has been lost these days, with every disappointment, every mishap and every bad hair day branded a 'tragedy'.

A tragedy is really only one thing: a serious play in which a flaw in the protagonist's nature or action creates his/her own downfall (i.e. death). Anything outside of this definition, however unpleasant, painful or traumatic, is not a tragedy.

The aforementioned flaw in the protagonist's character is often down to hubris, or, excessive pride (see also 'Macbeth'). And in the very worst cases, the mistake made by the protagonist results in disproportionate calamity (i.e. what he/she did was pretty bad but the playwright gives him/her a far worse ending than the audience might think justified). The reason for including these points about tragedy here is simple: the principles of the tragedy that originated in ancient Greece remain in place even today, in contemporary drama, and have been through the ages. So any play you study, unless it's a comedy, will be based on many of these principles.

The chorus

An essential element in Greek dramas is the role of the chorus, comprising a group of individuals but, traditionally, acting and speaking as one 'character'. The chorus has several functions:

- it comments on the action for, and on behalf of, the audience;
- it offers advice or warnings of impending doom to key characters;
- it laments loudly on behalf of the audience when things go horribly wrong.

A very important thing the chorus does is fill in the blanks for the audience, i.e. just as with flashbacks in a film it will offer some context or reminders of what brought the audience, and the action, to this point. This is very relevant to what we see of the chorus in the extract here.

5.5 Learning point: central conflict

You will already have learned that the entire point of a play is that there is a problem or crisis that needs to be resolved. The word 'conflict' appears in many a Higher English question paper, mostly in the Drama section, and we will extend this here. The conflict is generally between two or more characters or between a character and something more abstract: 'wider society' and 'religion' ('The Crucible') or the notion of 'justice' and what this means ('View from the Bridge').

In this sense, the drama isn't merely about two 'people' having a problem but about a human representation conflicting with society. This extension allows the audience to place themselves in the shoes of the character(s) and think: *what would I do?*

Arthur Miller was a master of this theme of 'individual versus society'. We can all identify with his everyday figure of Eddie Carbone. From his 'simple' point of view:

- who wouldn't want to protect their niece from a layabout?
- who wouldn't want to challenge the law when it doesn't work in their favour?
- who wouldn't take matters into their own hands in utter desperation?

The trick, for the playwright, is to introduce the conflict (or tension, or crisis) early on in the play; after all, there is only limited time in which to develop and resolve it. The tension can be hinted at, built-up or indeed suddenly introduced by the playwright - it all depends on the play. The point of the extract in this section is for us to recognise how and where Sophocles introduces the tension in the opening scenes.

5.6 Extract from drama: Worked example

The following extract is taken from the start of the play 'Antigone' (pronounced An-ti-guh-nee) by Sophocles.

Antigone starts where a major battle in the Theban war finishes, in which our protagonist, Antigone, and her sister, Ismene, lose both their brothers. The brothers (Eteocles and Polynices) fought on opposing sides in the war and actually killed one another. Creon has just been crowned King and, because Polynices fought on the opposing side (the Argives) Creon has decreed that only Eteocles is to receive a proper burial while Polynices is to be left to the animals. Anybody defying this order, or anybody mourning him openly, is to be punished by death.

It is at this point the play begins.

Exhibit 20: Extract one from 'Antigone'

Characters:
Ismene and Antigone - daughters of Oedipus
Creon, King of Thebes
Chorus of Theban elders

Scene:
Before the Palace at Thebes

Enter ISMENE from the central door of the Palace. ANTIGONE follows, anxious and urgent; she closes the door carefully, and comes to her sister.

ANTIGONE: O sister! Ismene dear, dear sister Ismene!
You know how heavy the hand of God is upon us;
How we who are left must suffer for our father, Oedipus.
There is no pain, no sorrow, no suffering, no dishonour
We have not shared together, you and I.
And now there is something more. Have you heard this order,
This latest order that the King has proclaimed to the city?
Have, you heard how our dearest are being treated like enemies?

ISMENE: 'I have heard nothing. about any of those we love,
Neither good nor evil - not, I mean, since the death
Of our two brothers, both fallen in a day.
The Argive army, I hear, was withdrawn last night.
I know no more to make me sad or glad.

ANTIGONE: I thought you did not. That's why I brought you out here,
Where we shan't be heard, to tell you something alone.

ISMENE: What is it, Antigone? Black news, I can see already.

ANTIGONE: O Ismene, what do you think? Our two dear brothers...
Creon has given funeral honours to one,
And not to the other; nothing but shame and ignominy.
Eteocles has been buried, they tell me, in state,
With all honourable observances due to the dead.
But Polynices, just as unhappily fallen - the order
Says he is not to be buried, not to be mourned;
To be left unburied, unwept, a feast of flesh

© HERIOT-WATT UNIVERSITY

For keen-eyed carrion birds. The noble Creon!
It is against you and me he has made this order.
Yes, against me. And soon he will be here himself
To make it plain to those that have not heard it,
And to enforce it. This is no idle threat;
The punishment for disobedience is death by stoning.
So now you know. And now is the time to show
Whether or not you are worthy of your high blood.

ISMENE: My poor Antigone, if this is really true,
What more can I do, or undo, to help you?

ANTIGONE: Will you help me? Will you do something with me? Will you?

ISMENE: Help you do what, Antigone? What do you mean?

ANTIGONE: Would you help me lift the body ... you and me?

ISMENE: You cannot mean ... to bury him? Against the order?

ANTIGONE: Is he not my brother, and yours, whether you like it
Or not? I shall never desert him, never.

ISMENE: How could you dare, when Creon has expressly forbidden it?

ANTIGONE: He has no right to keep me from my own.

ISMENE: O sister, sister, do you forget how our father
Perished in shame and misery, his awful sin
Self-proved, blinded by his own self-mutilation?
And then his mother, his wife - for she was both...
Destroyed herself in a noose of her own making.
And now our brothers, both in a single day
Fallen in an awful exaction: of death for death,
Blood for blood, each slain by the other's hand.
Now we two left; and what will be the end of us,
If we transgress the law an defy our king?
O think, Antigone; we are women; it is not for us
To fight against men; our rulers are stronger than we,
And we must obey in this, or in worse than this.
May the dead forgive me, I can do no other
But as I am commanded; to do more is madness.

ANTIGONE: No; then I will not ask you for your help.
Nor would I thank you for it, if you gave it.
Go your own way; I will bury my brother;
And if I die for it, what happiness!
Convicted of reverence - I shall be content
To lie beside a brother whom I love.
We have only a little time to please the living,
But all eternity to love the dead.
There I shall lie forever. Live, if you will;
Live, and defy the holiest laws of heaven.

ISMENE: I do not defy them; but I cannot act

Against the State. I am not strong enough.

ANTIGONE: Let that be your excuse, then. I will go
And heap a mound of earth over my brother.

ISMENE: I fear for you, Antigone; I fear -

ANTIGONE: You need not fear for me. Fear for yourself

ISMENE: At least be secret. Do not breathe a word.
I'll not betray your secret.

ANTIGONE: Publish it
To all the world! Else I shall hate you more.

ISMENE: Your heart burns! Mine is frozen at the thought.

ANTIGONE: I know my duty, where true duty lies.

ISMENE: If you can do it; but you're bound to fail.

ANTIGONE: When I have tried and failed, I shall have failed.

ISMENE: No sense in starting on a hopeless task.

ANTIGONE: Oh, I shall hate you if you talk like that!
And he will hate you, rightly. Leave me alone
With my own madness. There is no punishment
Can rob me of my honourable death.

ISMENE: Go then, if you are determined, to your folly.
But remember that those who love you... love you still.

ISMENE goes into the Palace. ANTIGONE leaves the stage by a side exit.

Enter the CHORUS of Theban elders.

CHORUS: Hail the sun! the brightest of all that ever
Dawned on the City of Seven Gates, City of Thebes!
Hail the golden dawn over Dirce's river
Rising to speed the flight of the white invaders
Homeward in full retreat!

The army of Polynices was gathered against us,
In angry dispute his voice was lifted against us,
Like a ravening bird of prey he swooped around us
With white wings flashing, with flying plumes,
With armed hosts ranked in thousands.

At the threshold of seven gates in a circle of blood
His swords stood round us, his jaws were opened against us;
But before he could taste our blood, or consume us with fire
He fled, fled with the roar of the dragon behind him
And thunder of war in his ears.

The Father of Heaven abhors the proud tongue's boasting;
He marked the oncoming torrent, the flashing stream
Of their golden harness, the clash of their battle gear;
He heard the invader cry Victory over our ramparts,

And smote him with fire to the ground.
Down to the ground from the crest of his hurricane onslaught
He swung, with the fiery brands of his hate brought low:
Each and all to their doom of destruction appointed
By the god that fighteth for us.

Seven invaders at seven gates seven defenders
Spoiled of their bronze for a tribute to Zeus; save two
Luckless brothers in one fight matched together
And in one death laid low.

Great is the victory, great be the joy
In the city of Thebes, the city of chariots.
Now is the time to fill the temples
With glad thanksgiving for warfare ended;
Shake the ground with the night-long dances,
Bacchus afoot and delight abounding.

But see, the King comes here,
Creon, the son of Menoeceus,
Whom the gods have appointed for us
In our recent change of fortune.
What matter is it, I wonder
That has led him to call us together
By his special proclamation?

The central door is opened, and CREON enters.

CREON: My councilors: now that 'the gods have brought our city
Safe through a storm of trouble to tranquillity, [sic]
I have called you especially out of all my people
To conference together, knowing that you
Were loyal subjects when King Laius reigned,
And when King Oedipus so wisely ruled us,
And again, upon his death, faithfully served
His sons, till they in turn fell - both slayers, both slain,
Both stained with brother-blood, dead in a day -
And I, their next of kin, inherited
The throne and kingdom which I now possess
No other touchstone can test the heart of a man,
The temper of his mind and spirit, till he be tried
In the practice of authority and rule.
For my part, I have always held the view,
And hold it still, that a king whose lips are sealed
By fear, unwilling to seek advice, is damned.
And no less damned is he who puts a friend
Above his country; I have no good word for him.
As God above is my witness, who sees all,
When I see any danger threatening my people,
Whatever it may be, I shall declare it.
No man who is his country's enemy
Shall call himself my friend. Of this I am sure -

Our country is our life; only when she
Rides safely, have we any friends at all.
Such is my policy for our common weal.
In pursuance of this, I have made a proclamation
Concerning the sons of Oedipus, as follows:
Eteocles, who fell fighting in defence of the city,
Fighting gallantly, is to be honoured with burial
And with all the rites due to the noble dead.
The other - you know whom I mean - his brother Polynices;
Who came back from exile intending to burn and destroy
His fatherland and the gods of his fatherland,
To drink the blood of his kin, to make them slaves -
He is to have no grave, no burial,
No mourning from. anyone; it is forbidden.
He is to be left unburied, left to be eaten
By dogs and vultures, a horror for all to see.
I am determined that. never, if I can help it,
Shall evil triumph over good. Alive
Or dead, the faithful servant of his country
Shall be rewarded.

CHORUS: Creon, son of Menoeceus,
You have given your judgment for the friend and for the enemy.
As for those that are dead, so for us who remain,
Your will is law.

CREON: See then that it be kept.

CHORUS: My lord, some younger would be fitter for that task

CREON: Watchers are already set over the corpse.

CHORUS: What other duty then remains for us?

CREON: Not to connive at any disobedience.

CHORUS: If there were any so mad as to ask for death

CREON: Ay, that is the penalty. There is always someone
Ready to be lured to ruin by hope of gain.

He turns to go. A SENTRY enters from the side of the stage.
CREON pauses at the Palace door

Read the extract carefully, twice, and make sure you understand it: write down any points you think are interesting and any questions you have. When you're ready, read the annotated extract - Exhibit 21 in the 'Annotated extracts' section at the end of this topic - and complete the following questions.

Extract from 'Antigone'

Q1: The possibility of tension

Jot down some thoughts about how Sophocles introduces the possibility of tension here in the opening stage directions.

....

Q2: Hubris

"And now is the time to show Whether or not you are worthy of your high blood." Note Antigone's language and think about what you've learned about hubris. If we consider this line to be an early indication of Antigone's hubris (pride, arrogance) find further, increasingly dramatic and alarming, evidence of this throughout the extract.

....

Q3: Stage directions

"ISMENE goes into the Palace. ANTIGONE leaves the stage by a side exit." Discuss how the stage directions here highlight the sisters' differences; their respective allegiances.

....

Q4: Tone and features of language

"Hail the sun! the brightest of all that ever Dawned on the City of Seven Gates, City of Thebes." How does the tone contrast with the sisters' previous dialogue and what features of the language contribute to this? (Support note: the Chorus is celebrating their city's recent victory in battle, to remind the audience of the context.)

....

Q5: Aspects of language

"The army of Polynices was gathered against us, In angry dispute his voice was lifted against us," What aspects of the language make it more 'formally poetic'? Why would this be the case? (Think of the Chorus' dramatic function.) Discuss the features of language here: consider structure, imagery and word choice.

....

Q6: Voice of reason

Find examples in the extract where Ismene is the voice of reason.

5.6.1 Features of language

Some of the features of *the sisters' language* in this extract - Exhibit 21 - can be identified as:

- exclamation;
- repetition;
- rhetorical question;
- statement;
- reasoning;
- command;
- juxtaposition (when two contrasting words/ideas are placed near each other for heightened effect or drama).

With this in mind, try the following activities.

Features of language

Find examples of (some of) the features of language in the sisters' speech. Comment on the purpose and effect of these features.

For example, what is the purpose of the repetition of "hate" in lines 101, 107 and 108? What is the effect of this repetition and how does this link with your other work on detailed analysis of aspects of the extract?

Characters' language

Consider the various characters' language in this opening extract - Exhibit 20 - and make a detailed analysis of the ways in which:

Q7: The *sisters' language* shows the differences in their characters.

....

Q8: The *central conflict* of the play is introduced (Antigone vs. Creon).

....

Q9: The *nature of the tragedy* is established.

The chorus

Q10: Consider the *language* of the chorus, both prior to and following Creon's arrival, and discuss how it helps you understand the chorus's *dramatic function*.

5.6.2 Choose an extract

Choose an extract

A final exercise you could do is take the learning from this section and apply it to your reading of another extract. Choose an extract of approximately the same length as those used in the SQA Textual Analysis exam paper. So:

- identify and recognise the *dramatic function* of other characters you know;
- if the extract is a tragedy, consider the nature of the *tragedy* in other plays you know;
- find the *central conflict* in other plays and discuss how it arises, develops and is resolved.

For any of these you could try a detailed analysis which, of course, involves a very close look of the *language and techniques* employed by the playwright.

5.7 Annotated extracts

Extract one from 'Antigone' - annotated

Exhibit 21: Extract one from 'Antigone' - annotated

The following text is an annotated extract from Sophocles' 'Antigone', published in 441BC.

Characters:
Ismene and Antigone - daughters of Oedipus
Creon, King of Thebes
Chorus of Theban elders

Scene:
Before the Palace at Thebes

Enter ISMENE from the central door of the Palace. ANTIGONE follows, anxious and urgent; she closes the door carefully, and comes to her sister.[1]

ANTIGONE: O sister! Ismene dear, dear sister Ismene!
You know how heavy the hand of God is upon us;
How we who are left must suffer for our father, Oedipus.
There is no pain, no sorrow, no suffering, no dishonour
We have not shared together, you and I.
And now there is something more. Have you heard this order,
This latest order that the King has proclaimed to the city?[2]
Have, you heard how our dearest are being treated like enemies?

ISMENE: 'I have heard nothing. about any of those we love,
Neither good nor evil - not, I mean, since the death

Of our two brothers, both fallen in a day.
The Argive army, I hear, was withdrawn last night.
I know no more to make me sad or glad.

ANTIGONE: I thought you did not. That's why I brought you out here,
Where we shan't be heard, to tell you something alone.

ISMENE: What is it, Antigone? Black news, I can see already.

ANTIGONE: O Ismene, what do you think? Our two dear brothers...
Creon has given funeral honours to one,
And not to the other; nothing but shame and ignominy.
Eteocles has been buried, they tell me, in state,
With all honourable observances due to the dead.
But Polynices, just as unhappily fallen - the order
Says he is not to be buried, not to be mourned;
To be left unburied, unwept, a feast of flesh
For keen-eyed carrion birds. The noble Creon!
It is against you and me he has made this order.
Yes, against me. And soon he will be here himself
To make it plain to those that have not heard it,
And to enforce it. This is no idle threat;
The punishment for disobedience is death by stoning.
So now you know. And now is the time to show
Whether or not you are worthy of your high blood.[3]

ISMENE: My poor Antigone, if this is really true,
What more can I do, or undo, to help you?

ANTIGONE: Will you help me? Will you do something with me? Will you?

ISMENE: Help you do what, Antigone? What do you mean?

ANTIGONE: Would you help me lift the body ... you and me?

ISMENE: You cannot mean ... to bury him? Against the order?[4]

ANTIGONE: Is he not my brother, and yours, whether you like it
Or not? I shall never desert him, never.

ISMENE: How could you dare, when Creon has expressly forbidden it?[5]

ANTIGONE: He has no right to keep me from my own.

ISMENE: O sister, sister, do you forget how our father
Perished in shame and misery, his awful sin
Self-proved, blinded by his own self-mutilation?
And then his mother, his wife - for she was both...[6]
Destroyed herself in a noose of her own making.
And now our brothers, both in a single day
Fallen in an awful exaction: of death for death,
Blood for blood, each slain by the other's hand.[7]
Now we two left; and what will be the end of us,
If we transgress the law an defy our king?

O think, Antigone; we are women; it is not for us
To fight against men; our rulers are stronger than we,
And we must obey in this, or in worse than this.
May the dead forgive me, I can do no other
But as I am commanded; to do more is madness.

ANTIGONE: No; then I will not ask you for your help.
Nor would I thank you for it, if you gave it.
Go your own way; I will bury my brother;
And if I die for it, what happiness!
Convicted of reverence - I shall be content
To lie beside a brother whom I love.
We have only a little time to please the living,
But all eternity to love the dead.
There I shall lie forever. Live, if you will;
Live, and defy the holiest laws of heaven.

ISMENE: I do not defy them; but I cannot act
Against the State. I am not strong enough.

ANTIGONE: Let that be your excuse, then. I will go
And heap a mound of earth over my brother.

ISMENE: I fear for you, Antigone; I fear -

ANTIGONE: You need not fear for me. Fear for yourself

ISMENE: At least be secret. Do not breathe a word.
I'll not betray your secret.

ANTIGONE: Publish it
To all the world! Else I shall hate you more.

ISMENE: Your heart burns! Mine is frozen at the thought.

ANTIGONE: I know my duty, where true duty lies.

ISMENE: If you can do it; but you're bound to fail.

ANTIGONE: When I have tried and failed, I shall have failed.

ISMENE: No sense in starting on a hopeless task.

ANTIGONE: Oh, I shall hate you if you talk like that!
And he will hate you, rightly. Leave me alone
With my own madness. There is no punishment
Can rob me of my honourable death.

ISMENE: Go then, if you are determined, to your folly.
But remember that those who love you... love you still.

ISMENE goes into the Palace. ANTIGONE leaves the stage by a side exit.

Enter the CHORUS of Theban elders.[8]

CHORUS: Hail the sun! the brightest of all that ever
Dawned on the City of Seven Gates, City of Thebes![9]
Hail the golden dawn over Dirce's river
Rising to speed the flight of the white invaders
Homeward in full retreat!

The army of Polynices was gathered against us,
In angry dispute his voice was lifted against us,[10]
Like a ravening bird of prey he swooped around us
With white wings flashing, with flying plumes,
With armed hosts ranked in thousands.

At the threshold of seven gates in a circle of blood
His swords stood round us, his jaws were opened against us;
But before he could taste our blood, or consume us with fire
He fled, fled with the roar of the dragon behind him
And thunder of war in his ears.

The Father of Heaven abhors the proud tongue's boasting;
He marked the oncoming torrent,[11] the flashing stream
Of their golden harness, the clash of their battle gear;
He heard the invader cry Victory over our ramparts,
And smote him with fire to the ground.

Down to the ground from the crest of his hurricane onslaught
He swung, with the fiery brands of his hate brought low:
Each and all to their doom of destruction appointed
By the god that fighteth for us.

Seven invaders at seven gates seven defenders
Spoiled of their bronze for a tribute to Zeus; save two
Luckless brothers in one fight matched together
And in one death laid low.

Great is the victory, great be the joy
In the city of Thebes, the city of chariots.
Now is the time to fill the temples
With glad thanksgiving for warfare ended;
Shake the ground with the night-long dances,
Bacchus afoot and delight abounding.[12]

But see, the King comes here,
Creon, the son of Menoeceus,[13]
Whom the gods have appointed for us
In our recent change of fortune.[14]
What matter is it, I wonder
That has led him to call us together
By his special proclamation?[15]

The central door is opened, and CREON enters.

CREON: My councilors: now that 'the gods have brought our city
Safe through a storm of trouble to tranquillity, [sic]
I have called you especially out of all my people
To conference together, knowing that you
Were loyal subjects when King Laius reigned,
And when King Oedipus so wisely ruled us,
And again, upon his death, faithfully served
His sons, till they in turn fell - both slayers, both slain,
Both stained with brother-blood, dead in a day -
And I, their next of kin, inherited
The throne and kingdom which I now possess
No other touchstone can test the heart of a man,
The temper of his mind and spirit, till he be tried[16]
In the practice of authority and rule.
For my part, I have always held the view,
And hold it still, that a king whose lips are sealed
By fear, unwilling to seek advice, is damned.
And no less damned is he who puts a friend
Above his country; I have no good word for him.
As God above is my witness, who sees all,
When I see any danger threatening my people,
Whatever it may be, I shall declare it.
No man who is his country's enemy
Shall call himself my friend. Of this I am sure -
Our country is our life; only when she
Rides safely, have we any friends at all.
Such is my policy for our common weal.
In pursuance of this, I have made a proclamation
Concerning the sons of Oedipus, as follows:
Eteocles, who fell fighting in defence of the city,
Fighting gallantly, is to be honoured with burial
And with all the rites due to the noble dead.
The other - you know whom I mean - his brother Polynices;
Who came back from exile intending to burn and destroy[17]
His fatherland and the gods of his fatherland,
To drink the blood of his kin, to make them slaves -
He is to have no grave, no burial,
No mourning from. anyone; it is forbidden.
He is to be left unburied, left to be eaten
By dogs and vultures, a horror for all to see.
I am determined that. never, if I can help it,
Shall evil triumph over good. Alive
Or dead, the faithful servant of his country
Shall be rewarded.

CHORUS: Creon, son of Menoeceus,
You have given your judgment for the friend and for the enemy.
As for those that are dead, so for us who remain,
Your will is law.

TOPIC 5. DRAMA

CREON: See then that it be kept.

CHORUS: My lord, some younger would be fitter for that task

CREON: Watchers are already set over the corpse.

CHORUS: What other duty then remains for us?[18]

CREON: Not to connive at any disobedience.

CHORUS: If there were any so mad as to ask for death

CREON: Ay, that is the penalty. There is always someone
Ready to be lured to ruin by hope of gain.

*He turns to go. A SENTRY enters from the side of the stage.
CREON pauses at the Palace door*

Notes:

[1] The very first moment of the play.
[2] Further suggestion of tension/crisis in the protagonist's very first speech.
[3] Note Antigone's language and think about what you've learned about hubris.
[4] Here we see, in the opening minutes of the action, where the central conflict **begins**: two sisters taking differing views on how to respond to a King's order.
[5] Ismene's dramatic function here is to offer the voice of reason.
[6] In addition to offering the voice of reason, Ismene's dramatic function here is to remind the audience of the tragedy of their parents: Oedipus, their father, killed his own father (not knowing it was his father) then married his own mother (not knowing she was his mother), bringing plague and death to his city as the gods disapproved. He blinded himself and Jocaste (his wife) hung herself, to break the curse on their community. This function of 'filling in the blanks' is also done by the Chorus a little later on.
[7] This is the first time the audience learns the brothers killed each other.
[8] The Chorus in Greek tragedies played the part of both observer/audience and participant; both within and outside of the action. Here, the Chorus comprises a group of men addressed by Creon as "my councilors". They are both advisors to Creon and commentators for the Audience.
[9] The language in the Chorus' opening lines.
[10] Tragedies were written in verse until the roughly the 18th century. We see this in the sisters' language, but this bit from the Chorus appears to be more 'formally poetic' than the sisters'.
[11] Here the Chorus continue to function as Commentator for the audience's benefit, relaying the story of the recent war over Thebes that ended in Thebes' victory. Note the subjectivity in the CHORUS! This is not an objective, impartial observer - the Chorus 'works for' the king and 'speaks for' the people.
[12] Bacchus was the god of late nights and parties - a very important god ;-)
[13] Announcing the arrival of a key character: the Chorus' dramatic function is about to change from one of Observer/Commentator to being a character integrated into the action.
[14] Creon only recently became King following the battle over Thebes that cost him

his two nephews
[15] The Chorus prepares the audience for Creon's order - which the audience already knows about from Antigone - heightening the drama.
[16] Creon's fairly straightforward justification for the order that follows.
[17] Here is the order against Polynices' burial - confirming what the audience learned from Antigone and cementing our understanding the central conflict.
[18] Here we see the Chorus at the service of Creon: compliant, a voice for the audience. The Chorus functions as a character in its own right.

5.8 Learning points

Summary

You will now have a better understand the development of:

- dramatic function;
- the language in drama;
- the central conflict in drama.

Unit 2 Topic 6

Conclusions and consolidation

Contents

6.1 Conclusions 140
6.2 Checklist: Questions to ask yourself 140
6.3 Advice: Hold back 140
6.4 Advice: Annotation, annotation, annotation 141
6.5 Other resources to help you 141
6.6 Learning points 141

Learning objective

By the end of this topic you will have:

- reflected on the extent of your own progress;
- considered your current levels of skill and confidence;
- identified what further practice you can continue to undertake.

6.1 Conclusions

By the end of this section, you should have increased your understanding about, and confidence in, the demands of this part of the course.

It is hoped that the extracts, annotated notes, questions and detailed, suggested answers have done their job, which was to offer you some new angles on textual analysis whilst complementing the learning you've already undertaken. Equally importantly is the hope that you've enjoyed discovering:

- new texts and authors;
- new themes and ideas;
- new explorations and approaches.

6.2 Checklist: Questions to ask yourself

When you feel ready, you could undertake a reflective exercise to gauge your own level of confidence about the demands of textual analysis. It is still likely there will be variation in your preferences regarding genres, features and techniques, but it is also hoped that certain gaps in your understanding and level of skill have been reduced significantly by working through the topics here.

Ask yourself the following questions.

1. Am I clear about what have I gained from these topics and the work here?
2. Do I feel more confident about the demands of textual analysis?
3. Can I identify my current strengths and areas for improvement?
4. Do I feel able to tackle any aspects I still don't feel all that confident about?
5. Do I feel ready for the exam?
6. Do I understand how to continue practising my skills using further resources?

If you can answer "yes" to most of these questions, then you would seem to have made the most of this resource. If not, this is a good opportunity to revisit areas or topics that perhaps you've not focused on enough yet.

6.3 Advice: Hold back

There is no need to panic, so try to resist the urge to head straight for what you think will be your genre and extract of preference, and be open to pleasant surprises.

As discussed in the 'Prose non-fiction' topic, it pays to examine the extract's title, subject matter and first paragraph or two to see whether any of it is accessible and interesting or obscure and confusing. If you find it obscure and confusing: drop it, even though you're a fan of non-fiction, and move on to see what the others have to offer. You may find, to your surprise, that the poem presented has lots to offer you or that the drama extract is by your favourite playwright.

6.4 Advice: Annotation, annotation, annotation

As soon as you have found the passage of your dreams, the one you want to commit the next hour and a half of your life to, start reading with your pen in hand and scribble in the margins anything that seems remotely interesting or appropriate for analysis. For example, the narrator might have a specific way of speaking; the poem may have some striking imagery or use of sound; a character in the drama extract might actually have no speech, only silence; the prose piece might be remarkably fast-paced and action-packed.

Jot it all down so that, when you really get down to composing an answer that is focused on the demands of the question (as per the expectations for a response worth about 20 marks) you have already gathered a lot of points to discuss.

6.5 Other resources to help you

You'll find valuable resources such as past exam papers and detailed marking instructions on SQA's website (http://bit.ly/29RhLfp).

If you have access to Glow, go into Education Scotland's section of resources and look for their Advanced Higher English document from 2015. On page 69 you'll find "an example of a high-quality textual analysis of poetry" based on the 2012 exam.

The internet is awash with readings, lectures, clips, blogs, authors' interviews, poetry and all other imaginable means to stimulate, inspire and help you with aspects of textual analysis.

6.6 Learning points

Summary

You should now have:

- reflected on the extent of your own progress;
- considered your current levels of skill and confidence;
- identified what further practice you can continue to undertake.

Unit 2 Topic 7
Textual analysis test

Textual analysis test

Q1: Make a detailed study of the ways in which Walt Whitman presents the central concern of 'This Compost' (Exhibit 22).

You may consider:

- structure;
- sound;
- any other feature you consider significant.

Exhibit 22: 'This Compost' by Walt Whitman

1

Something startles me where I thought I was safest;
I withdraw from the still woods I loved;
I will not go now on the pastures to walk;
I will not strip the clothes from my body to meet my lover the sea;
I will not touch my flesh to the earth, as to other flesh, to renew me.

O how can it be that the ground does not sicken?

How can you be alive, you growths of spring?
How can you furnish health, you blood of herbs, roots, orchards, grain?
Are they not continually putting distemper'd corpses within you?

Is not every continent work'd over and over with sour dead?

Where have you disposed of their carcasses?
Those drunkards and gluttons of so many generations;
Where have you drawn off all the foul liquid and meat?
I do not see any of it upon you to-day—or perhaps I am deceiv'd;
I will run a furrow with my plough—I will press my spade through the sod, and turn it up underneath;
I am sure I shall expose some of the foul meat.

2

Behold this compost! behold it well!

Perhaps every mite has once form'd part of a sick person—Yet behold!
The grass of spring covers the prairies,

The bean bursts noiselessly through the mould in the garden,
The delicate spear of the onion pierces upward,
The apple-buds cluster together on the apple-branches,
The resurrection of the wheat appears with pale visage out of its graves,
The tinge awakes over the willow-tree and the mulberry-tree,
The he-birds carol mornings and evenings, while the she-birds sit on their nests,
The young of poultry break through the hatch'd eggs,

The new-born of animals appear—the calf is dropt from the cow, the colt from the mare,
Out of its little hill faithfully rise the potato's dark green leaves,
Out of its hill rises the yellow maize-stalk—the lilacs bloom in the door-yards;
The summer growth is innocent and disdainful above all those strata of sour dead.

What chemistry!
That the winds are really not infectious,
That this is no cheat, this transparent green-wash of the sea, which is so amorous after me,
That it is safe to allow it to lick my naked body all over with its tongues,
That it will not endanger me with the fevers that have deposited themselves in it,
That all is clean forever and forever,
That the cool drink from the well tastes so good,
That blackberries are so flavorous and juicy,
That the fruits of the apple-orchard, and of the orange-orchard—that melons, grapes, peaches, plums, will none of them poison me,
That when I recline on the grass I do not catch any disease,
Though probably every spear of grass rises out of what was once a catching disease.

3

Now I am terrified at the Earth! it is that calm and patient,
It grows such sweet things out of such corruptions,
It turns harmless and stainless on its axis, with such endless successions of diseas'd corpses,
It distils such exquisite winds out of such infused fetor,
It renews with such unwitting looks, its prodigal, annual, sumptuous crops,
It gives such divine materials to men, and accepts such leavings from them at last.

Q2: Prose fiction

Make a detailed study of the means used by Neil M. Gunn to present the significance of the natural world in this extract from Butcher's Broom (Exhibit 23).

Exhibit 23: Extract from 'Butcher's Broom'

The extract below is from the opening pages of Neil M. Gunn's novel 'Butcher's Broom', in which the reader is immediately introduced to the main character, Mairi, an old woman and a highly-respected healer in her remote Highland community.

The old woman stood on the Darras, the doorway, between the bright sea and the dark hills; and when at last she turned from the sea and lifted her burden to her back, the door closed behind her. But the vacant glitter remained in her eyes and they held their stare until the valley began to pour slowly into them its dark comfort. For a long time she was like one who had turned into her own house and found it empty, and walked in a silence that was a hearkening to presences withdrawn beyond the walls and fading away.

Every now and then there was a glint in this vagueness, for she had been born by the sea, and sea-water readily curls over and breaks on the shore of the mind. Looked at from a great distance childhood is little more than the breaking of small bright waves on a beach. And whatever of pain and coldness there may have been, the brightness keeps a certain wild strangeness, a restless fly-away, that the hills do not know and never quite conquer.

The sea had been in a good mood that morning, had had that pleasant scent that is the breath of fine weather. A person could always tell what the weather is to be by smelling the sea. There is the grey dark smell, cold inside the nostrils, ominous; the damp raw smell, husky to the throat, unsettled; the keen dry lifting tang of wind; but when good weather has newly come, how the sea brims and sways and breathes its sweet fragrance on the air! This morning, too, there had been the extra exhilaration of autumn, that indescribable quickening that the skin takes in a shiver.

All of that sea she now carried in her basket as she went back among the companionable hills. For in addition to fish, she had many kinds of weed and shell. The clear pink dulse , gathered not off other sea-plants but off the rocks, was one of her most useful specifics. Eaten raw, it had a cleansing effect; boiled, with a pinch of butter added to the infusion, it acted as a tonic, bracing the flesh, making it supple, and drawing taut the muscles of the stomach. It could be preserved, too, by drying. A man working in a field could put a dry blade or two in his mouth and chew away at them. At first they were tasteless as gristle, but in a very short time they yielded back their juices, which began to run about the gums and fill the whole mouth with a richness that had to be frequently swallowed. When the dried dulse was ground into a powder and taken fasting, it sickened and expelled worms. Other ailments, like the stone and colic, yielded to it.

Linarich, slake, and sea-tangle had also their many uses; though she had not much of each with her now, for slake was mostly needed in the spring, when, after the rigour of winter, the cattle were weak and costive. Linarich, perhaps, was more useful at any time. It helped to soothe and heal the skin after a blister plaster. In the case of sciatica, for example, the ancient custom was to cut spirewort into small pieces, pack them in a limpet shell, and fasten the shell to the thigh-bone in order to raise a big blister, from which the watery matter could be drained away. After the third draining, a linarich plaster dried and healed the wound.

It was in her nature not to return home without such gifts. She had spent two days with a relative by marriage whose husband had been suffering from a mysterious fever and could not sweat. They had sent for her, for Dark Mairi of the Shore. She had a reputation for healing among the people of that land. She was a small woman, roundly built, deep-chested and straight, yet she did not give an impression of bodily strength so much as of something delicate and hardy that persists evenly. Her skin was pale and little wrinkled; her eyes dark, and of a jewelled smallness. But perhaps the suggestion of persistence, of abidingness, that was the silent note struck by her person, was sustained most distinctly by the cheek-bones that did not obtrude in round knobs but ran straight back towards her ears, each in a visible ridge. These ridges drew the skin taut and gave the frontal expression a curious flattened steadiness. Her hair was black and coarse-grained, with grey strands showing here and there in a good light. It was drawn firmly back from her forehead, tautening the skin at the temples, as the cheek-bones tautened it down the sides of her face. Her head was raised in a watchfulness that was sometimes direct and glimmering and sometimes staring-blind.

This 'blindness' in her expression had often the air of unintelligence, and when she smiled it could be seen as a sort of weakness running thinly all over her face. To move her out of her unthinking self seemed to expose her, to show that apart from what she was unthinkingly she was very little. One might as well have exposed a stone by causing it to smile or a piece of a mountain. Indeed, in her steady unthinking darkness, she might have walked out of a mountain and might walk into it again, leaving no sign.

The sick man had looked at her with expectation. She asked him questions quietly. She smiled her small weak smile. She put her hand on his forehead. Her hand was very cold. Her smile did not touch her eyes at all. She was not concerned. She would soon put him all right. Oh yes. She did not even say what was wrong with him. And the doubt that had clouded the man's eyes faded out, not into eagerness or impatience, but into an almost stupid peace. She prepared her drink and gave it to him. It was hot and harsh to the throat as oily sea-water. "It's strong," he said. "Strong enough," she answered and packed the extra clothes around him. "Strong," he muttered, and his body shuddered as under a convulsion and settled down into the bed, fatally accepting what was coming to it. When it relaxed from its next shudder there was a crawling warmth under the skin. The warmth grew; it became a glowing live heat. Soon his whole body was a white dry furnace. He was being consumed, burnt up. Out of that heat the storm burst. The drops ran into runnels. These runnels tickled his face and his chest, and made his eyes water. "God, I'm sweating!" he gasped. "Sweat you," said she. When she saw his hair steaming, she turned away and began asking his wife the news of the place. The two women sat down and told each other all they knew of everybody, so that their neighbours in their lives and their actions were brought clearly before them. In this way the wife became happy and greatly moved towards Dark Mairi, to whom she unburdened herself, enjoying now what had been her saddest moments. In the morning the man was quite spent, but his eyes and his mind were clear and steady. "I'm weak as a fly," he jested. "You'll be strong as a horse," she replied. Whereupon the strength of the horse began to trickle into him. "God's blessing with you," he said. "And with yourself," she answered, looking at him a moment then turning away.

Q3: Prose non-fiction

In a detailed analysis, discuss in what ways, and how effectively, Emmeline Pankhurst conveys how the Hyde Park demonstration defied Gladstone's assertion that "it is not to be expected that women can assemble in such masses" in this extract from 'My Own Story' (Exhibit 24).

Exhibit 24: Extract from 'My Own Story'

The following extract is from Emmeline Pankhurst's memoir 'My Own Story'. Here, the organisation she leads (the Women's Social and Political Union) plans and carries out its biggest demonstration thus far, in Hyde Park, London.

"Of course," added Mr Gladstone, "it is not to be expected that women can assemble in such masses, but power belongs to masses, and through this power a Government can be influenced into more effective action than a Government will be likely to take under present conditions."

The Women's Social and Political Union determined to answer this challenge. If assembling in great masses was all that was necessary to convince the Government that woman suffrage had passed the academic stage and now demanded political action, we thought we could undertake to satisfy the most skeptical [sic] member of the Cabinet. We knew that we could organise a demonstration that would out-rival any of the great franchise demonstrations held by men in the thirties, sixties, and eighties. The largest number of people ever gathered in Hyde Park was said to have approximated 72,000. We determined to organise a Hyde Park demonstration of at least 250,000 people. Sunday, June 21, 1908, was fixed for the date of this demonstration, and for many months we worked to make it a day notable in the history of the movement. Our example was emulated by the non-militant suffragists, who organised a fine procession of their own, about a week before our demonstration. Thirteen thousand women, it was said, marched in that procession.

On our demonstration we spent, for advertising alone, over a thousand pounds, or five thousand dollars. We covered the hoardings of London and of all the principal provincial cities with great posters bearing portraits of the women who were to preside at the twenty platforms from which speeches were to be made; a map of London, showing the routes by which the seven processions were to advance, and a plan of the Hyde Park meeting-place were also shown. London, of course, was thoroughly organised. For weeks a small army of women was busy chalking announcements on sidewalks, distributing handbills, canvassing from house to house, advertising the demonstration by posters and sandwich boards carried through the streets. We invited every¬body to be present, including both Houses of Parliament. A few days before the demonstration Mrs Drummond and a number of other women hired and decorated a launch and sailed up the Thames to the Houses of Parliament, arriving at the hour when members entertain their women friends at tea on the terrace. Everyone left the tables and crowded to the water's edge as the boat stopped, and Mrs Drummond's strong, clear voice pealed out her invitation to the Cabinet and the members of Parliament to join the women's demonstration in Hyde Park. "Come to the park on Sunday," she cried. "You shall have police protection, and there will be no arrests, we promise you." An alarmed someone telephoned for the police boats, but as they appeared, the women's boat steamed away.

What a day was Sunday, June 21st-clear, radiant, filled with golden sunshine! As I advanced, leading, with the venerable Mrs Wolstenholm-Elroy, the first of the seven processions, it seemed to me that all London had turned out to witness our demonstration. And a goodly part of London followed the processions. When I mounted my platform in Hyde Park, and surveyed the mighty throngs that waited there and the endless crowds that were still pouring into the park from all directions, I was filled with amazement not unmixed with awe. Never had I imagined that so many people could be gathered together to share in a political demonstration. It was a gay and beautiful as well as an awe-inspiring spectacle, for the white gowns and flower-trimmed hats of the women, against the background of ancient trees, gave the park the appearance of a vast garden in full bloom.

The bugles sounded, and the speakers at each of the twenty platforms began their addresses, which could not have been heard by more than half or a third of the vast audience. Notwithstanding this, they remained to the end. At five o'clock the bugles sounded again, the speaking ceased, and the resolution calling upon the Government to bring in an official woman-suffrage bill without delay was carried at every platform, often without a dissenting vote. Then, with a three-times-repeated cry of "Votes for Women!" from the assembled multitude, the great meeting dispersed.

The London Times said next day: "Its organisers had counted on an audience of 250,000. That expectation was certainly fulfilled, and probably it was doubled, and it would be difficult to contradict anyone who asserted that it was trebled. Like the distances and the number of the stars, the facts were beyond the threshold of perception."

The Daily Express said: "It is probable that so many people never before stood in one square mass anywhere in England. Men who saw the great Gladstone meeting years ago said that compared with yesterday's multitude it was as nothing."

We felt that we had answered the challenge in Mr Gladstone's declaration that "power belongs to the masses," and that through this power the Government could be influenced; so it was with real hope that we despatched [sic] a copy of the resolution to the Prime Minister, asking him what answer the Government would make to that unparalleled gathering of men and women.

Q4: Drama

In a detailed analysis of the extract from Sophocles' 'Antigone' (Exhibit 25) discuss how the **dramatist** develops the conflict between Antigone and Creon. In your answer you should take into account the use of:

- language;
- dramatic function;
- any other dramatic device you consider to be important.

Exhibit 25: Extract from Antigone

CREON (to the SENTRY): You - you may go. You are discharged from blame.

Exit SENTRY.

Now tell me, in as few words as you can,
Did you know the order forbidding such an act?

ANTIGONE: I knew it, naturally. It was plain enough.

CREON: And yet you dared to contravene it?

ANTIGONE: Yes.
That order did not come from God. Justice,
That dwells with the gods below, knows no such law.
I did not think your edicts strong enough
To overrule the unwritten unalterable laws
Of God and heaven, you being only a man.
They are not of yesterday or to-day, but everlasting,
Though where they came from, none of us can tell.
Guilty of their transgression before God
I cannot be, for any man on earth.
I knew that I should have to die, of course,
With or without your order. If it be soon,
So much the better. Living in daily torment
As I do, who would not be glad to die?
This punishment will not be any pain.
Only if I had let my mother's son
Lie there unburied, then I could not have home it.
This I can bear. Does that seem foolish to you?
Or is it you that are foolish to judge me so?

CHORUS: She shows her father's stubborn spirit: foolish
Not to give way when everything's against her.

CREON: Ah, but you'll see... The over-obstinate spirit
Is soonest broken; as the strongest iron will snap
If over-tempered in the fire to brittleness.
A little halter is enough to break
The wildest horse. Proud thoughts do not sit well
Upon subordinates. This girl's proud spirit
Was first in evidence when she broke the law;
And now, to add insult to her injury,
She gloats over her deed. But, as I live,
She shall not flout my orders with impunity.
My sister's child - ay, were she even nearer,
Nearest and dearest, she should not escape
Full punishment - she, and her sister too,
Her partner, doubtless, in this burying.
Let her be fetched! She was in the house just now;
I saw her, hardly in her right mind either.
Often the thoughts of those who plan dark deeds
Betray themselves before the deed is done.
The criminal who being caught still tries.
To make a fair excuse, is damned indeed.

ANTIGONE: Now you have caught, will you do more than kill me?

CREON: No, nothing more; that is all I could wish.

ANTIGONE: Why then delay? There is nothing that you can say
That I should wish to hear, as nothing I say
Can weigh with you. I have given my brother burial.
What greater honour could I wish? All these
Would say that what I did was honourable,
But fear locks up their lips. To speak and act
Just as he likes is a king's prerogative.

CREON: You are wrong. None of my subjects thinks as you do.

ANTIGONE: Yes, sir, they do; but dare not tell you so.

CREON: And you are not only alone, but unashamed.

ANTIGONE: There is no shame in honouring my brother.

CREON: Was not his enemy, who died with him, your brother?

ANTIGONE: Yes, both were brothers, both of the same parents.

CREON: You honour one, and so insult the other.

ANTIGONE: He that is dead will not accuse me of that.

CREON: He will, if you honour him no more than the traitor.

ANTIGONE: It was not a slave, but his brother, that died with him.

CREON: Attacking his country, while the other defended it.

ANTIGONE: Even so, we have a duty to the dead.

CREON: Not to give equal honour to good and bad.

ANTIGONE: Who knows? In the country of the dead that may be the law.

CREON: An enemy can't be a friend, even when dead.

ANTIGONE: My way is to share my love, not share my hate.

CREON: Go then, and share your love among the dead.
We'll have no woman's law here, while I live.

Enter ISMENE from the Palace.

CHORUS: Here comes Ismene, weeping
In sisterly sorrow; a darkened brow,
Flushed face, and the fair cheek marred
With flooding rain.

CREON: You crawling viper! Lurking in my house
To suck my blood! Two traitors unbeknown
Plotting against my throne. Do you admit
To a share in this burying, or deny all knowledge?

ISMENE: I did it - yes - if she will let me say so.
I am as much to blame as she is.

ANTIGONE: No.
That is not just. You would not lend a hand
And I refused your help in what I did.

ISMENE: But I am not ashamed to stand beside you
Now in your hour of trial, Antigone.

ANTIGONE: Whose was the deed, Death and the dead are witness.
I love no friend whose love is only words.

ISMENE: O sister, sister, let me share your death,
Share in the tribute of honour to him that is dead.

ANTIGONE: You shall not die with me. You shall not claim
That which you would not touch. One death is enough.

ISMENE: How can I bear to live, if you must die?

ANTIGONE: Ask Creon. Is not he the one you care for?

ISMENE: You do yourself no good to taunt me so.

ANTIGONE: Indeed no: even my jests are bitter pains.

ISMENE: But how, O tell me, how can I still help you?

ANTIGONE: Help yourself. I shall not stand in your way.

ISMENE: For pity, Antigone - can I not die with you?

ANTIGONE: You chose; life was your choice, when mine was death.

ISMENE: Although I warned you that it would be so.

ANTIGONE: Your way seemed right to some, to others mine.

ISMENE: But now both in the wrong, and both condemned.

ANTIGONE: No, no. You live. My heart was long since
So it was right for me to help the dead.

CREON: I do believe the creatures both are mad;
One lately crazed, the other from her birth.

ISMENE: Is it not likely, sir? The strongest mind
Cannot but break under misfortune's blows.

CREON: Yours did, when you threw in your lot with hers.

ISMENE: How could I wish to live without my sister?

CREON: You have no sister. Count her dead already.

ISMENE: You could not take her - kill your own son's bride?

CREON: Oh, there are other fields for him to plough.

ISMENE: No truer troth was ever made than theirs.

CREON: No son of mine shall wed so vile a creature.

ANTIGONE: O Haemon, can your father spite you so?

CREON: You and your paramour, I hate you both.

CHORUS: Sir, would you take her from your own son's arms?

CREON: Not I, but death shall take her.

CHORUS: Be it so. Her death, it seems, is certain.

CREON: Certain it is.
No more delay. Take them, and keep them within -
The proper place for women. None so brave
As not to look for some way of escape
When they see life stand face to face with death.

The women are taken away.

Unit 2 Topic 8

Acknowledgements

- *William Shakespeare*, Sonnet 116
- *John Keats*, When I Have Fears
- *Robert Browning*, The Lost Leader
- *Robert Browning*, My Last Duchess
- *Walt Whitman*, This Compost
- *William Blake*, The Tyger
- *Robert Burns*, To A Mouse, On Turning Her Up in Her Nest With The Plough
- *Ella Wheeler Wilcox*, Inevitable
- *William Knox*, Mortality
- *Neil M. Gunn*, Butcher's Broom
- *Emmeline Pankhurst*, My Own Story
- *Jackie Kay*, Red Dust Road
- *Sophocles*, Antigone

Portfolio

1	**Introduction**	**157**
	1.1 Overview and requirements	158
	1.2 Genres of writing	158
	1.3 Planning	159
	1.4 Referencing and bibliography	165
	1.5 Learning points	166
2	**Discursive writing**	**167**
	2.1 Overview	168
	2.2 Persuasive writing	169
	2.3 Argumentative writing	175
	2.4 Informative writing	181
	2.5 Learning points	187
3	**Creative writing**	**189**
	3.1 Overview	190
	3.2 Reflective writing	190
	3.3 Poetry	194
	3.4 Prose fiction	198
	3.5 Drama	202
	3.6 Annotated extracts	207
	3.7 Learning points	213
4	**Annotated exemplars**	**215**
	4.1 Essay one: Persuasive writing	217
	4.2 Essay two: Argumentative writing	222
	4.3 Essay three: Short story	226
	4.4 Essay four: Reflective	230
5	**Acknowledgements**	**237**

Unit 3 Topic 1

Introduction

Contents

- 1.1 Overview and requirements ... 158
- 1.2 Genres of writing ... 158
- 1.3 Planning ... 159
  - 1.3.1 Mind map ... 160
  - 1.3.2 Paragraph plan ... 161
  - 1.3.3 Series of images ... 163
  - 1.3.4 Flowchart ... 164
  - 1.3.5 Sticky notes ... 165
- 1.4 Referencing and bibliography ... 165
- 1.5 Learning points ... 166

Learning objective

By the end of this topic you will:

- understand the skills required to complete the portfolio;
- have a clear understanding of the requirements of the folio;
- be aware of the different types of writing that can be included in your portfolio;
- understand some of the methods that can be used to plan a piece of writing;
- have an awareness of the requirements to reference work and create a bibliography.

1.1 Overview and requirements

The Advanced Higher portfolio-writing is the part of the course where you are able to showcase your skills in writing: skills you have already begun to demonstrate in your work for the Higher portfolio and will now develop further. These include being able to:

- show how well you can use and understand complex language in a variety of contexts;
- create arguments using critical thinking skills;
- use creative thinking skills to produce original work;
- research effectively, selecting relevant material from a variety of sources;
- structure work to create a significant impact;
- use references effectively or create a bibliography;
- create and sustain a clear mood or tone;
- critically reflect on your own work;
- redraft your writing based on your reflections.

The Advanced Higher portfolio consists of two pieces of writing, each of which is worth 15 marks. This means that 30% of your final Advanced Higher English grade is generated by the work you put into this section of the course.

How is this different from Higher?

The requirements of an Advanced Higher portfolio differ in a number of important ways from the portfolio you submitted at Higher.

1. Genres of writing - you can choose to do any two different genres. There is no requirement to have a creative and a discursive piece.
2. Content - the level of language used, structure and subject matter all need to be more complex and more sophisticated than that which is required at Higher.
3. Length - each piece of writing should be at least 1000 words. Poetry is the exception here; it can be shorter.

1.2 Genres of writing

It is important that you are aware of the genres of writing that you are best at so that you are giving yourself the best chance to score high marks in this section of the course. Think about writing you have done in the past: which did you enjoy the most? Which provided you with the best feedback? Which audience do you prefer to write for? You should also consider the genres which will provide you with the best opportunities to be original and skilful in terms of language, theme and structure.

You can choose from the following genres:

- persuasive;
- informative;
- argumentative;
- reflective;
- poetry;
- prose fiction;
- drama.

You should be familiar with these from your previous study in English and each is explored in more detail throughout this section.

The most effective way to ensure that you are submitting your best work is to produce writing in a variety of genres for different audiences and share it with classmates and teachers.

1.3 Planning

Writing is a process which begins with effective planning, regardless of genre. You are very likely to have planned writing in the past, so use the planning method that works best for you, whether it be one of the following ideas or something completely different.

Start by thinking about what interests you. Is it issues connected to young people and their experiences? Perhaps you have an interest in politics? It might be that your own personal experience has sparked the urge to write reflectively. One way to begin planning is to start with a broad topic and brainstorm your knowledge. This can be done on your own or with others: sometimes it helps to talk through your ideas!

There are a variety of ways to plan a piece of writing, such as using:

- a mind map;
- a paragraph plan;
- a series of images;
- a flowchart;
- sticky notes.

1.3.1 Mind map

One way to plan is to use a mind map around a single idea or theme.

An example of using a mind map in planning

You can hand write your mind map or use an electronic version. XMind (http://www.xmind.net/) is a popular free and open source tool and there are several other high quality mind mapping options, both free and paid apps, such as those listed on the Mind mapping software blog (http://bit.ly/1Wo4Ndc)

Some things to consider when creating a mind map include:

- use a landscape rather than portrait layout and start in the middle. If you are hand writing your mind map, use a blank piece of paper;
- you can use an image or picture for the main focus rather than words, if you prefer;
- each branch of your mind map should have a different colour theme. Your brain will remember this type of distinctive difference, helping you to separate ideas;
- use lines (straight or curved) to link ideas. This helps to create and maintain a structure;
- write as little as possible. This is about connecting ideas, not writing!

1.3.2 Paragraph plan

A paragraph plan showing the development of an argument, story or experience can help if you need to see the structure clearly before you begin.

> ***Ready for renewables?***
>
> Introduction
>
> - No. of wind farms (on and off-shore) as example of growth of renewable energy
>
> Scot Govt. position on renewable energy
>
> - Find statistics/dates/quotations to show positives and to show history of renewables in Scotland.
> - Govt. supportive of becoming totally renewable
> - Question about commitment - where is the investment?
>
> Different methods of generating power
>
> - Begin with renewables and link to previous paragraph
> - Wind, hydro, wave and tidal
> - Cost-efficient?
> - Environmental costs?
> - Jobs?
>
> Less environmentally friendly methods
>
> - Fracking
> - North Sea oil and gas
> - Nuclear
> - See questions for previous section
>
> Recent extension of nuclear power station's lifespan
>
> - Link back to end of previous paragraph
> - Shows lack of commitment OR lack of alternative? Which one?
> - Official govt. position - opposed, winding down

Conclusion

- Couple of sentences recapping main types of energy and their advantages and disadvantages
- My stance - ideologically opposed
- Responsibility as humans to extend life of the planet
- Reframe evidence of dangers of fracking and nuclear waste

TOPIC 1. INTRODUCTION

1.3.3 Series of images

This can work particularly well with poetry. Images can help you to think more clearly about language and the kind of atmosphere you hope to create.

Look at each photo: what kind of mood or atmosphere is suggested in each one?

© HERIOT-WATT UNIVERSITY

1.3.4 Flowchart

With flowcharts, structure is the greatest focus. This planning method is particularly helpful when it comes to persuasive, argumentative or informative writing.

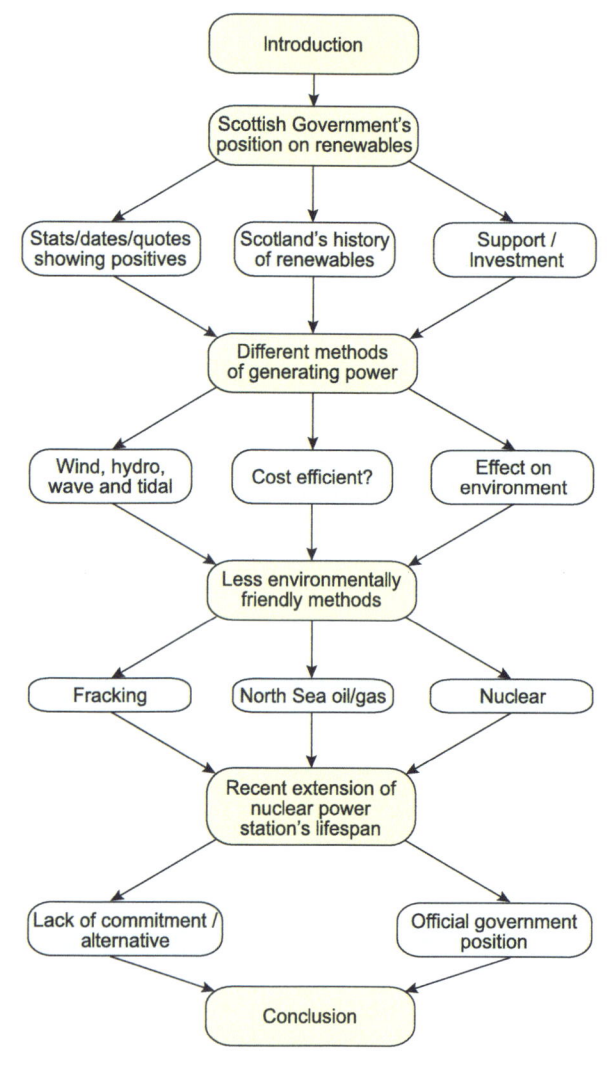

```
Introduction
    ↓
Scottish Government's position on renewables
    ↓
Stats/dates/quotes showing positives    Scotland's history of renewables    Support / Investment
    ↓
Different methods of generating power
    ↓
Wind, hydro, wave and tidal    Cost efficient?    Effect on environment
    ↓
Less environmentally friendly methods
    ↓
Fracking    North Sea oil/gas    Nuclear
    ↓
Recent extension of nuclear power station's lifespan
    ↓
Lack of commitment / alternative    Official government position
    ↓
Conclusion
```

An example of using a flowchart in planning

1.3.5 Sticky notes

Using sticky notes is helpful if you feel more comfortable physically moving things around into place. It allows for changing your mind, too!

An example of using sticky notes in planning

The plans shown here are fairly basic: yours will have much more detail, including statistics and quotations, for example. It is important to remember that plans are fluid; they can change as you write. If you need to add something, take something out or play about with the structure, you should. Your essay could change shape as you write it.

1.4 Referencing and bibliography

It is important to acknowledge sources correctly in your writing, particularly in persuasive, argumentative or informative writing. This can be done through footnotes in the body of your essay and by including a reference list or bibliography on a separate sheet at the end.

The SQA makes clear recommendations when it comes to referencing and how to lay out a bibliography. These can be accessed on the SQA's website or through your teacher.

1.5 Learning points

Summary

You should now feel more confident about beginning your folio and have a clear understanding of the following:

- the skills required to complete the portfolio;
- the requirements of the folio;
- the different types of writing that can be included in your portfolio;
- some of the methods that can be used to plan a piece of writing;
- the requirements to reference work and create a bibliography.

Unit 3 Topic 2

Discursive writing

Contents

2.1	Overview	168
2.2	Persuasive writing	169
	2.2.1 Topic, title, audience and purpose	169
	2.2.2 Introduction	170
	2.2.3 Constructing an argument	172
	2.2.4 Conclusion	173
	2.2.5 Persuasive style	174
2.3	Argumentative writing	175
	2.3.1 Topic, title, audience and purpose	175
	2.3.2 Introduction	177
	2.3.3 Constructing an argument	178
	2.3.4 Conclusion	179
	2.3.5 Argumentative style	180
2.4	Informative writing	181
	2.4.1 Topic, title, audience and purpose	181
	2.4.2 Introduction	182
	2.4.3 Structure	183
	2.4.4 Conclusion	185
	2.4.5 Informative style	186
2.5	Learning points	187

Learning objective

By the end of this topic, you will have a clear understanding of the following for persuasive, argumentative and informative writing:

- appropriate topics and how to choose a title;
- audience and purpose;
- the appropriate structure(s) to use;
- the type of language suited to audience and purpose and how to use it effectively;
- how to incorporate facts, statistics, anecdotal evidence, charts, tables, diagrams.

2.1 Overview

This topic is concerned with the types of writing which can be categorised as discursive writing:

- persuasive;
- argumentative; and
- informative.

These are written in continuous prose and there are many similarities in the ways in which you can tackle them. For each one it is important to consider:

- the *purpose and audience* of the essay;
- the best *structure* to make a significant impact;
- how to use *language* effectively to engage your audience.

Of course, *technical accuracy* is also important: you cannot afford to have more than a few errors in this area and through the redrafting process, you have the opportunity to eradicate them completely.

Topic choice

The topic you choose is, of course, vitally important to the success of your writing. It is always best to strive for originality: fresh ideas or an unusual angle will make sure that you have the best chance of doing well. The types of topics you consider are likely to be similar to those you may have thought about at Higher but your treatment of them will differ in the complexity of the language you use, the careful selection of appropriate evidence and your ability to structure your work in an innovative or insightful way.

Use a topic that you have not tackled before: adapting a piece of Higher work is unlikely to be successful as the requirements at Advanced Higher are much more stringent. Go for something completely fresh which interests you: give yourself the best chance to do well! Think about your concerns and interests: it could be debating the merits of rugby league and rugby union or discussing the dangers of the Isle of Man TT. Avoid websites promising 100 great discursive writing topics: these are often overdone or cliched.

There are areas of similarity between genres, especially between persuasive and argumentative writing, but it is important that you read each section carefully so that you are fully aware of the differences, too!

Reading

A great way to prepare for writing your portfolio essays is to read as widely as possible in as many different genres as you are interested in: it is an easy way to look at good practice and maybe even find some helpful tips on using language and structure to your advantage.

For example, if you are interested in reading articles debating the latest political and financial issues, you might read 'The Economist'; if you are interested in learning more about how to write creatively, you might read the work of Doris Lessing or Ray Bradbury to learn more. Remember that you must reference clearly the words, ideas and information of others or risk being accused of plagiarism. Look again at the SQA's advice on how to do this as you are writing.

Planning

As discussed in the introduction, planning is vital to the production of an Advanced Higher English essay. Decide on the style of planning which suits you best, referring to the introduction for tips on how to use the planning method you choose most effectively. Ensuring that you have planned and researched fully will allow you to focus your attention on how to write the essay with style and originality.

2.2 Persuasive writing

The persuasive writing genre is used frequently by journalists to encourage readers to consider and support their thinking.

2.2.1 Topic, title, audience and purpose

Topic and title

The essay should aim to be original but the topic doesn't always have to be. You can write in an innovative way about a popular topic: you just need to think of an interesting or unusual angle and ensure that you use language, structure and tone to create an original piece of work. Your title is also important as it sets the tone for the essay: for example, is it humorous/outraged/sympathetic? It shouldn't be too long (you want to attract the reader's attention) but avoid tabloid-type headlines: your writing is going to be **complex and sophisticated** after all!

Audience

This will be dependent on the topic. For example, an essay which aims to persuade the reader that the continued development of technology is essential to the evolution of mankind will be aimed at those who need convincing. What age are they? What kind of lifestyles might they have? What are their interests?

Purpose

The underlying purpose of persuasive writing is always to encourage the reader to finish the essay agreeing with your point of view. It is your job to use the techniques discussed in the rest of this section to do this.

Here is a small selection of the kind of ideas you might consider. Remember, these are topics, not titles.

1. The current crisis in the NHS is the first step on the road to privatisation.

2. The increasing awareness of mental health issues is leading to a sympathy vacuum.

3. We need to change the language we use if we want to eradicate insulting gender stereotypes.

4. Online gaming is creating a subculture of social misfits.

Persuasive writing: Topic titles

Come up with titles for the following topics, remembering to think about the tone each piece of writing could have. There is more than one viewpoint for each one: make sure your title hints at yours.

1. The current crisis in the NHS is the first step on the road to privatisation.
2. The increasing awareness of mental health issues is leading to a sympathy vacuum.
3. We need to change the language we use if we want to eradicate insulting gender stereotypes.
4. Online gaming is creating a subculture of social misfits.

Persuasive writing: Audiences

Identify potential audiences for each of the following titles. Who are you trying to convince? Think about lifestyle, age, interests, etc.

1. The current crisis in the NHS is the first step on the road to privatisation.
2. The increasing awareness of mental health issues is leading to a sympathy vacuum.
3. We need to change the language we use if we want to eradicate insulting gender stereotypes.
4. Online gaming is creating a subculture of social misfits.

2.2.2 Introduction

The introduction to your persuasive essay needs to:

- engage the reader;
- explain the topic;
- set out your position.

The introduction to any piece of work is where you set out what you are going to do and this is no different. What is different about the introduction to a piece of persuasive writing is, however, that you want to influence the reader to listen to your point of view from the first word. You can start in a number of ways, including:

- a large or shocking statistic, e.g. two-thirds of British 12-15 year olds have a smart phone and send an average of 200 messages per week;
- a contentious statement, e.g. smart phones are destroying the mental health of today's teenagers;

TOPIC 2. DISCURSIVE WRITING

- a question, e.g. do we really want the next generation to grow up lacking even basic social skills?

Your use of language can influence the reader from the very beginning. Of course, you could be setting the reader up: perhaps your view is the opposite and you can spend the remainder of your essay proving that these shocking statistics and bold statements are misleading.

Short overview

Next, you need to provide a short overview of the subject. This should demonstrate your understanding of both sides of the issue, so that your reader is curious to find out how you are going to come to a conclusion.

Example topic: Social media is destroying essential social skills

Look closely at any gaggle of teenagers and it seems that they are hostage to their mobile phones. They are often reading messages, watching videos, posting pictures and responding to comments rather than interacting with the live human beings who make up their immediate vicinity. To an observer, conversation is piecemeal and constantly interrupted by chirps, beeps and whistles which gain their attention instantly in a way that an 'Excuse me,' from a stranger is unlikely to do. From inside the group, however, the experience is a very different one. Brains are buzzing and energy levels feel stratospheric, stimulated by the constant flow of information, visuals and interaction provided by friends and acquaintances both present and electronically connected.

This outlines the main crux of the argument: are social skills disappearing or are they as alive as ever, just exhibited differently?

Stance

Before you end the introduction you must ensure that the reader knows what your stance is. Rather than stating it explicitly, use tone, vocabulary, sentence structure or imagery (or all of them!) to do just that. Make this clear as it will help the reader to follow your argument.

The real question is, do we want in on[1] the most exciting development in human social interaction for decades or would we rather be left lagging in a Victorian parlour[2] full of social mores that are fast losing their relevance[3]?

Notes:

[1] The phrase 'want in on' is informal and, teamed with the positive connotations of 'most exciting', implies that the writer is on the side of youth and technology.
[2] The imagery of 'a Victorian parlour' is one of strictures and rules, where behaving in a manner dictated by polite society is more important than anything else. It is made clear that social skills as they stand are of questionable 'relevance'. It also shows clearly that the writer thinks that bygone days should be exactly that: it is time to move on.
[3] The negative connotations are clear, demonstrating that being 'in on' this is where the reader should want to be.

Ending your introduction with a question can be useful as a method of linking to the main body of your essay but you don't have to end it this way: you can state your stance in any way you choose.

Persuasive writing: Introduction

Write a basic introduction for each of the topics below.

1. The current crisis in the NHS is the first step on the road to privatisation.
2. The increasing awareness of mental health issues is leading to a sympathy vacuum.
3. We need to change the language we use if we want to eradicate insulting gender stereotypes.
4. Online gaming is creating a subculture of social misfits.

Don't worry too much about facts and statistics: think about how to use language to persuade the reader to hear you out and remember what you need to include in an effective persuasive introduction.

2.2.3 Constructing an argument

You should plan your essay so that the points you make increase in impact as it progresses, ending with the most potent argument in your arsenal. Remember, you are not limited by the same word count as you had in Higher so you can afford to provide comprehensive and wide-ranging arguments.

Each paragraph or section of your essay is likely to contain the following:

- a clear point in favour of your stance;
- clear links to the paragraph(s) before and/or after;
- evidence such as facts, statistics or anecdotal evidence to back up your stance;
- acknowledgement of the argument that could be provided by opponents of your stance and an attempt to disprove or discredit it with a solid argument of your own.

Persuasive writing: Constructing an argument

Brainstorm or research the topics below and come up with a list of arguments for and against each one and decide how you would structure the essays if you were to write them.

1. The current crisis in the NHS is the first step on the road to privatisation.
2. The increasing awareness of mental health issues is leading to a sympathy vacuum.
3. We need to change the language we use if we want to eradicate insulting gender stereotypes.
4. Online gaming is creating a subculture of social misfits.

2.2.4 Conclusion

The conclusion of your persuasive essay must:

- provide a summary of some of your main points;
- use language to convince any readers who still require it that your stance is the right one;
- finish with a bold/strong statement reiterating your position, perhaps linking back to language or ideas you used in your introduction.

Example topic: Social media is destroying essential social skills

It appears, then, that the question of whether or not mobile phones and smart technology are destroying what many consider to be important social skills is moot. Social skills, by definition, are the actions and interactions appropriate to the society in which we live. We no longer use 'snail mail' for the majority of our communication and the art of face-to-face conversation is not the only way to connect with those around us. Communicating electronically is natural for the vast majority of young people: this is the society in which we live. The gentle 'excuse me' is making way for the thrilling chirps, beeps and whistles: it's time for everyone to get on that information super-highway and experience the world the way it really is now.

Persuasive writing: Conclusion

Write a conclusion for each of the topics below, thinking about what you should include and looking back at the introductions you wrote earlier.

1. The current crisis in the NHS is the first step on the road to privatisation.
2. The increasing awareness of mental health issues is leading to a sympathy vacuum.
3. We need to change the language we use if we want to eradicate insulting gender stereotypes.
4. Online gaming is creating a subculture of social misfits.

2.2.5 Persuasive style

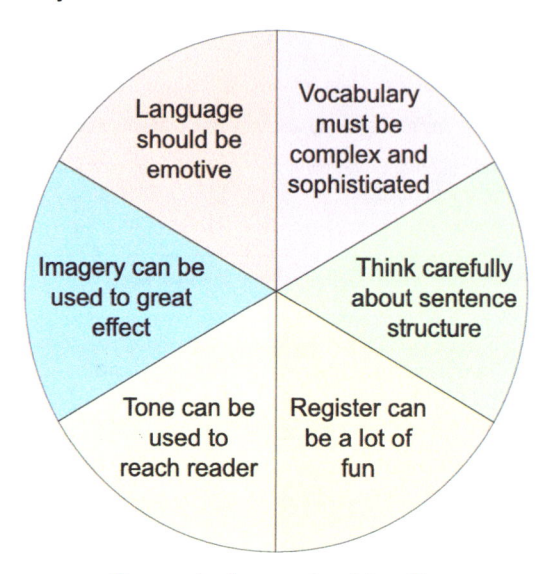

Six aspects of persuasive style writing

Language should be emotive: you feel strongly about this subject and it is important that your reader is given the opportunity to feel as outraged/upset/horrified/convinced as you do.

Vocabulary must be complex and sophisticated: spend time looking over sections of your essay as you write it and highlight or underline the words and phrases that could be improved.

Think carefully about your sentence structure: is it varied? Have you used sentence structure to add impact to your argument?

The register of a persuasive essay can be a lot of fun: it can be informal, engaging, conversational or challenging, for example.

Likewise, the tone is something you can use throughout to reach the reader: you can be humorous, sarcastic or outraged, among others.

Effective persuasive essay writing is also able to use imagery to great effect. Creating and developing an extended metaphor helps to develop a mood or tone. You could, for example, refer to the advent of smart-phone technology using imagery that calls to mind great explorers, searching out new frontiers.

> **Persuasive writing: Persuasive style**
>
> Read the following paragraph and decide how it could be improved, either by using more complex and sophisticated vocabulary, changing sentence structure or using some imagery to create mood and/or tone.
>
> Older people do not understand the excitement of instant responses to queries or questions, or the fact that any piece of information you want is out there waiting to be discovered at the touch of your fingertips. They grew up in a society where mail was something you could hold and a reply took days to find you. Imagine having to leave the house to check your bank balance or go to the library to find out the GDP of the USA for your Modern Studies homework.

2.3 Argumentative writing

An argumentative essay is one that clearly explores both sides of an issue, giving equal weight to both.

Your stance is important but you must ensure that both sides of the argument are well-represented.

2.3.1 Topic, title, audience and purpose

Topic and title

Your argumentative essay should aim to be original but the topic doesn't always have to be. You can write in an innovative way about a popular topic: you just need to think of an interesting or unusual angle, for example, when writing about feminism, focus on one aspect like the language traditionally used to refer to women and their experiences rather than writing broadly about it.

If you choose to write about the role of the police in the UK, think about the possibility of arming them, rather than focussing broadly on how effective they are. Ensure that you use language, structure and tone to create an original piece of work.

Your title is also important as it sets the tone for the essay: for example, is it humorous/outraged/sympathetic? It shouldn't be too long (you want to attract the reader's attention) but avoid tabloid-type headlines: your writing is going to be complex and sophisticated after all!

Audience

This will be dependent on the topic. For example, an essay which is discussing the importance of trade unions in modern British industry may appeal to a different audience than an essay on the introduction of an opt-out organ donor scheme. What age are they? What kind of lifestyles might they have? What are their interests?

Purpose

The underlying purpose of argumentative writing is to discuss a topic in depth and detail, providing well-researched information while making clear your line of thought or stance on the issue. It must be well-balanced, with equal weight given to both sides of the argument. It is your job to use the techniques discussed in the rest of this section to do this.

Here is a small selection of the kind of ideas you might consider:

- Are we filming too much?
- Gender and sexuality: should we change the language?
- Should police in the United Kingdom be armed?
- Should bullying be criminalised?
- Should fracking be banned?

Remember, these are topics, not titles.

Argumentative writing: Topic titles

Come up with titles for the topics below, remembering to think about the tone each piece of writing could have.

1. Are we filming too much?
2. Gender and sexuality: should we change the language?
3. Should police in the United Kingdom be armed?
4. Should bullying be criminalised?
5. Should fracking be banned?

Argumentative writing: Audiences

Identify potential audiences for each of the titles below, thinking about who you are trying to convince (lifestyle, age, interests, etc.).

1. Are we filming too much?
2. Gender and sexuality: should we change the language?
3. Should police in the United Kingdom be armed?
4. Should bullying be criminalised?
5. Should fracking be banned?

2.3.2 Introduction

The introduction to your argumentative essay needs to:

1. Engage the reader;
2. Explain both sides of the topic;
3. Let the reader know what your position is going to be.

The introduction to any piece of work is where you set out what you are going to do and this is no different. It is your opportunity to use language and content to interest the reader. You can start in a number of ways, including:

- a large or shocking statistic, e.g. less than one-third of today's children play outside unsupervised, compared with more than half of parents;
- a contentious statement, e.g. we are raising a generation of indoor children who risk social awkwardness and serious ill health;
- a question, e.g. do you remember playing outside as a child, lost in games of hide-and-seek or cycling around local streets, trying to drum up enough participants for a game of football?

Your use of language can influence the readers from the very beginning, encouraging them to become involved in the topic. Use the first thing you write as a hook to reel them in.

Short overview

Next, you need to provide a short overview of the subject. This should demonstrate your understanding of both sides of the issue, to show the reader that you are aware of its controversial or contentious nature.

Example topic: Does modern culture have a detrimental effect on childhood?

It appears as if those days are disappearing as children spend more and more of their leisure time indoors, meeting friends online instead of at the park and watched protectively by anxious parents instead of discovering the pitfalls of outdoor play unfettered by worries and concern. Parents' worries about stranger danger and an increasing focus on health and safety may well have their part to play here but perhaps the increasing availability of electronic devices and hundreds of television channels, not to mention YouTube, Netflix and their contemporaries, are actually a more attractive option for today's children. The real question is, does today's society really have a detrimental effect on young people? Or were we just lucky to have made it this far without lasting damage?

The two sides of the issue are clear here: is modern society damaging to the experience of childhood or not? Some of the points discussed in the rest of the essay are included here, such as spending time online, excessive use of electronics, protective parents and the perceived increased threat of abduction. The end of the introduction shows that there is another side to this argument: the dangers were always there.

Argumentative writing: Introduction

Write a basic introduction for each of the topics below.

1. Are we filming too much?
2. Gender and sexuality: should we change the language?
3. Should police in the United Kingdom be armed?
4. Should bullying be criminalised?
5. Should fracking be banned?

Don't worry too much about facts and statistics: think about how to use language to persuade the reader to hear you out and remember what you need to include in an effective persuasive introduction.

2.3.3 Constructing an argument

You should plan your essay so that the points you make increase in impact as it progresses, ending with the most potent argument in your arsenal. Remember, you are not limited by the same word count as you had in Higher so you can afford to provide comprehensive and wide-ranging arguments.

Each paragraph or section of your essay is likely to contain the following:

- a clear point in favour of your stance;
- clear links to the paragraph(s) before and/or after;
- evidence such as facts, statistics or anecdotal evidence to back up your arguments.

Argumentative writing: Constructing an argument

Brainstorm or research the topics below and come up with a list of arguments for and against each one and decide how you would structure the essays if you were to write them.

1. Are we filming too much?
2. Gender and sexuality: should we change the language?
3. Should police in the United Kingdom be armed?
4. Should bullying be criminalised?
5. Should fracking be banned?

2.3.4 Conclusion

The conclusion of your argumentative essay must:

- provide a summary of some of your main points;
- use language to convince readers to come down on one side or the other;
- finish with a statement reiterating your position, perhaps linking back to language or ideas you used in your introduction.

Example topic: Does modern culture have a detrimental effect on childhood?

There is no doubt that childhood is enormously different for today's youngsters but that doesn't mean it is worse. Their young lives are filled with a level of privilege and entitlement that today's older generation could only imagine: electronic gadgets; an ambrosial assortment of snacks and food; anything they could ever ask for to view at the tap of a screen and the ability to connect instantly with friends and family anywhere on the planet. That doesn't sound too terrible, surely? All those hours of playing in the sunshine, coming home when the street lights went on and knocking on the door of a friend's house in eager anticipation were wonderful, of course, but who's to say these experiences are not still waiting for our children of today? If children want to play outside, they will. If they want to cycle, they will. If they want to talk to friends lying on the floor of the hall because the telephone cord doesn't stretch to their bedroom, well, I suppose they'll just have to do without that particular joy: I think they'll cope.

Argumentative writing: Conclusion

Write a conclusion for each of the topics below, thinking about what you should include and looking back at the introductions you wrote earlier.

1. Are we filming too much?
2. Gender and sexuality: should we change the language?
3. Should police in the United Kingdom be armed?
4. Should bullying be criminalised?
5. Should fracking be banned?

2.3.5 Argumentative style

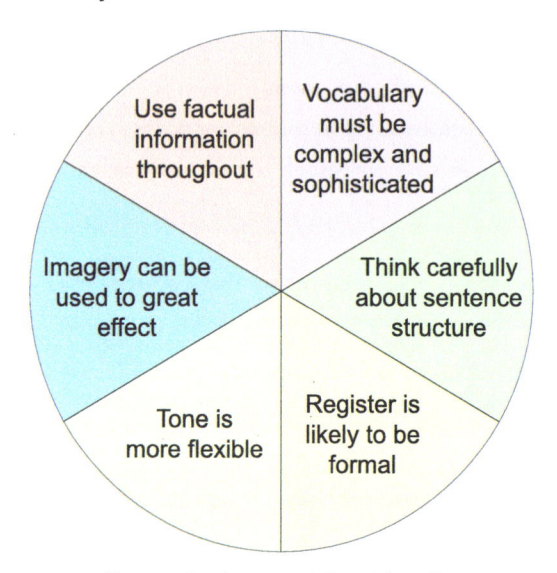

Six aspects of argumentative style writing

You must use factual information throughout the essay: argumentative essays without fact are simply a series of opinions. Statistics, anecdotal evidence and quotations are all useful ways to include the facts required to lend weight to the arguments.

Vocabulary must be complex and sophisticated: spend time looking over sections of your essay as you write it and highlight or underline the words and phrases that could be improved.

Think carefully about your sentence structure: is it varied? Have you used sentence structure to add impact to your argument?

The register of an argumentative essay is likely to be formal, depending on the issue.

The tone is more flexible: you could use humour in places but the whole essay is unlikely to rely on humour. Your tone can challenge, imply outrage or anger or suggest fear, among others.

Effective argumentative essay writing is also able to use imagery to great effect. Creating and developing an extended metaphor helps to develop a mood or tone. You could, for example, refer to the advent of smart-phone technology using imagery that calls to mind great explorers, searching out new frontiers.

> **Argumentative writing: Argumentative style**
>
> Read the following paragraph below and decide how it could be improved, either by using more complex and sophisticated vocabulary, changing sentence structure or using some imagery to create mood and/or tone.
>
> Children these days are exposed to lots of material online that wasn't available to many adults when they were small. From sexually explicit song lyrics to violent scenes and skinny supermodels, their experiences are wider and happen earlier. It is easy to imagine that it will have a negative effect on at least some of them as they grow up.

2.4 Informative writing

Informative writing is exactly what it sounds like: an essay that relays information about a particular topic, albeit in a complex and sophisticated manner.

2.4.1 Topic, title, audience and purpose

Topic and title

Your informative essay should aim to be original but the topic doesn't always have to be. You can write in an innovative way about a popular topic: you just need to think of an interesting or unusual angle and ensure that you use detail and data to help create an original piece of work. Your title is also important as it sets out clearly what the essay will be concerned with. It shouldn't be too long (you want to attract the reader's attention) but avoid tabloid-type headlines: your writing is going to be complex and sophisticated after all!

Audience

This will be dependent on the topic. For example, an essay which is discussing the importance of trade unions in modern British industry may appeal to a different audience than an essay on the introduction of an opt-out organ donor scheme. What age are they? What kind of lifestyles might they have? What are their interests?

Purpose

The underlying purpose of informative writing is to provide information about a topic in depth and detail, showing evidence of research while making clear your line of thought or stance on the issue. It is your job to use the techniques discussed in the rest of this section to do this.

Here is a small selection of the kind of ideas you might consider:

- The importance of the European Union
- The impact of the No vote on those living in poverty in Scotland
- The impact of a university degree on future earnings

> **Informative writing: Topic titles**
>
> Read some online or broadsheet articles and write out how their titles would sound if they were simply giving information.

2.4.2 Introduction

The introduction to your argumentative essay needs to:

1. Make clear exactly what the purpose and topic of your essay are;
2. Mention some of the detail that will be included;
3. Let the reader know what your stance is on the topic.

The introduction to any piece of work is where you set out what you are going to do and this is no different. It is your opportunity to use language and content to interest the reader. You can start in a number of ways, including:

- a statistic which informs the reader of the over-riding concern of your essay, for example:

    In the first six months of 2014 renewable energy provided the single largest source of electricity to Scotland, for the first time ever.

- a statement giving an overview of the essay's main concerns, for example:

    There is no question that Scotland's ability to produce renewable energy is an extremely important political and social concern.

Your introduction should also explain why this is your focus: what makes it important and worth writing about?

> **Example topic: The plausibility of renewable energy sources in Scotland**
>
> Given depleting fossil fuel resources and the controversy over nuclear power, the push to enable Scotland to produce its energy through clean, renewable means such as wind farms and hydro power plants is discussed with regularity in the Scottish parliament. However, the desire to do this and the country's facility for making it happen are completely different conversations: do we really have the capacity to become a leader in renewable energy?

This explains why renewable energy is an important topic at the moment and outlines the purpose of the essay: to demonstrate whether or not it is a feasible proposition for Scotland. The use of the rhetorical question at the end of the introduction is really the only place in an informative essay that you want to use one: engagement with the reader is generally one way in this type of writing, with information passing from you to the reader.

TOPIC 2. DISCURSIVE WRITING

> **Informative writing: Introduction**
>
> Look at the topics below and write a basic introduction for each one to help you get used to writing the introductions for this type of essay.
>
> 1. The importance of the European Union.
> 2. The impact of the No vote on those living in poverty in Scotland.
> 3. The impact of a university degree on future earnings.

2.4.3 Structure

The structure of an informative essay is logical and information is laid out in discrete sections in a careful order. Unlike persuasive and argumentative essays, you are not setting out to convince the reader to agree with your point of view: you might have one, and it might be evident in your writing, but your job is to lay out the relevant information for the reader to peruse.

Planning is still important: make sure you have researched thoroughly so that you can structure your essay appropriately. Some of it will be chronological, for example, information about the origins of renewable energy in Scotland will be close to the beginning. Other sections will be separated simply by content.

> **Informative writing: Structure**
>
> Look at the list below and decide in which order you would put them in an essay. Practise your research skills by looking for information on each one, including charts, diagrams, tables and/or graphs.
>
> 1. The position of the Scottish government on renewable energy.
> 2. The financial benefits/disadvantages of nuclear power.
> 3. The different methods through which Scotland generates its power.
> 4. The position of the Scottish government on nuclear power.
> 5. Scotland's environment and the effects of non-renewable energy.
> 6. Scotland's environment and the effects of renewable energy.

Here is an example of how you might incorporate a table into an informative essay.

It is clear that the introduction of renewables as a viable energy source has made great strides in Scotland in recent years as the table below demonstrates :

© HERIOT-WATT UNIVERSITY

Exhibit 26: Renewable electricity generated (GWh) in Scotland 2000-2015

Year	Wind[1]	Hydro	Wave/Tidal	Solar PV	Landfill	Sewage	Other Biofuels	TOTAL	Gross Consumption	Renewables as a % of gross consumption
2000	216.7	4,665.3	-	-	68.5	-	21.1	4,971.6	40,801	12.2%
2001	245.2	3,737.5	-	-	109.3	-	110.4	4,202.4	40,446	10.4%
2002	406.1	4,455.4	-	-	157.0	-	80.1	5,098.7	41,619	12.3%
2003	448.9	2,902.0	0.0	-	228.0	-	145.5	3,724.4	41,238	9.0%
2004	848.4	4,474.8	0.0	-	339.2	-	169.8	5,832.2	41,364	14.1%
2005	1,280.9	4,612.2	0.0	-	395.4	-	197.2	6,485.7	41,923	15.5%
2006	2,022.9	4,224.9	0.0	-	424.0	-	283.7	6,955.6	41,309	16.8%
2007	2,644.0	4,692.9	0.0	-	486.5	-	179.8	8,003.2	40,718	19.7%
2008	3,360.1	4,700.6	0.0	0.0	501.7	20.3	479.0	9,061.8	41,049	22.1%
2009	4,553.9	4,856.7	0.1	0.0	533.8	25.8	616.1	10,586.4	38,852	27.2%
2010	4,921.9	3,255.5	0.0	0.8	529.1	31.9	725.5	9,464.8	39,571	23.9%
2011	7,099.5	5,319.3	0.4	8.3	509.4	35.3	714.0	13,686.3	37,804	36.2%
2012	8,294.3	4,838.3	0.5	67.2	547.1	35.4	902.0	14,684.9	37,641	39.0%
2013	11,133.3	4,362.7	2.5	90.7	562.8	30.2	766.5	16,948.6	38,148	44.4%
2014	11,664.1	5,435.8	2.1	131.7	533.5	28.2	1,166.5	18,961.9	38,115	49.7%
2015	14,046.5	5,779.8	2.0	187.4	503.4	26.2	1,336.6	21,882.0	-	57.4%[r]

1 Between 2000 and 2008 the wind generation figure may include a small quantity of wave, tidal and solar.

We can see from the information above that the use of renewable energy sources has grown substantially in the last few years and, according to these figures from the Scottish Government, they now account for more than half of Scotland's gross consumption of energy as a nation. This would certainly seem to suggest that the country is capable of providing energy without recourse to oil, gas and coal and gives renewable energy activists every reason to hope for a brighter future. The use of wind, tidal/wave, solar and other renewable energy sources is increasing year on year. It is important to look carefully at how the consumption of renewable energy breaks down, however. In 15 years, consumption of wind energy has increased by more than 64, reaching a massive 14,046.5 Gigawatts (Gwh) in 2015. This is very impressive and no-one would argue that reducing reliance on fossil fuels is a hugely positive step but what this table does not demonstrate is the country's capacity for producing energy harnessed through wind turbines. According to figures from the European Wind Energy Association, Scotland is set to be the most crowded country in the world for wind turbines with 2,683 in operation, 282 under construction and 2,202 currently working through the process for planning consent. There will come a time when the building of turbines is no longer a viable option.

Informative writing: Positives and negatives

Look at the information in the above table (Exhibit 26).

What else stands out? Pick out the positives and any negatives that you can find. Being able to analyse information in this kind of format is important when it comes to writing an informative essay.

Have a look at some of the other information on the Scottish Government's website and see what information you can extract from it - http://bit.ly/2fxv07j.

Informative writing: Information sources

The following information sources come from the Scottish Government website:

- Renewables policy (http://bit.ly/2btNZxn)
- 2020 Routemap For Renewable Energy in Scotland (http://bit.ly/2bb3I6D)
- Latest Energy Statistics for Scotland (http://bit.ly/2bwearT)
- Climate Change (http://bit.ly/2bG4hnj)

Using the information you can find in these pages, practise writing about the tables, data, statistics, charts etc. in the same way as the table above. Analyse the information looking for what it doesn't show, as well as what it does!

2.4.4 Conclusion

Your conclusion will be a summary of the points you have made and should leave the reader in no doubt that you have explored the issue in a detailed way. It is less about convincing the reader, as in a persuasive essay, and more about reminding them of the important things to remember when discussing this topic. Your own point of view can be included here.

Informative writing: Conclusion

Write a conclusion for the essay on renewable energy that you structured. Some of the possible sections of the essay are listed below.

1. The position of the Scottish government on renewable energy.
2. The financial benefits/disadvantages of nuclear power.
3. The different methods through which Scotland generates its power.
4. The position of the Scottish government on nuclear power.
5. Scotland's environment and the effects of non-renewable energy.
6. Scotland's environment and the effects of renewable energy.

2.4.5 Informative style

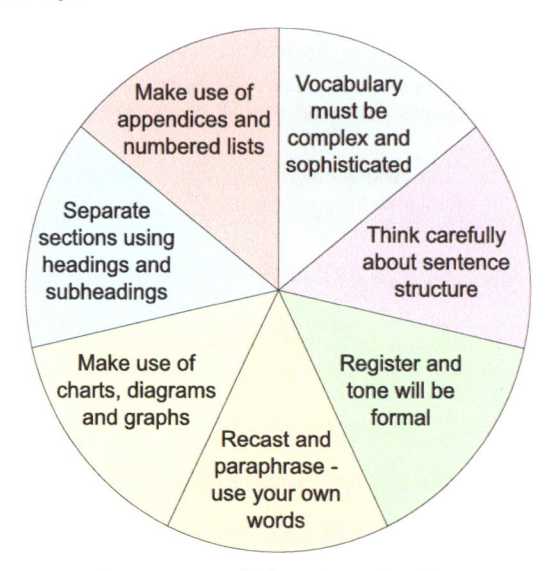

Seven aspects of informative style writing

- Vocabulary must be complex and sophisticated
- Think carefully about sentence structure
- Register and tone will be formal
- Recast and paraphrase - use your own words
- Make use of charts, diagrams and graphs
- Separate sections using headings and subheadings
- Make use of appendices and numbered lists

Vocabulary must be complex and sophisticated: spend time looking over sections of your essay as you write it and highlight or underline the words and phrases that could be improved.

Think carefully about your sentence structure: is it varied? Have you used sentence structure to add impact to your writing?

The register and tone of an informative essay will be formal.

The importance of recasting and paraphrasing the information you include cannot be overstressed. You must ensure that you are using your own words and conveying the information in your own way.

It is likely that you will make use of data such as charts, diagrams and graphs to illustrate your work and add conviction to your words. Make sure that they are appropriately placed and do, in fact, add something: choose this type of information carefully, ensuring that you understand clearly what each piece is saying.

Each section should be separated clearly using headings and sub-headings, if appropriate.

You can make use of appendices and numbered lists, too: make sure you are confident about when to do this. One way to do this is to look at other texts to find the best practice. Perhaps you are required to do this in other subjects: the same rules apply!

TOPIC 2. DISCURSIVE WRITING

> **Informative writing: Informative style**
>
> Look back at your structure for the essay on renewable energy. Thinking carefully about the advice on style in informative writing, choose one section and write it out.
>
> Let your peers and/or teacher have a look at it and give you some feedback.

2.5 Learning points

> **Summary**
>
> You should now feel more confident about discursive writing and have a clear understanding of the following:
>
> - appropriate topics and how to choose a title;
> - audience and purpose;
> - the appropriate structure(s) to use;
> - the type of language suited to audience and purpose and how to use it effectively;
> - how to incorporate facts, statistics, anecdotal evidence, charts, tables, diagrams.

© HERIOT-WATT UNIVERSITY

Unit 3 Topic 3

Creative writing

Contents

3.1 Overview 190
3.2 Reflective writing 190
    3.2.1 Structure 190
    3.2.2 Introduction 191
    3.2.3 Language 192
    3.2.4 Conclusion 193
3.3 Poetry 194
    3.3.1 Subject and theme 194
    3.3.2 Structure and form 194
    3.3.3 Types of poetry 195
    3.3.4 Language 196
    3.3.5 Symbolism 197
3.4 Prose fiction 198
    3.4.1 Subject and theme 198
    3.4.2 Structure 199
    3.4.3 Characterisation 199
    3.4.4 Setting 200
    3.4.5 Language 200
3.5 Drama 202
    3.5.1 Subject, plot and theme 203
    3.5.2 Dialogue and characterisation 204
    3.5.3 Elements of stagecraft 205
3.6 Annotated extracts 207
3.7 Learning points 213

Learning objective

By the end of this topic, you will:

- understand and be able to use the conventions of reflective writing, poetry, prose fiction and drama at Advanced Higher;
- be aware of the importance of redrafting.

3.1 Overview

You will already be familiar with broadly creative writing and its requirements from your folio at Higher. The best way to prepare for this type of writing is, of course, to read! Reading lots of different examples of each genre is not only hugely enjoyable, it provides you with the chance to gather ideas for your own writing: style, tone, use of language, topic or subject.

For annotated examples of some of these types of writing, go to the 'Annotated exemplars' topic in this section.

It is important to note that you must constantly review and revise your work. Read and reread what you have written, looking at the information and activities contained in this topic to guide your judgement. Redrafting your work is part of the writing process, along with looking at other examples of the genres you have chosen to write about.

3.2 Reflective writing

This type of writing is personal and requires you to write in prose about your own thoughts and/or experiences. You are likely to centre your writing around an experience, idea or insight that has had an effect on how you feel about or react to things now.

As in discursive writing, you are aiming to be original here and should avoid commonly tackled subjects unless you are confident that your approach will be sufficiently innovative to give the writing a new twist. Potential ideas include:

- revisiting an important moment in your childhood and discussing its long-lasting impact;
- thinking about a pivotal relationship and its effect on you, in the past and/or present;
- a moment or event that prompted a realisation or self-discovery.

The possibilities for reflective writing are enormous: almost any small, everyday, apparently insignificant event can be the catalyst for a moment of realisation!

3.2.1 Structure

Think carefully about how you will structure your writing, referring back to the 'Introduction' topic in this section for the different methods you can use to do this. It is important to strive for originality and/or a structure that enables you to unfold your ideas/experience effectively.

For example, you could describe the most poignant moment of your experience in a single paragraph at the beginning of the essay, then revisit it as you work your way through the narrative. Or, an account of watching the relentless nature of a honey bee as it works or the labour of a colony of ants could lead to a questioning of your place in a system, be it school, family or society at large.

Reflective writing: Structure

Look again at the approaches suggested in the previous topic and choose one:

- revisiting an important moment in your childhood and discussing its long-lasting impact;
- thinking about a pivotal relationship and its effect on you, in the past and/or present;
- a moment or event that prompted a realisation or self-discovery.

How would you begin this essay? What could you do that would engage your reader from the very beginning? Think about language and tone: what do you want your reader to feel at this stage?

Ask a classmate or your teacher to look at what you have written and give you feedback.

3.2.2 Introduction

The introduction must engage the reader immediately and provide a glimpse of the rest of your essay. Will it be humorous? Outraged? Morose?

Reflective writing: Introduction 1

Read the introduction below and when you're ready read the annotated version - Exhibit 27 in the 'Annotated extracts' section at the end of this topic .

As I watched the bee hover over flower after flower, single-mindedly gathering its store of pollen, my mind wandered to the queen, waiting in royal expectation for her orders to be fulfilled by the unquestioning subjects of her adoring hive. Did she wonder about their loyalty? Were there factions filled with dissatisfied minions waiting for their opportunity to stage a carefully planned coup and dethrone her? Unlikely, given their lack of independent thought and centuries of genetic programming. The entourage of which I was a member, however, was subject to a different kind of programming: our hive was not full of brainwashed bees, but scheming teenage girls.

Reflective writing: Introduction 2

Think of an event from your life so far which has taught you something about yourself, or someone else, or some aspect of life as a teenager. How could you introduce it, using the same type of introduction? What innocuous, everyday occurrence could lead into it? How could you use a motif to introduce the main concerns?

Write the introduction and let others have a look at it and ask for feedback. Would they like to read on?

3.2.3 Language

You must engage the reader in reflection in this type of writing, encouraging him or her to share your experience or consider how a similar experience has affected him or her. This can be achieved through a combination of techniques, including imagery, sentence structure, sound, word choice and, as mentioned before, the use of motifs and tone.

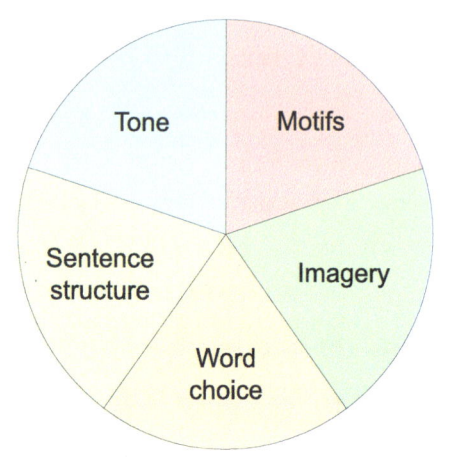

Techniques to engage the reader in reflection

Tone

Your tone ought to be personal: it can be amused, upset, incensed, confidential, anxious or any other appropriate tone, depending upon the subject matter.

Motifs

Motifs can be used to emphasise an important idea, recurring throughout the essay to keep focus on the theme or main concerns. Examples of motifs could include repeated reference to a clock to convey the idea of time passing or water dripping to refer to the idea of a constant pressure or stress.

Imagery

Imagery (metaphor, simile and personification) and sound (onomatopoeia, alliteration and assonance) are used to great effect by writers in all genres: just because you are not writing fiction doesn't mean you shouldn't take advantage of all the wonderful techniques that are available. They allow you to describe, for example, a scene, person, event or feeling in such a way that the reader is able to visualise it or is inspired to feel how you felt: they can be very powerful, used well. At this level, it is important to be original, however: hackneyed, overused similes are not allowed!

Word choice

Your word choice must be carefully considered at every point in your essay: remember, at Advanced Higher you are often using complex and sophisticated language . Think carefully about your vocabulary. This does not mean that using simple vocabulary cannot be effective, however: think carefully about the effect you are hoping to create at each point in your writing and use language that is appropriate.

Sentence structure

Your use of sentence structure is also very important as it can be used as effectively as imagery and word choice to create atmosphere. Think about the effect you want to create and consider how best to convey them: short sentences to convey shock or panic? Repetition to drive home a particular feeling? Inversion to subvert the reader's expectations? A long, rambling sentence to emphasise confusion?

> **Reflective writing: Language**
>
> Identify any language features used in this short paragraph and think about whether or not they are effective. Explain your thoughts: compare with a peer.
>
> An annotated version can be found in the 'Annotated extracts' section at the end of this topic - Exhibit 28.
>
>> Approaching the school building, at the centre of a buzzing group of drones, I felt the familiar stirrings of irritation, ennui and envy. I could hardly bear another day of fawning over someone as vacuous as our fearless leader, watching from the ranks as she drawled orders: our Cleopatra, whose every whim must be obeyed. I looked around at my companions: they exuded excitement and anticipation, surely due to the upcoming social event of the year. Well, the month at least. Which shoes to wear? Which dress? Which lipstick? Hardly questions to tax the intellects of the exceptional students we were supposed to be.

3.2.4 Conclusion

This should tie together the main points of your essay: emphasise again what it is you feel has been important in this experience. Although your feelings about and reactions to the subject of your essay should be clear throughout, this is where you have a real opportunity to reflect properly on it.

> **Reflective writing: Conclusion**
>
> What do you think of this conclusion? What is good about it? What is missing, or not as well-developed as it could be? Explain your thoughts: compare with a peer.
>
> An annotated version can be found in the 'Annotated extracts' section at the end of this topic - Exhibit 29.
>
>> My brief dalliance into the upper echelons of school society had left me disillusioned and ostracised. Visions of ruling the social elite and commanding the allegiance of a band of beauties lay scattered before me, shrapnel from a pointless war. The hard lesson of the value of substance before appearance had been learned and it stays with me: I regret every day the casual abandonment of true friends for nothing more than an illusory victory. It turns out it's not really winning when the prize is worthless.

3.3 Poetry

Poetry requires you to use your skills with language in a very different way from prose or drama. Its form, the way in which you use language and its effect on the reader are all likely to require different skills from writing prose or drama. Its purpose can often be to encourage the reader to view an idea in a new way, through your use of a variety of techniques, including form, structure, rhythm, rhyme and language. Familiarise yourself with a variety of poets, styles and subjects by reading lots of poetry before you begin to write.

Below are a couple of websites containing hundreds of poems for you to read:

- Poetry Foundation (http://www.poetryfoundation.org/browse/)
- Poem Hunter (http://www.poemhunter.com/)

Remember, you are required to write one poem: a group of poems on a similar theme is not a good idea. One single poem is more likely to be successful.

3.3.1 Subject and theme

Think carefully about what you could write about: the possibilities are unlimited! It could be a person or a place, a mood or experience: anything at all.

> **Poetry: Subject and theme**
>
> Jot down a list of possible subjects for your poetry and see which jump out at you as being the most exciting, interesting or attractive to write about. It could be an unexpected meeting with an old friend, prompting reflections on the past; a view from your local area and a comment on the beauty of nature; a nerve-wracking experience or a comment on technology's rise. What is important is that your poem's message is conveyed clearly through the poetic techniques you use.

3.3.2 Structure and form

There is a variety of ways in which you can structure your poem, depending on the type of poetry you choose to write. As you already know, poetry is structured in lines and, often, stanzas. Whether or not you decide to use stanzas will depend on your subject and how you want to convey your message. For example, you can use separate stanzas to address the different stages of an experience; to describe elements of a person or animal or to move from one stage in time to another.

TOPIC 3. CREATIVE WRITING 195

Poetry: Structure and form

Read the poem below and comment on its division into stanzas. Why is the poem separated? How does this improve the poem?

After reading and making your own observations, read the annotated text - Exhibit 30 in the 'Annotated extracts' section at the end of this topic .

Siegfried Sassoon 'Suicide in the Trenches'

I knew a simple soldier boy
Who grinned at life in empty joy,
Slept soundly through the lonesome dark,
And whistled early with the lark.

In winter trenches, cowed and glum,
With crumps and lice and lack of rum,
He put a bullet through his brain.
No one spoke of him again.

You smug-faced crowds with kindling eye
Who cheer when soldier lads march by,
Sneak home and pray you'll never know
The hell where youth and laughter go.

3.3.3 Types of poetry

There are many types of poems and they all use rhythm and rhyme in differing ways. Some examples include:

- **sonnet** - describes a thought or idea in 14 lines. Each line is 10 syllables long. Sonnets follow one of two rhyme schemes: Italian (abba abba cdecde) or English (abab cdcd efef gg);

- **ballad** - a poem that tells a story, often a love story. Ballads were traditionally set to music in many cases due to the rhyming couplets in which they were often written;

- **ode** - these use similes and metaphors throughout and are written as a tribute to a particular person or object;

- **free verse** - this has no set rhythm. This type of poetry can rhyme but often does not;

- **villanelle** - a French verse form consisting of five three-line stanzas and a final quatrain, with the first and third lines of the first stanza repeating alternately in the following stanzas. These two refrain lines form the final couplet in the quatrain.

Your poem can conform to one of these styles or not: it is entirely up to you. Think about your theme and main ideas and which suits it best, as well as which you feel most comfortable with. Perhaps you could try a parody or pastiche of the type of poetry you have been working with in the literary study!

If you want to know more about particular types of poetry, try the Young Writers website (http://bit.ly /27RfUQh).

© HERIOT-WATT UNIVERSITY

Remember, how far you decide to use a particular style of poetry, or rhythm or a rhyme scheme is up to you and dependent on your own style of writing. Poetry does not have to rhyme to be successful!

3.3.4 Language

Use of language is key in poetry: it is more economical and descriptive than prose or drama writing and often uses word choice, word order, **enjambment**, **imagery** and **sound** in innovative and unusual ways. Again, the best way to understand this is to read lots of poetry!

Look again at the first stanza of Sassoon's poem, 'Suicide in the Trenches':

> I knew a simple soldier boy
> Who grinned at life in empty joy,
> Slept soundly through the lonesome dark,
> And whistled early with the lark.

If it had been written in prose it might look something like this:

> Before the war he was a lovely, cheerful soul who was able to find happiness in everything. He laughed, sang and whistled his way through life and never had a moment's worry.

Poetry: Language

Take the following sentences and rewrite them as lines of poetry:

1. I watched the waves crashing relentlessly across the shore as I contemplated the terrible pain of losing her.

2. The sound of the children's laughter echoed throughout the house and I looked forward to years of the same sound punctuating my life for years to come.

3. The garden sparkled after the rain: flowers, grass and even weeds seemed otherworldly.

Share your responses with classmates and ask for feedback: listening to what others think is a great way to improve your writing! Think about the following before you start:

- What imagery could you use?

- How can you use word order and/or enjambment to ensure that the key messages of each line are clear?

- Can you use sound to convey the messages clearly?

- Think about word choice: ensure that your vocabulary is carefully chosen to create a particular mood/tone.

- Remove any unnecessary words from the paragraph: poetry uses far fewer words to convey messages.

3.3.5 Symbolism

Many poets use symbolism as a means of conveying an important theme. For example, in 'The Flea', John Donne uses a flea to represent the idea of sexual love, where the mingling of the couple's blood in the flea is used to attempt to persuade the woman to begin a physical relationship with the persona. This is effective as a flea is not a traditionally romantic notion conveying Donne's main idea that the act of sex is no more important or noteworthy than being bitten by a flea.

After reading the following text and making your own observations, read the annotated text - Exhibit 31 in the 'Annotated extracts' section at the end of this topic .

John Donne 'The Flea'

Mark but this flea, and mark in this,
How little that which thou deniest me is;
It sucked me first, and now sucks thee,
And in this flea our two bloods mingled be;
Thou know'st that this cannot be said
A sin, nor shame, nor loss of maidenhead,

> Yet this enjoys before it woo,
> And pampered swells with one blood made of two,
> And this, alas, is more than we would do.

Oh stay, three lives in one flea spare,
Where we almost, nay more than married are.
This flea is you and I, and this
Our marriage bed, and marriage temple is;
Though parents grudge, and you, w'are met,
And cloistered in these living walls of jet.

> Though use make you apt to kill me,
> Let not to that, self-murder added be,
> And sacrilege, three sins in killing three.

Cruel and sudden, hast thou since
Purpled thy nail, in blood of innocence?
Wherein could this flea guilty be,
Except in that drop which it sucked from thee?
Yet thou triumph'st, and say'st that thou
Find'st not thy self, nor me the weaker now;

> 'Tis true; then learn how false, fears be:
> Just so much honor, when thou yield'st to me,
> Will waste, as this flea's death took life from thee.

If you decide to use symbolism in your writing, whether it be poetry or another genre, try to use something unusual, too: originality of ideas will help you to achieve a better mark.

3.4 Prose fiction

There is a variety of suggestions from the SQA for the type of prose writing you can undertake for the portfolio, including:

- a short story;
- an extract, such as the opening, the conclusion or a key episode from a novel;
- a focused piece of characterisation;
- a monologue or dialogue;
- a detailed description of an imaginary setting;
- a series of diary entries or an exchange of letters.

Think carefully about the type of prose writing with which you have been successful in the past as well as the type of writing you enjoy and feel comfortable producing.

Regardless of the type of prose fiction you choose to create, there are particular points to note in all of the cases above and these are clearly specified by the SQA. You must have a clear plot, featuring characters whose traits are clearly identifiable and show development. There must be a denouement, bringing the plot to some kind of close or resolution and a defined structure which adds to the thematic concerns and the content of the writing. Dialogue, imagery and symbolism must also be included, as well as a stance, or tone, which shows your skills in this type of writing.

3.4.1 Subject and theme

You subject can be anything at all: there is no limit to where and when it is set, who is featured and what happens. However, be aware that this is Advanced Higher and you must strive to be innovative. A ghost story set in a graveyard is a little too clichéd, as is a romance set in a high school. Think about short stories you have read which deal with an issue or the development of a character which drives the action.

There is a plethora of modern and more established short story writers out there: read some stories to see how the professionals achieve originality. Useful websites include:

- Book Trust (https://www.booktrust.org.uk/booklists/s/short-stories-ya/)
- American Literature - 100 Great Short Stories (http://bit.ly/239SnaP)

> **Prose fiction: Subject and theme**
>
> Make a list of anything at all that you are interested in writing about, e.g. people, places, incidents, memories, relationships, issues, news items.
>
> Once you have made the list, think about the type of prose fiction you are most keen to undertake and identify the topics/subjects that would let you explore it best. This is a good way to get started with your writing. You should, however, be prepared to begin more than one piece of writing: you don't have to finish a piece of work if you feel it isn't going the way you want it to!

3.4.2 Structure

The structure of prose fiction is vital to its success. Your writing should intrigue the reader and keep them guessing, or build tension, or subvert their expectations.

Think about the following:

- the plot of your writing must be worked out in advance: only then can your structure be effective;
- the structure guides your reader towards the denouement of your writing, foreshadowing incidents and building characterisation as appropriate;
- the ending is likely to leave the reader with work to do: it must not be explicit;
- different sections could be narrated by different characters;
- you could employ the technique of flashback, if appropriate.

3.4.3 Characterisation

The development of character is of vital importance in prose fiction. Characters must be credible and behave/speak consistently in order to achieve this.

Think about the following when you are developing your character(s):

- Are they trustworthy?
- How do they react to the situations or events in the writing?
- How do they speak? How often do they speak?
- How do they interact with and react to the other characters?
- Are their personalities clear?

By considering these questions whenever characters appear, they are more likely to develop into well-rounded, credible representations who will aid in the development of your themes and main concerns.

Many writers also think about the previous existence of their character(s) before they begin to help them to understand how they would react or behave in particular situations. Questions like where were they born; what were their parents like; who were their best childhood friends and what did they do for fun can all help you to develop more rounded characters.

Prose fiction: Characterisation

Consider the following three characters:

- an old man whose wife has recently died;
- the youngest child from a large family;
- a teenager.

How would the characters above react to these three events?

1. Being ignored by a friend
2. Being involved in a car accident
3. The first morning at a new job

Write a paragraph or two giving an account of each character's reaction, thinking about the questions above. Do this with a peer and then make comments on each other's responses. If the feedback is positive and you feel inspired develop the paragraph(s) further: it could make a successful folio piece!

3.4.4 Setting

It is important to note that the setting in time and place of your prose fiction will be influenced by its subject matter but it can still have a major effect on the success of your writing. Described (or alluded to) skilfully, setting is often the strongest contributor to atmosphere. Use language to render your setting(s) as realistic as possible.

Prose fiction: Setting

Write a paragraph describing the following scenarios, thinking about the atmosphere you hope to create in each one:

1. Waking up on an empty train
2. A hospital room
3. A picnic by the river

Play around with these: you could subvert expectations, creating an unexpected atmosphere. As always, avoid cliché!

3.4.5 Language

How you choose to use language in prose fiction depends on the genre you choose but you must use it carefully: there are no 'spare' words in a short story. Every word, phrase, sentence and paragraph has a purpose, whether it be to further the plot or show character development and this means that your choice of language is vitally important. As with all writing, you will use a combination of techniques, including imagery, sentence structure, sound, word choice and, as mentioned before, the use of motifs and tone.

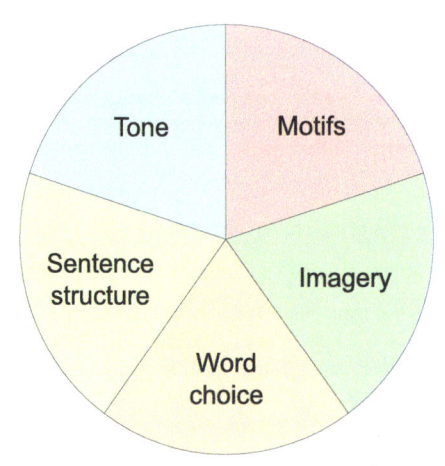

Techniques of language used in prose fiction

Tone

Tone will vary throughout the writing, depending on who is narrating and what is happening.

Motifs

Motifs can be used to emphasise an important idea, recurring throughout the writing to keep focus on the theme or main concerns. Examples of motifs could include repeated reference to a clock to convey the idea of time passing or water dripping to refer to the idea of a constant pressure or stress.

Imagery

Imagery (metaphor, simile and personification) and sound (onomatopoeia, alliteration and assonance) are used to great effect by writers in all genres. They allow you to describe, for example, a scene, person, event or feeling in such a way that the reader is able to visualise it or is inspired to feel how your characters feel: they can be very powerful, used well. At this level, it is important to be original, however: hackneyed, overused similes are not allowed!

Word choice

Your word choice must be carefully considered at every point in your writing: what are you conveying? What atmosphere are you creating? Again, remember that this is Advanced Higher: complex and sophisticated!

Sentence structure

Your use of sentence structure is also very important as it can be used as effectively as imagery and word choice to create atmosphere. Think about the effects you want to create and consider how best to convey them: short sentences to convey shock or panic? Repetition to drive home a particular feeling? Inversion to subvert the reader's expectations? A long, rambling sentence to emphasise confusion?

> **Prose fiction: Language**
>
> Look at the options below and write a few paragraphs for each one. Use language to create atmosphere, play around with vocabulary and sentence structure and include some dialogue to convey a sense of character. Remember to use what you have already learned about setting and character.
>
> 1. An unknown visitor arrives at the protagonist's home
> 2. Your main character arrives at work/a party/home and no-one recognises him/her
> 3. An argument between two main characters (not just dialogue)
>
> Share your writing with your peers and teacher: feedback on your writing is important for its development.

3.5 Drama

This genre differs significantly from the others in a number of ways. Chief among these is the fact that you are writing for an audience who are expected to watch or listen to the action of your drama rather than read it and therefore they must have something to watch or listen to: every movement, piece of dialogue and facial expression ought to be designed to elicit a reaction from the audience and add to their appreciation of the drama.

Dialogue will form the majority of your writing and is vital to how your characters are perceived, along with their facial expressions and movements on stage. This does not mean that you should underestimate the power of the other aspects of stagecraft, however: stage directions, lighting, music, props and costume can all have an important part to play in creating a drama.

There are many types of drama that you could choose to create for your portfolio of writing. Some of these, listed by the SQA, include:

- a dramatic monologue;
- an opening scene of a play;
- a complete one-act play;
- a play for radio;
- a television sit-com;
- a storyboard, shooting script, a film script;
- a documentary drama.

It is possible that you will choose to stick with what you know best, writing the type of drama you have encountered in your study of literature: drama designed to be performed on a stage. However, you may choose to write a play for radio or television, or a film script. If you do, make sure that you research these styles of writing fully before you embark upon your writing. The BBC Writer's Lab website (http://bbc.in/1RDVnDl) is a good place to start.

TOPIC 3. CREATIVE WRITING

Regardless of the type of drama you decide to write, the SQA is clear about what you must do in order to be successful:

- create characters who are credible, interesting and capable of provoking in the reader an intellectual and/or emotional response;
- make effective use of dialogue - and other modes of communication (including non-verbal modes such as gesture, body-language);
- establish a setting in which, and a situation out of which, the drama will arise;
- develop and communicate a recognisable theme, a centre of interest that will give point to the script;
- produce a particular effect, mood or atmosphere;
- demonstrate familiarity with the requirements of script layout and presentation;
- convince the reader of the potential of the script for dramatic realisation in an appropriate medium, ensuring always that stage directions, technical effects and other production notes are directly linked to the action.

3.5.1 Subject, plot and theme

When considering what to write about, remember that many dramas are centred around the idea of conflict, especially if you choose to write a complete play or script. The conflict can be related to something minor, like an argument between siblings or friends, a lost ticket or a missed opportunity or it may be concerned with a larger issue, perhaps something topical, like the arrival of refugees in the country or domestic abuse. In the latter case, use your characters and how they behave to explore this on a smaller scale rather than a national one. Whatever you choose, make sure that your treatment of it is well-researched and realistic.

Planning the shape of your drama is very important:

- How will it begin?
- How will the possibility of conflict or the issue be introduced?
- What will you do develop your theme and keep the audience entertained?
- If you are writing a one-act play, with a beginning, middle and end, how will it end?

In fact, even if you are writing part of a drama, you ought to know how it would end so that your work looks as if it will continue.

Drama: Subject, plot and theme

Make a list of current issues that you might be inspired to explore in a drama. Look at news websites for ideas. Explore their potential by considering the following:

- Where and when would it be set?
- Who would your characters be?

© HERIOT-WATT UNIVERSITY

- What kind of thing is likely to happen?
- How might you resolve the situation, or draw it to a close?

If you are finding it difficult to come up with responses to these questions, it probably isn't the topic for you!

3.5.2 Dialogue and characterisation

This is how the action of the drama really comes alive: the words your characters speak are the most important aspect of the writing. It must be realistic and appropriate to the setting and the characters that you have created, as well as advancing the plot. Think about characters you have encountered in plays you have studied: how well does the dialogue they speak help you to understand the type of person he or she is?

Cassie in 'Bold Girls', for example, is exactly that: bold and outrageous, and the way she speaks emphasises this. The character of Romeo is an incurable, lovesick romantic and his use of romantic imagery underlines this clearly. Your characters should be equally clear to see through the words they speak.

Drama: Dialogue and characterisation

Consider the following scenarios:

1. Two friends discover that they are about to be interviewed for the same job.
2. A mother and daughter meet their new neighbours: a refugee family fleeing from the conflict in Syria.
3. Two men hear sounds of what seems to be a struggle coming from inside a parked van.

Look at the characters below and use some of them to write dialogue for one or more of the scenarios:

- a married man who works in a local garage;
- a teacher in a secondary school;
- an elderly woman who has a very old secret;
- an IT expert;
- a new mother;
- a man who has just discovered that he is ill.

Develop the type of people they are through what they say and how they say it, building on the information supplied. You could work with a partner, taking a character each. You can incorporate other elements of stagecraft but they are not essential: demonstrating your skills of characterisation is what is important here!

3.5.3 Elements of stagecraft

The most commonly used of these include stage directions, lighting, music, costume and props. These elements of drama writing are all used to great effect by a variety of playwrights but they are not all always included in a drama script. They are used for a variety of reasons, including to indicate setting. Just as with prose fiction, setting in time and place is important when planning your writing here. Deciding this will, of course, be part of the planning process and should be considered throughout. What is different in drama is that you need to consider how to move from one setting to another, for example, from inside to outside or from one room to another.

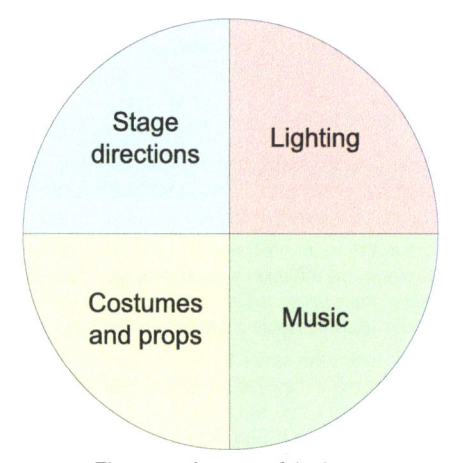

Elements of stagecraft in drama

Stage directions

Different playwrights use stage directions to varying extents. Shakespeare used them to signal when characters entered or left the stage and for very little else: Tennessee Williams' and Arthur Miller's stage directions, on the other hand, are much more prescriptive, detailing where a character might stand or sit, the volume they should speak at, their tone and, often, what they might wear. They were frequently very clear about stage sets and how they ought to look and what music should be heard.

What is important for you to remember is that you are creating a piece of drama and you are likely to have clear ideas, over and above the plot and characters you create, about how it should look and sound. Include as much detail as you feel is important but remember not to overshadow the dialogue: this must take precedence over everything else.

Lighting

Lighting can be used in drama for a variety of purposes: to highlight (or hide!) the presence of a particular character or characters; to create a mood or atmosphere; to change scene, moving the focus from one part of the stage to another or simply to recreate the type of lighting found in a particular setting.

Music

Used cleverly, music can add a great deal to a piece of drama. Tennessee Williams uses a recurring polka to highlight the fracturing of Blanche Dubois' psyche as the play progresses: it becomes a very stylistic motif. Music, like lighting, can also be used to create a mood or atmosphere that adds to the action of the play or the development of a character.

Costumes and props

Some playwrights can be very specific about costumes and props: they are regarded as vital to the setting and theme of the play. Think about where your drama is set and what the plot and theme are. Is specifying what characters are wearing and what kind of electronic device they are holding important? If not, use dialogue and action to convey these.

Drama: Elements of stagecraft

Read this short piece of prose and transform it from prose into a drama script, considering how you will use elements of stagecraft and dialogue to create a similar atmosphere. You could continue the writing further, if inspiration strikes!

As the sun set, the light in the room grew dim and my mood lowered with it. Glancing despondently out at the street, my attention was absorbed by the sight of a grubby toddler sitting alone on the patchy grass verge, sniffling piteously. There was no sign of anyone else and I began to feel the uncomfortable stirrings of anxiety.

Pulling open the door, I scanned the street for someone to take the responsibility I was beginning to fear might become mine. I crossed the road and knelt beside the child, whose clothes were grimier than I had at first realised. I smiled tentatively and gently said, "Hello, what are you doing here?" She looked at me and changed from sniffling to outright howling. "No, don't do that!" I implored, startled, as a voice shouted from behind me, "Come here! Where have you been? What have I told you about wandering off?" Turning, I was confronted with an accusatory glare as a small woman scooped up the child, roughly shaking her.

Her appearance was only marginally more presentable than that of the toddler, whose howling continued unabated. "Mind your own business!" the woman snarled, as she turned to leave.

"Mummy! I want mummy!"

"I'm here," the woman replied, in an attempt at a soothing tone.

"I want mummy!" screamed the hysterical little girl. "Mummy!"

3.6 Annotated extracts

Reflective writing: Introduction - annotated

Exhibit 27: Reflective writing: Introduction - annotated

The text below is an example of a reflective writing introduction.

> As I watched the bee hover over flower after flower[1], single-mindedly gathering its store of pollen[2], my mind wandered to the queen, waiting in royal expectation for her orders to be fulfilled by the unquestioning subjects of her adoring hive. Did she wonder about their loyalty? Were there factions filled with dissatisfied minions waiting for their opportunity to stage a carefully planned coup and dethrone her?[3] Unlikely, given their lack of independent thought and centuries of genetic programming. The entourage of which I was a member, however, was subject to a different kind of programming[4] : our hive was not full of brainwashed bees, but scheming teenage girls[5].
>
> **Notes:**
>
> [1] The initial tone is contemplative.
> [2] This introduction uses a small, everyday event to introduce the main idea.
> [3] Language is used to create the idea of a monarch and her subjects, as well as the political image of a leader being deposed in a coup. These could run throughout the essay as motifs, or an extended metaphor, helping to convey the theme.
> [4] Although it is not clear yet exactly what it is, a personal experience is certainly on its way.
> [5] The tone now gives way to an element of humour: it may not be a particularly serious subject.

Reflective writing: Language - annotated

Exhibit 28: Reflective writing: Language - annotated
The text below is an example of the language used in reflective writing.

> Approaching the school building, at the centre of a buzzing group of drones[1], I felt the familiar stirrings of irritation, ennui and envy. I could hardly bear another day of fawning over someone as vacuous as our fearless leader[2], watching from the ranks as she drawled orders: our Cleopatra[3], whose every whim must be obeyed. I looked around at my companions: they exuded excitement and anticipation, surely due to the upcoming social event of the year. Well, the month at least[4]. Which shoes to wear? Which dress? Which lipstick?[5] Hardly questions to tax the intellects of the exceptional students we were supposed to be.[6]
>
> **Notes:**
>
> [1] Continuation of the bee motif, with a suggestion of the military language introduced previously.
> [2] The mocking tone gives away the narrator's real feelings, along with the lexical choice of 'vacuous'.
> [3] The use of this image suggests both beauty and power and, along with 'every whim', also has connotations of someone who misuses these because she can.
> [4] The mocking tone is continued: the narrator clearly believes that this is not worth becoming quite so excited about.
> [5] The repeated use of questions here mimics the excited and repetitive chatter of the girls.
> [6] The final sentence here continues the mocking tone, letting the reader know that the narrator considers herself to be above these frivolous concerns and that she is considers herself and her friends to be 'exceptional'.

Reflective writing: Conclusion - annotated

Exhibit 29: Reflective writing: Conclusion - annotated
The text below is an example of a reflective writing conclusion.

My brief dalliance into the upper echelons of school society had left me disillusioned and ostracised[1]. Visions of ruling the social elite and commanding the allegiance[2] of a band of beauties lay scattered before me, shrapnel from a pointless war[3]. The hard lesson of the value of substance before appearance had been learned and it stays with me: I regret every day the casual abandonment of true friends for nothing more than an illusory victory. It turns out it's not really winning when the prize is worthless[4].

Notes:

[1] The use of vocabulary - 'brief dalliance', 'echelons' and ostracised' - points to the social sphere that the narrator aspired to.
[2] Continues the military references begun in the introduction.
[3] More military language.
[4] This piece of reflection at the end of the essay sums up the narrator's feelings about the whole affair. It was not worth it - friends are more important than social status, which is, in fact, intangible and unimportant in comparison.

Siegfried Sassoon 'Suicide in the Trenches' - annotated

Exhibit 30: Siegfried Sassoon 'Suicide in the Trenches' - annotated

The following annotated poem is Siegfried Sassoon's 'Suicide in the Trenches', published in 1918.

I[1] knew a simple[2] soldier boy
Who grinned at life in empty joy[3],
Slept soundly[4] through the lonesome dark,
And whistled[5] early with the lark.

In[6] winter trenches[7], cowed and glum[8],
With crumps and lice and lack of rum[9],
He put a bullet through his brain[10].
No one spoke of him again[11].

You[12] smug-faced[13] crowds with kindling eye
Who cheer[14] when soldier lads march by,
Sneak[15] home and pray you'll never know
The hell where youth and laughter go[16].

Notes:

[1] The first stanza provides a clear picture of a young, carefree and secure young man.
[2] He is uncomplicated, as is his life, presumably.
[3] The phrase 'grinned at life' conveys the kind of cheerfulness that comes with a life unfettered by negativity or unhappiness. The phrase 'empty' suggests, again, that his life is a straightforward, pleasant one, free of worry or concern.
[4] He has no concerns or troubles at this point.
[5] Another example of his happiness and carefree attitude.
[6] The second stanza deals with the state of his living conditions and his mind after going to war.
[7] The atmosphere changes immediately: no larks or sound sleeping. The springlike tone of the first stanza is exchanged for the harshness of 'winter'.
[8] Another change: he is no longer the happy and confident whistler but unhappy and afraid.
[9] A list of the privations he has to suffer in the trenches: again, very negative in contrast to the first stanza.
[10] A shocking change in tone from the first stanza. His life is so awful in the trenches he would rather die than continue to go through the experience.
[11] The potential and joy of his former self is immediately negated.
[12] The persona addresses the reader, the public, with an accusatory tone in this stanza, showing his contempt for those who send the youth of the country to suffer and die in these hellish conditions.
[13] An unflattering and condemnatory use of word choice, demonstrating the

persona's anger towards those who encourage young men to join up.
[14] Shows the support and encouragement given to those who are going to fight.
[15] Another unflattering connotation: those who have been cheering 'sneak' off to safety, while 'lads' go off to fight and die.
[16] The poem ends with a clear demonstration of the persona's main concern: that young boys, full of 'youth and laughter', are being sent to face unimaginable horrors.

John Donne 'The Flea' - annotated

Exhibit 31: John Donne 'The Flea' - annotated
The following annotated poem is John Donne's 'The Flea', published in 1633.

Mark but this flea, and mark in this,
How little that which thou deniest me is;
It sucked me first, and now sucks thee,
And in this flea our two bloods mingled be;[1]
Thou know'st that this cannot be said
A sin, nor shame, nor loss of maidenhead,[2]

    Yet this enjoys before it woo,
    And pampered swells with one blood made of two,
    And this, alas, is more than we would do.[3]

Oh stay, three lives in one flea spare,
Where we almost, nay more than married are.
This flea is you and I, and this
Our marriage bed, and marriage temple is;[4]
Though parents grudge, and you, w'are met,
And cloistered in these living walls of jet.

    Though use make you apt to kill me,
    Let not to that, self-murder added be,
    And sacrilege, three sins in killing three.

Cruel and sudden, hast thou since
Purpled thy nail, in blood of innocence?
Wherein could this flea guilty be,
Except in that drop which it sucked from thee?
Yet thou triumph'st, and say'st that thou
Find'st not thy self, nor me the weaker now;

    'Tis true; then learn how false, fears be:
    Just so much honor, when thou yield'st to me,
    Will waste, as this flea's death took life from thee.[5]

Notes:

[1] The flea has bitten both of them and now their blood is mixed within it.
[2] The persona argues that being bitten in this way does mean that either of them has done anything wrong: it is not as serious as loss of virginity may be considered to be.
[3] He goes on to argue that the flea has achieved more intimacy with both than they have enjoyed with each other.
[4] He compares the flea to a 'marriage bed', again suggesting a level of intimacy hardly less than having sex.
[5] The poem ends with his argument that her 'honor', or the importance of her

> virginity, will seem as insignificant as her killing of the flea when she finally 'yields' to him.

3.7 Learning points

Summary

You should now feel more confident about tackling these types of writing and have a clear understanding of the following:

- understand and be able to use the conventions of reflective writing, poetry, prose fiction and drama at Advanced Higher;
- be aware of the importance of redrafting.

Unit 3 Topic 4

Annotated exemplars

Contents

4.1 Essay one: Persuasive writing 217
4.2 Essay two: Argumentative writing 222
4.3 Essay three: Short story 226
4.4 Essay four: Reflective 230

Read through the essays contained in this section to see some examples of good writing. Many of the skills mentioned in this section are exemplified and it will help you to see how you can use these skills when it comes to your own writing.

Not all genres are included here: if you don't see the genre you are interested in, do more reading. You can find endless examples of writing in magazines, newspapers, on the internet, in collections of poetry, short stories or drama: read as much as you can and look for where writers have used the techniques discussed in this section.

At the end of each piece is a comment with a suggested mark: read them along with the SQA marking instructions to get a sense of what markers are thinking when they mark your work - http://bit.ly/2bQjWSL.

4.1 Essay one: Persuasive writing

Is technology detrimental to the world of literature?[1]

Walk into[2] your nearest Starbucks or another chain coffee shop. Do a quick headcount. How many of the patrons are reading?[3] A fair amount, I would imagine. Okay, okay[4] - now count the number of people reading from a physical copy of a book? Hardly any is my guess. Alright, so how many of the customers are reading from an eBook or an e-Reader? Well, I wager that the majority of people in that shop would be perusing the latest exploits of Katniss Everdeen or Christian Grey on some sort of technological device. And why wouldn't they be? In recent years, technology has advanced in key aspects of our lives, such as transport, food, and housing. Of course it had to at some point be utilised to advance our reading habits![5] However, the burning question remains; did our reading habits need advancement at all? It can be argued that the whole concept of downloading books is effectively killing the book industry by eliminating the entire magical premise of entering a bookstore, stopping, and breathing in the beautiful smell of new books, freshly delivered from the smoking pens of literary geniuses[6]. But with high-street bookstores charging extortionate prices in a time where people are struggling to pay for necessities, let alone the luxury of a paperback, has the arrival of reading technology helped the world of literature, or in fact hindered it?[7]

The enthusiastic proponents of purchasing real books boast of the advantages of doing so online, including the cost, or lack of[8]. It is often either cheaper or the same price to buy books online and large online book-sellers such as Amazon or Play.com often offer free delivery and usually have 3 for 2 deals on certain books. Delivery from these kinds of websites is frequently very good, aiming to deliver in less than a week, although you can request faster delivery at extra cost, with the main attraction of ordering online being the fact that one doesn't have to leave the sofa to purchase the desired reading matter, in a tried and tested format. Equally however, downloading books onto an e-Reader can be just as cheap and, with a good broadband connection, extremely fast. In a world where people have limited time to race through an unlimited number of activities, having a portable device which can instantly download literature and hold over 300,000 books is admittedly much easier than hauling round an entire library in your handbag[9].

In[10] fact, due to the introduction of the e-Book, not only is it easier to read books, but there are also more opportunities for self-publishing, which allows for a wider range of amateur authors to reach an audience with their material, many of whom would have been rejected by more conventional publishing methods, such as through an agent. In 2011 an American called John Locke became the first self-published author to be really successful in exploring the amazing possibilities of the electronic frontier[11], selling over one million Kindle books by using Amazon Kindle Direct Publishing, a service where authors are able to publish their material directly to Amazon Kindle Apps. Mr Locke is now a New York Times best-selling author, and the first self-publishing author to reach number one on the Amazon booklist. Not only is this assistance beneficial for authors who fail to attract the attention of more traditional publishers, but it allows enthusiastic readers to immerse themselves in a varied choice of literature. Of course, connoisseurs of literature[12] should be immensely grateful for the rigorous policing of literary boundaries[13] carried out by agents and publishers who still largely work within the print industry. While Mr. Locke's hugely successful foray into the world of literature has provided a popular product, the advent of online self-publishing has also spawned legions of hellish tales[14], penned by people with little talent and even less self-awareness (as well as a disturbing lack of acquaintances courageous enough to review their loved ones' literary attempts with anything approaching honesty[15]). In these busy times, who has the energy or hours required to trawl through tripe hoping for an undiscovered gem?[16]

One of the more controversial arguments surrounding e-Readers is its "eco-friendly" status. No paper is required since the reading material is downloaded and stored on the device, meaning that fewer trees have to be cut down. Studies have also shown that driving to a bookshop and purchasing a physical book creates double the carbon dioxide emissions than those created by someone purchasing a book online, suggesting that e-Readers are far better for the planet than printed books[17]. However[18], because lumber companies plant two trees for every one they cut down, the first point must be considered moot. Furthermore, the same studies have shown that an Amazon Kindle produces around 168 kg of carbon dioxide in its life cycle, around 23 times more than the amount of carbon dioxide produced by a single physical book. There is also the toxicity of the heavy metals used in reading devices and their batteries to take into consideration, difficult to recycle and certainly not environmentally kind. Add to this the fact that the average life-cycle of most e-Readers is two years, whereas a book can last for generations if looked after well, and the eco argument loses much of its power. So, where a paper book can be recycled after an extensive period of time, potentially giving pleasure over and over, e-Readers and their components are destined to rot in landfill after a couple of years' use.[19]

In recent years we have seen the effects of the 'technologising' of books on Britain's high streets. Borders was once a massive UK book store, a large enterprise with sales of literature spanning worldwide. Yet the company was unable to combat the fierce competition from the online book industry, and in November 2009 admitted defeat[20] and entered administration. Although we can largely blame the Internet for the downfall of such a major store, the company itself was also at fault. At a time where there was a gap in the market for buying music and film online, Borders instead focussed on expanding their sub-sections of CD, DVDs, and video games, whereas other bookshops such as Barnes & Noble adapted to the increasing interest in reading electronically by introducing their own digital bookstore app in the battle to keep up with the modern market of book-selling. But in the end, it was the daily barrage from the world of online retail and lack of strategic planning in the technology department which made Borders just another victim of the recession. The idea of losing such places of relaxation and refuge is a difficult one to stomach, however, contributing as they do to the whole experience of reading. In the war between physical and electronic books, stores such as Borders must embrace technology in order to survive.

It[21] is not only the customer who is likely to suffer when the flow of the sale of books diminishes to a sorry trickle, however. Due to the current ease of self-publication previously mentioned, publishing agencies and professional proof-readers are also at risk of finding themselves out of work, meaning that this sector of work may well be losing many of its employees. The lumber industry is likely to suffer also; fewer trees will have to be cut down to provide printed books if the majority of books are stored online and technological devices. In a time when the threat of deforestation is constantly assuaged by valiant attempts at reforestation, those who work in the industry will suffer more than the environment. In addition, other high street bookshops are also beginning to feel the pressure from online sellers. Recently Waterstones were forced to axe up to 650 jobs as a result of cost-cutting measures, and have closed branches up and down the country. Though many jobs have been and will be created during this transition to the technological era of civilisation, there are far more jobs that will be lost: is it really worth it?

I[22] am perfectly willing to admit that technology does have its advantages, and I for one do love most aspects of this new age of laptops, phones and video games. But I will say one thing to the creators of the latest technological devices: leave my books alone![23] As an avid reader from a young age, not once have I thought to myself 'I wish I could turn a page by sliding my hand across the screen'. That is the whole point of literature, trembling[24] as you turn the page to a dramatic part of your book, or inserting a bookmark, promising to pick up where you left off as soon as you can. And of course I was heartbroken when Borders shut down, as that shop contained everything that a book-lover would need: stationery, GAME, Starbucks, and obviously the books! I could spend hours perusing through the shop; visiting the different floors was like entering different chapters of the same novel. And my favourite part of the buying experience was the first time I opened up a new book and breathed in all the hours spent writing, all the ideas turned into a paperback by the author. If the big companies such as Amazon or Apple steal this from me, I will be devastated. If it is within this lifetime that we see books and bookshops replaced by soulless, money-driven e-Readers and their online sellers, then this is the wrong lifetime for me[25].

Notes:

[1] The subject matter is stated clearly.
[2] The use of the imperative engages the reader immediately, and continues to do so throughout the next few sentences.
[3] The questions in this paragraph also engage the reader, encouraging them to think about the use of e-Readers.
[4] The tone is informal: conversational and friendly. Again, the reader is encouraged to become engaged in thinking about the topic.
[5] This comment introduces one side of the argument: that technology's advance into how we read was unavoidable and, implicitly, a positive step.
[6] The opposing argument is introduced: reading in this way means losing some of the 'magic' of the activity. Word choice is used to hint at the writer's point of view: 'killing' and 'eliminating' align the e-readers with destruction while 'magical' and 'beautiful' invite the reader to appreciate the experience of buying and reading a new book.
[7] Including a question at the end of the introduction is another technique which not only engages the reader but also offers an insight into what is coming next: in this case, a discussion of whether or not technology benefits literature.
[8] This paragraph discusses the merits of online shopping for reading matter and contains points which advance both arguments for both physical books and e-Readers.
[9] The tone here is humorous, further engaging the reader.
[10] This paragraph inverts the format of the previous paragraph, arguing for e-Readers first. This ensures that the essay is less formulaic and reads more smoothly than simply using the same structure repeatedly.
[11] The language used here encourages the reader to think about John Locke as an adventurer: someone who was able to discover uncharted territory. The word choice of 'exploring' and 'frontier' help to achieve this.
[12] The word 'connoisseurs' implies taste and a broad knowledge of the subject,

suggesting that what comes next is the opinion of experts in the field.
[13] The word choice here of 'policing' and 'boundaries' suggests authority, giving this argument more gravitas than the previous one.
[14] The imagery here is reminiscent of hell itself, creating a clear picture of some very, very bad writing indeed.
[15] A humorous tone again, balancing out the critical comments made about self-published authors. This further engages the reader.
[16] A summarising sentence which makes clear the candidate's stance for this section of the argument, at least.
[17] A strong, unequivocal argument in favour of e-Readers.
[18] The rest of this paragraph manages to discredit the eco argument entirely, using statistics.
[19] Again, word choice is used to suggest the candidate's viewpoint: 'pleasure' is positive and 'destined to rot' is most decidedly not.
[20] The word choice of 'combat' and 'defeat' is used to convey the idea of a battleground, along with 'battle', 'barrage' and 'war' later in the paragraph.
[21] This paragraph and the previous one are entirely focussed on the disadvantages of electronic reading, as the candidate moves towards the conclusion, demonstrating his or her own point of view without doubt.
[22] The conclusion to this essay is effective for a number of reasons, beginning with the move from third person to first person narration, signalling that the reader is going to hear the candidate's own point of view now.
[23] This imperative begins to show the candidate's strength of feeling on the matter.
[24] Word choice also conveys strength of feeling: 'trembling', 'heartbroken' and 'devastated'.
[25] Overall, the conclusion to this essay demonstrates the candidate's point of view clearly through word choice, tone and ideas.

Reference list

- Los Angeles Times 'E-books are good news for the literary world' (http://lat.ms/2gBTFN0)
- Allison's Blog 'Electronic Literature: Good or Bad?' (http://bit.ly/2gv22sv)
- Activity Press eReport 'Hard questions for booksellers as ebook efforts face setbacks' (http://bit.ly/2eYxwa8)
- The Guardian 'Amazon Publishing bookshop boycott grows' (http://bit.ly/2gaLQw8)
- The Wire 'Don't Feel Too Bad About Borders' (http://bit.ly/2eYDpnG)
- The Christian Science Monitor 'Bad news for independent bookstores: Is Google becoming 'another Amazon'?' (http://bit.ly/2fhJVRM)
- The Guardian 'Online retail sales hit £50bn' (http://bit.ly/2fKOIVs)
- BBC 'The rise of the indie author' (http://bbc.in/2geqk7t)
- Author John Locke 'Fathers and Daughters' (http://www.donovancreed.com/)
- The Guardian 'The ecological case for ebooks' (http://bit.ly/2fhUDYL)
- Teleread 'Are e-books more eco-friendly than paper books?' (http://bit.ly/2fKMU9z)

Mark range

This persuasive essay is likely to be placed in the 15-13 mark range as it displays:

- sustained thoughtfulness and insight;
- committed and clear stance;
- skilful shaping;
- skilful use of style, technique and language.

4.2 Essay two: Argumentative writing

Gas Fracking: The Way Ahead, Or a Road to Nowhere?[1]

It[2] has been clear for a while now that our energy systems need serious updating. The lack of remaining resources alone is a major issue, not to mention the environmental impact our current methods have. Although the majority of people understand that the ultimate goal is to crawl out of our caves and embrace the renewable energies of our planet[3], our technology is still decades, if not centuries, away from allowing us to have one hundred percent clean energy. In the short term new ways must be found to harvest the subterranean resources we so desperately rely on to keep our Neolithic societies functioning[4].

One proposed method has caused much controversy amongst members of the energy community, offering access to previously inaccessible fossil fuel reserves; but posing the risk of fairly substantial environmental damage[5]. This[6] method is known as 'fracking' (or 'hydraulic fracturing'), which involves the extraction of natural gas from black shale reserves; which - conveniently - are found all over the British Isles. The process involves drilling[7] deep holes into the dense shale rock, before pumping an extremely high pressure mixture of water, sand and chemicals into the opening, causing small fissures which allow natural gas to escape from the rock and travel up the drill hole, to be collected and piped away.

Many people are concerned about the effects of this supposedly 'next generation'[8] technique. One - which actually led to the temporary banning of fracking in the UK - is the risk of induced seismic activity. In 2011, the area around and including Blackpool was hit by two earthquakes, of magnitudes 2.5 and 1.5, which were considered reason enough to halt the process[9]. The United Kingdom only recently lifted the aforementioned ban, after long deliberations with the government over the dangers of fracking, one of which was this risk of these seismic events. This led to new precautions being introduced; a cap on the seismic activity being among them, with anything above a magnitude of 0.5 being deemed unsafe. However, this doesn't necessarily mean that there is no risk of damage to small villages, as a sudden quake could, theoretically, strike at any time.

This risk is not actually as serious as you may think[10]. Anything below a magnitude of 2.0 isn't likely to be felt by the majority of people. Only seismographs and very sensitive individuals would notice the quake, so we must ask ourselves: is this really a good enough reason to turn down an enterprise which could potentially allow us run our caveman-style society for the foreseeable future[11]? The use of indigenous natural gas could drastically reduce the amount of fossil fuel we need to import, making us far less dependent on other countries. It would also result in a lower carbon footprint for the UK as we would not be responsible for the massive tanker journeys from distant places such as the Middle East and America. These benefits for the economy certainly state a case for fracking as a viable source of fuel, even with the risks it carries[12].

The job market would also experience a noticeable boost, with thousands of new jobs created by the proposed propagation of the new technique. As a country with roughly 8% unemployment (amongst the economically active population) the UK would definitely benefit from the influx of career opportunities[13].

Nevertheless, the economic benefits of the practice are quite quickly levelled out by the impact it can have on the environment. The concoction of water, sand and chemicals that is used to fracture the rock can cause complications. The mixture was, until recently, a closely guarded secret of the energy companies, but recently the British firm 'Cuadrilla', revealed the contents of their mining fluid. The chemicals they use could pose a serious threat to local wildlife if they were to leak into the water table, due to their toxicity. Approximately 40 000 gallons of chemicals are used during each 'fracturing', a mixture which can contain up to 600 different chemicals, including known toxins and carcinogens such as lead, mercury, ethylene glycol, methanol, hydrochloric acid and formaldehyde[14]. This creates further opposition to the technique, on behalf of conservationists, who are concerned about the wellbeing of animals and plants in the surrounding area. However, many of the claims of drilling well contamination are unsubstantiated; with a lot of arbitrary figures or assumed information. This does not, however, detract from the need to ensure no such leaks ever occur; should fracking become a popular process.

Even though with proper procedure, and monitoring, the risk to wildlife could be prevented, the 'dirty water' must still be disposed of. Currently, the wastewater is dealt with in a few, quite simple, ways; which are causing some distress amongst environmentalists. One of the methods is to pump the residual fluids into waste wells, much like those used for the actual fracturing process, where they will be left and sealed; a glorified landfill really. This obviously raises concerns about the long term effect of these wells, both on the surrounding above ground areas and - perhaps more importantly - on the geological environment found deep down in the wells, which some people worry will cause instability in the rock; increasing the risk of quakes.

The second method carries less risk, but creates even more concern due, mostly, to its somewhat unsightly nature. In a nutshell the plan would be to store the residue in tanks, either above ground or sunk into it, which would be covered over and treated - to ensure the mixture is safe - before it is pumped back into rivers and into the sea. The treatment plants, used to process the waste, would take up a great deal of land (something not exactly in abundance in the British Isles), as well as peppering the idyllic countryside with what can only be described as a series of industrial eyesores. It is probable that this would have a negative effect on local communities; with property prices likely to fall, as well as damage to tourist related income.

Nonetheless, we must make an effort to prioritise what is truly important. Yes, clean energy would be great, and yes, we don't want to have to look at tumours on our treasured rural areas, and yes, we want our shores to be desirable for residents and tourists alike[15]; but maybe that's just the price we will have to pay to maintain our archaic way of living[16].

After all, the overwhelming argument for the introduction of fracking is the same as that of any other proposed energy source; we don't really have another option at the moment. With our current technology, we are entirely dependent on the production of electricity to continue to function, and although wind, solar, hydroelectric and numerous other renewable energies are coming on in leaps and bounds, we must realise that our lavish lifestyles are supported by the dirtier, uglier energy our axe-swinging, mammoth slaying, forefathers[17] thought up. Progress will happen, and I believe at some point we will be able to live in a far more sustainable way, but for the meantime we will just have to accept that we are reliant on the that most famous caveman discovery; fire.

It[18] is perfectly clear then, that necessity justifies risk in this instance; with the proposed benefits to the economy, to world fuel reserves and to the job market easily outweighing the limited associated risk and the aesthetic impact of fracking in the UK. To reiterate, the idea of clean energy is very pretty and pleasant, but the reality of our limited technology and dwindling resources delay the proliferation of such ideal energy sources until such a time as the situation permits it. For the meantime, fracking will allow the UK to function more independently, boost our economy and job market, and help to alleviate the overbearing problem of the world's waning fuel reserves; which I believe will play an increasingly pivotal part in world politics in the coming years, as they begin to run out...

Notes:

[1] A clear indication of the topic to be discussed.
[2] The overall tone of this paragraph is fitting for an argumentative essay: it is formal and serious. This is appropriate for argumentative writing, unlike the conversational, sometimes humorous tone of the previous persuasive essay.
[3] This imagery of caveman moving into a new future is effective as it conveys an understanding that how we harvest energy now is not suitable for our future: we need to explore new methods, rather than relying on out-of-date approaches.
[4] The candidate's viewpoint seems to be expressed here: we may not have a choice when it comes to fracking.
[5] A brief summary of the main pros and cons of this area.
[6] A summary of how fracking works: brief and functional, the tone is neutral and explanatory.
[7] The process is explained using technical terms such as 'drilling', 'shale rock' and 'fissures', which demonstrate the candidate's understanding of the topic.
[8] The use of 'supposedly' and the inverted commas around 'next generation' convey a slightly mocking tone, suggesting that the candidate disagrees with those who show concern.
[9] An example of how the candidate's research is informing the essay, providing statistics that can then be discussed in more detail.
[10] Addressing the reader is a valid approach in argumentative and persuasive writing. In this case it encourages the reader to read on and discover the very facts that the candidate wants to stress.
[11] The use of 'we' and the subsequent question also engage the reader.
[12] A good concluding sentence: sums up the main points of the last couple of paragraphs and conveys the candidate's point of view.
[13] Although the candidate is making a good point, and one which supports fracking, this paragraph is quite short and lacks detail.
[14] Detailed statistics demonstrating evidence of research.
[15] This is an effective use of repetition: the candidate stresses that the negatives cannot be argued with, accepting that these points are valid.
[16] This paragraph and the next focus on the idea of fracking as the best way to create the energy we need for the foreseeable future: building up to the essay's conclusion which, given the language and structure of the essay so far, is likely to come down on the side of fracking.
[17] This word choice conveys the negative connotations of fracking: destructive and 'dirty'. This, however, does not detract from the candidate's argument that straits are so dire that this is likely to be our only option at the moment.
[18] A good conclusion, summarising some of the pros and cons and then coming to rest

clearly on the side of fracking. It finishes by implying that this issue is so important that it is not only fit for discussion in an English essay, but also on the world stage.

Mark range

This argumentative essay is likely to be placed in the 15-13 mark range as it displays:

- sustained thoughtfulness and insight;
- committed and clear stance;
- skilful shaping;
- skilful use of style, technique and language.

4.3 Essay three: Short story

Rendezvous

"So, how did it happen?" Her voice was tinged with both intrigue and a certain stern quality. "I need to know."

"I'll tell you how, from the very beginning; the whole story. Just don't interrupt..."

"My cynicism had largely consumed my day to day activities[1]. The vibrant colours which brought joy to others and still surrounded me had become grey to me[2], and I was becoming numb to the attempts of others to raise my spirits. There was one thing, and one thing alone, which gave me a reason to push onwards; a search. A daring quest I had been on for some time now, its only goal to find one man[3]. One man among millions. A man named Alec Saculara.

I had encountered him once before and was now compelled to seek him out. We had a connection, one I cannot begin to describe; like some sort of ethereal[4] rope tethering us together. He was the subject of almost all my dreams and his face seemed to appear everywhere I went. For an eternity the pursuit had been fruitless, but my luck shifted a few months ago, when I discovered the username 'SacularaA182' in one particular internet chat room.

All Saculara knew of me was that I was a 14 year-old girl, whose favourite pastimes were watching movies and playing volleyball (a useful lack of detail which could be attributed to the 20 word limit in the site's 'About Me' section). Coming across him was largely down to fate, out of my all-too-mortal hands[5], so I made sure to be online for at least an hour of every night, of every week, of every month[6]. At first the whole plan seemed to border on the obsessive, but as time went on my desire to find him grew, deepened, festered. Until one day, I finally found him, and the purgatory of waiting[7] seemed like nothing more than a lengthy inconvenience.

It was time to put my painstakingly conceived plan into action. Struck by the thunderous realisation that it was him, my hands shook and adrenaline insisted that I speak to him[8]. I had to meet with him. I just had to.

"Hey, nice to meet you, my name's Eleanor." Careful, I thought, you don't want to scare him.

"Hi, I'm Alec," his innocuous reply came, sealing the deal. There was now no doubt, this was what I had been searching for.

Over the course of the next five weeks, Alec and I spent many hours with each other online; becoming privy to each other's deepest thoughts and experiences, strengths and weaknesses; anything that would allow us to be closer and more open with each other. Many months passed, the evenings were long, and the conversations intricate and lengthy, but it finally paid off last night when he proposed a meeting in my local park, down by the weeping willow at the bottom of a long lane. Can you believe it?[9] After all that, he did the hard part himself. I[10] felt faint at the thought of seeing his face, as if the world was drifting away from me. The plan was in its closing stage, the final act.

"Sure, I'd love to meet you", the keys seemed heavy under my fingers; each letter was momentous. "When?"

"How about tonight, at ten?" I took a while to appreciate the moment. To appreciate the victory that had finally come. After all the misery that had befallen me, I had - at last - found some success. After one more, long, deep breath, I replied.

"I'll be there."

I carefully lowered the screen of the laptop until it clicked shut, and sat, just sat, for three hours, staring at the flickering digital clock on the table. Each minute seemed like a lifetime. The constant torrent of thoughts - which had bombarded my mind for the best part of two years - had subsided, replaced instead with absolute calm. However, this calm was not that of the white dove or the gates of heaven[11]. It was not some sort of nirvana that every person should aspire to, but instead the sort of harmony one might associate with death, an utterly peaceful acceptance. The sort that only one who has experienced great suffering can feel. Numbness. Complete and utter impartiality towards the world around me.

The clock ticked over to nine thirty; it was time. I rose to my feet and turned to the door, grabbing my jacket and scarf, throwing them on with a pre-emptive shiver, and wrapping my fingers around the handle of the carving knife I had sought out and secreted. I took a moment to inspect the razor sharp edge, shining with deadly purpose[12], before sliding it into my back pocket and stepping out of the door.

As it shut behind me there was a great sense of finality: the conclusion to this most miserable of tales was nearing. The cold, sharp wind against my skin, the thick mist, and the thin layer of snow that coated the ground[13] seemed to set the scene perfectly. It was reminiscent of the night this all began. When that fiend[14] took a beautiful little girl and ripped her away from her life of innocence, her dignity and, in the end, her life. She was my daughter, for God's sake[15]! I loved and cherished her, but an evil degenerate took advantage of her naivety to fulfil his own sick desires. I hadn't thought that some online chat with her friends would ever hurt her; but I was sadly and tragically mistaken. The judge and jury were powerless to exact any real revenge[16]. Apparently there 'wasn't any convincing evidence of his guilt', so he was let go; to flee into the ether, leaving nothing behind but malice and spite. Idiots! I knew it was him. I just knew it, deep down in my soul; and now I was prepared to make him pay.

There he was, standing under the weeping willow[17] tree as we had planned. The storm which had raged inside me for countless nights reached its peak. My hatred was total. I paced over, taking care not to let my emotions get the best of me. He didn't see me in the darkness, his eyes fixated on the glowing screen of his phone. As I covered more ground his eyes remained in their entranced state. I removed my scarf, clutching it in my free hand and came to an abrupt stop in front of my unsuspecting victim. He looked up from his hands and met my eye with a look of sheer terror. It was then I thrust the knife into his stomach, ramming my scarf down his throat as he doubled over. He tried with all his heart to scream for help, but his muffled wails could do little to help him now: his fate was sealed[18]. I pressed the blade against his throat and his eyes filled with panic and tears, revealing, but for a moment, a hint of remorse.

"Funny how the past comes back to haunt you, isn't it?" I slid the blade through his throat, relishing the feeling of redemption. At first he looked shocked as the blood spurted from the wound, but quickly the light left his eyes and he lay still. It was finally all over.

Then I walked here and turned myself in."

The detective leaned back from her perch on the edge of her chair and slumped back into it, letting out a long sigh.[19]

"That's all we needed to hear". Her empathy was obvious as she reached over and grabbed the voice recorder, which sat on the table between her and her suspect. She rose up to her feet and paced over to the door of the drab, concrete room. As she opened the door to leave, something brought her to a halt. She turned back towards the wreck of a man that sat in the centre of the room, stopping the recorder in her hand as she did.

"I'm sorry, truly I am."[20]

Notes:

[1] The structure of this story adds to its impact. The words in bold italics are clearly from the present and we are invited to listen to this character's story as he tells it to the listener. A sense of mystery is created.
[2] Use of contrast.
[3] Characterisation: the main character is determined and driven.
[4] This word choice adds to the mysterious atmosphere, as if there is something we cannot understand happening. It also begins to convey a sense of the afterlife, or heaven.
[5] More reference to the inexplicable.
[6] Use of repetition emphasises the character's fixation.
[7] Word choice: afterlife.
[8] Personification: this suggests that the character is not in control of his own actions.
[9] Conversational tone reminds us that we are hearing a first-hand account.
[10] 'I felt faint', 'each letter was momentous' and 'one more, long deep breath' in this and the next two paragraphs alert us to the fact that something of great importance is happening. The character is deeply affected by the idea of meeting with this man.
[11] More 'heavenly' word choice, along with 'nirvana' and the reference to death.
[12] This phrase alerts the reader to what is likely to happen next and brings into focus the language used so far, regarding death and heaven.
[13] Sets the atmosphere clearly: cold and inhospitable. The sharpness of the wind is reminiscent of the sharp knife the character is hiding.
[14] The word 'fiend' contrasts with the heavenly vocabulary used earlier in the story.
[15] The revelation that the character is not a 14 year-old girl after all, but an adult.
[16] The purpose of the character's befriending of this man is made clear: revenge.
[17] The symbolism of the tree becomes clearer, as it suggests to the reader the grief of this parent over the death of his or her daughter.
[18] A return to the idea of destiny introduced earlier in the story.
[19] The setting for the story's beginning is made clear. Our main character has murdered his daughter's killer and given himself up to the police: this is a confession.
[20] The story ends with a sympathetic gesture from the detective, feeling much as the reader does, perhaps.

TOPIC 4. ANNOTATED EXEMPLARS

Mark range

This short story is likely to be placed in the 12-10 mark range as it displays:

- shaping and sequencing which contributes to impact;
- confident use of style with a degree of originality.

4.4 Essay four: Reflective

As I watched the bee hover over flower after flower, single-mindedly gathering its store of pollen[1], my mind wandered to the queen, waiting in royal expectation for her orders to be fulfilled by the unquestioning subjects of her adoring hive. Did she wonder about their loyalty? Were there factions filled with dissatisfied minions waiting for their opportunity to stage a carefully planned coup and dethrone her?[2] Unlikely, given their lack of independent thought and centuries of genetic programming. The entourage of which I was a member, however, was subject to a different kind of programming[3]: our hive was not full of brainwashed bees, but scheming teenage girls[4].

Approaching the school building, at the centre of a buzzing group of drones[5], I felt the familiar stirrings of irritation, ennui and envy. I could hardly bear another day of fawning over someone as powerful as our fearless leader[6], watching from the ranks[7] as she drawled orders: our Cleopatra[8], whose every whim must be obeyed. I looked around at my companions: they exuded excitement and anticipation, surely due to the upcoming social event of the year. Well, the month at least[9]. Which shoes to wear? Which dress? Which lipstick?[10] Hardly questions to tax the intellects of the exceptional students we were supposed to be.

Watching[11] every American high school movie I could lay my impressionable hands on had furnished me with an unrivalled knowledge of the cliques that make up the population of every senior school: the jocks, the populars, the drama kids, the science nerds, the arty geeks and the misfits, all slotted together like pieces of an (admittedly hideously caste-like) jigsaw puzzle[12]. I had made my mind up that I would belong to the most popular group, the preening princesses who made plans to go to the mall and were, in equal measure, admired and desired by the rest of the school's population[13]. Arriving at our very Scottish school as an excitable first-year pupil, however, I realised that this system didn't quite fit with ours as neatly as I had anticipated: there were a few puzzle pieces missing and the ones we had were kind of tatty and difficult to slot in[14]. As I studied my fellow pupils with the kind of zeal that can collect A grades like popular American teenagers collect phone numbers, I became aware that our hierarchy was, disappointingly, much less glamorous.

I could see the geeks and nerds: they stood out a mile with their piles of books, spectacle-covered faces and serious conversations over the lunch tables. What I hadn't expected was that they would command such a loyal following: they seemed to have a never-ending supply of minions to run their errands - 'get me a bottle of water' - and fawn adoringly near them as they made clever comments and cutting remarks, usually about others' intelligence (or lack of). These were our leaders? With their mediocre make-up and safely styled hair?[15] Hmm. I would have to rethink my strategy for total school domination in light of this discovery[16].

The very second I was released from my final class of the day I made straight for home, my mind whirling with what I had learned. Even in my own classes I could see that the intellectuals were preparing for pole position: they were funny and confident and everyone was beginning to take notice of them. They were clever and they didn't care! This was not the world that 'Mean Girls' and 'High School Musical' had prepared me for but I knew what I was going to do: I would start my own clique and we would be all-powerful.

Every day, in every class, I slogged through lesson upon lesson of similes, fractions, historical dates and foaming scientific experiments, determined to ensure that I shone more brightly than the nearest star in our high school galaxy. If I was going to carve out a niche for the new leaders of the school, I was adamant that I would be our supergiant star, burning brightly and basking in the nervous thrall of anyone who was brave enough to come into my orbit. I even managed to recruit some willing participants to add to the constellation[17]. We were all high attaining, highly entertaining girls and we soon found ourselves to be the centre of attention: you might even say, the star attraction! Sorry, couldn't resist[18].

Over the next couple of years, we worked hard at everything: schoolwork, attracting the right kind of friends, being seen in the right places and, most importantly for me, wearing the right clothes and cosmetics. This was my cunning plan: to merge beauty and brains until we were invincible! As hard as I worked on creating the best brand for our clique, I was pleasantly surprised to discover that those of us who had gravitated towards each other had formed a strong and powerful bond of friendship[19]. There were three of us (as dictated by our holy text, 'Mean Girls') and we found each other to be not only hilarious and excellent company but also understanding and supportive. Jenna, Kelsey and I spent all of our time together, sharing problems with parents and evil siblings, make-up, video gems discovered online and our hopes for the future. My dream was simple: to rule the school, and I knew how lucky I was to have the support of these two behind me[20].

However[21], while it was true that we were rising through the ranks of the school, I found myself slowly but surely shunted sideways by the irresistible force that was Jenna. With her effortless beauty and practically superhuman intelligence, she was the one everyone wanted to be friends with, the one everyone asked for her opinion and then, imperceptibly, she became the one who made our decisions: where to go, what to wear, when to study and who to see[22]. It was agonising[23]. In fact, it was only palatable at all because it was entirely unintentional: it just happened that way. Even so, I found myself torn between running from the horror that someone else occupied my place as our leader and staying around to catch some of the reflected glory. Of course, I hung around: what else would I do? These girls were my best friends. They knew everything about me, every tiny detail and huge dream, and they wanted me around. The only thing that they didn't know was that I was becoming increasingly disaffected with my role: I didn't want to be anyone's second-in-command, even Jenna's.

I watched quietly for an opportunity to change the situation, hoping that she would make some horrific social gaffe or suffer a bout of amnesia that would prevent her from coming top in every single test we did. But she didn't - the closest she came was when she complimented Ella Davies on her radical new haircut without realising that her little sister had attacked her with blunt craft scissors. How very insensitive, no?[24] No - that was sweet: how kind of Jenna to try to make her feel better! Even increasing my own study time, without telling the girls, didn't work: no matter how much effort I put in, Jenna always beat me, irritatingly graciously. A plan began to formulate in my mind. I could see myself from an outsider's point of view - devious, envious and traitorous - but I couldn't do anything about it. I was too focussed on my dream of being the school's top dog to even consider backing out. If I didn't do it now, my whole life would be over.

We had a test coming up, a big one. The kind of test that decides which class you will be in the following year and, more importantly, would confirm (or upset) the status of those at the very top: Jenna and me. The only bright spot on the horizon was a party the following weekend, at which our attendance was mandatory: you don't keep your much-envied top spot in school by ignoring such important social events. It was a simple plan, really. Any fool could

© HERIOT-WATT UNIVERSITY

have thought it up but not just any fool could pull it off: it would need determination and a gift for acting that I wasn't sure I possessed. I would use social media and the inexhaustible teenage appetite for excellent gossip to destroy Jenna and then slide sweetly into her place, ready to rule the world of our school: the only world that mattered to me.

Studying became our top priority that week, with discussion of clothes, make-up and the guest list for that weekend's much-anticipated social event taking a poor second place. We worked and worked, determined to ensure that we held our hard-earned positions at the top of the table once the results came out. Of course, I was working on another project, too, and it was coming along nicely. The test came and went, and we all knew how well we had done as we moved into party mode. We exfoliated, tanned, took care of our talons at the local nail bar and arrived at school on the final morning of the week ready for whatever came our way, whatever it might be.

I[25] had a pretty good idea of what was about to happen: it was my plan after all.

As I walked into school that morning, then, mind ablaze with thoughts of coups and queens[26], I felt relaxed as I contemplated my weekend ahead, anticipating it ending in a very satisfactory manner indeed. Test scores were handed out and, unsurprisingly, Jenna and I came first and second, respectively. We were congratulated by everyone, some with gritted teeth, and began to think, in earnest, about the party that evening. I was less excited than usual and Jenna was concerned about me, going out of her way to make me laugh and compliment me on my sartorial choices for the evening, her generosity kindling a small fire of uncertainty that I extinguished[27] by imagining myself as our kind and selfless leader, popular, talented and uncontested.

A really successful coup has to be well-planned, with military precision[28], and it needs an iron will and nerves of titanium to see it through. I called on all of my reserves to see me through the evening and walked in, arm-in-arm with my best friends, the loveliest girls in the school. A wave of horror washed over me momentarily[29] as I anticipated what was about to happen, simultaneously excited and disgusted with myself. While the music didn't scratch to a halt at our entrance, the conversation certainly did, I was delighted to see. Jenna and Kelsey looked a little confused, used to extremes of attention but nothing quite this extreme. A faint whispering sounded from the back of the room, becoming louder as more people joined in the secretive conversations. I began to feel queasy with excitement as I realised that my plan had worked!

I had posted a picture on Snapchat earlier in the evening of Kelsey looking devastated, with the caption, 'Just found out Jenna cheated on test'. Not only had I posted it, but I was totally absolved of blame since I'd done it on Kelsey's phone while a dozen of us raced around Jenna's house putting the finishing touches to our glamorous looks. It could have been anyone! There was no way that Jenna could maintain her position now - she was a cheat and I was ready to step over the corpse of her good name[30] and assume my rightful position. Looking as confused as everyone else, I turned to the girls and whispered, 'What's going on?'

Their[31] stony faces sounded a loud warning bell: something had gone wrong.

'You are a backstabbing piece of scum!' Jenna spat venomously. I began to shake with dismay. How did she know it was me? I backed out of the room, turned and ran for the door, trying desperately to work out how she knew. Then I realised that if Jenna knew, everyone did, and that they had been whispering in those violent, judgemental undertones about me, not Jenna.

What had I done? How had it gone so wrong?[32] I desperately pulled my phone out of my bag and checked Snapchat for information. There it was. Immediately after my poisonous post was a picture that Jenna had taken of herself posing in the mirror. In the background, holding Kelsey's distinctive green phone case, was me. Typing. Caught.[33] I considered fleeing now more than ever but in an instant I realised that I couldn't retreat now, without going back and fighting for our friendship[34], a friendship I couldn't believe I had tried to destroy. Every ounce of the malice I had felt while conducting my campaign against Jenna melted away and I felt nothing but shame. I walked slowly back into the party, where the music was still playing, and stood in the doorway, watching as frenzied conversations took place, dissecting the events of the evening so far, dissecting my character and my motives. Gently, someone tugged at my arm.

'Hey.' Jenna was looking at me. Not accusingly or with rage but with pity and compassion. Suddenly, I was overcome and tears danced at the corner of each eye[35] as I looked back at my ally, my friend, my confidante.

'I'm sorry. I was jealous.' Even to me, the words sounded ridiculous. Why had I been so jealous? Faced with losing my friends, I couldn't have cared any less about being Cleopatra in the school's top clique. What an idiot!

Jenna put her arms around me and squeezed. 'Exam pressure,' she whispered gently. 'Forget about it.'

The most incredible thing about the whole humiliating experience is that she did. Forget about it, I mean. We never mentioned it again and once I had moved beyond my mean-spirited ambitions and thought about what my dreams really were, I was happier, kinder and just more fun to be around. My brief dalliance into the upper echelons of school society had left me disillusioned and ostracised. Visions of ruling the social elite and commanding the allegiance of a band of beauties lay scattered before me, shrapnel from a pointless war[36]. The hard lesson of the value of substance before appearance had been learned and it stays with me: I regret every day the casual abandonment of true friends for nothing more than an illusory victory. It turns out it's not really winning when the prize is worthless[37].

Notes:

[1] The initial tone is contemplative. This introduction uses a small, everyday event to introduce the main idea.
[2] Language is used to create the idea of a monarch and her subjects, as well as the political image of a leader being deposed in a coup. These could run throughout the essay as motifs, or an extended metaphor, helping to convey the theme.
[3] Although it is not clear yet exactly what it is, a personal experience is certainly on its way.
[4] The tone now gives way to an element of humour: it may not be a particularly serious subject.
[5] Bee imagery continued.
[6] A mocking tone. Word choice makes us think again about the imagery of a coup.
[7] Military language: this is found throughout the essay as the candidate keeps going the idea of a coup or battle in a war.
[8] This person is described in unflattering terms here: Cleopatra is used to describe

her ego and how others pander to her desires.
[9] Mocking tone here and in the final sentence of the paragraph.
[10] Use of repetition mimics the excitement of the pupils.
[11] Change of tone: more chatty and humorous than mocking. This is one of the ways in which the candidate signifies a change in focus, from the present to the past.
[12] Simile - quite a clichéd image but used less obviously further on in the paragraph.
[13] A small girl's admiration for these 'princesses' is made clear through word choice: 'princesses', 'admired' and 'desired'.
[14] See jigsaw comment above.
[15] Questions provide an insight into the narrator's mind.
[16] Entertaining, tongue-in-cheek tone.
[17] Extended metaphor used to emphasise the narrator's strong feelings. Stars are bright and well-admired: this is her dream.
[18] This piece of humour endears the reader to the narrator along with other attempts at a humorous, tongue-in-cheek or chatty tone.
[19] The reader discovers a little more about the narrator: while driven, she is not quite as single-minded as it seems.
[20] While this paragraph still has some elements of humour, there is more information about the narrator's life and her relationship with her friends.
[21] This paragraph moves on to discuss how the narrator felt about her dream of 'ruling the school' drifting further away.
[22] Two examples of repetition here, emphasising how overwhelmed the narrator is feeling.
[23] An effectively short sentence describing the intensity of her feelings.
[24] The narrator's personality is coming through with this humorous comment, in spite of her unkind thoughts.
[25] Effective use of the one sentence paragraph to signal the move from the chatty tone of party preparations to the more serious topic of 'the plan'.
[26] Nice link to the first two paragraphs and other examples of military imagery.
[27] Good use of metaphor to describe her feelings.
[28] More military language to introduce the effects of the narrator's attempted coup.
[29] Nice use of metaphor to describe her feelings, although waves are a little over-used.
[30] This metaphor is effective: it describes clearly and efficiently what the narrator hoped would happen.
[31] Again, good use of the one sentence paragraph, signalling a change in the narrative.
[32] Repeated use of questions mirrors the narrator's confusion.
[33] One word sentences reflect the narrator's panic.
[34] The military idea is continued, with a different focus.
[35] Personification here suggests that she is trying to hold back the tears.
[36] Good use of military language in this conclusion.
[37] The final sentence sums up the narrator's reflection. The conclusion is quite short but, along with descriptions of her feelings and reactions throughout the essay, the reflective nature of the essay is clear.

Mark range

This reflective essay displays:

- some thoughtfulness, insight and imagination (at this level);
- shaping and sequencing with some impact.

This suggests that this essay should be placed in the 9-7 range. There is, however, a confident use of style and language which might make a marker think about placing it in the next range up with a mark of 12-10.

Unit 3 Topic 5

Acknowledgements

- *Siegfried Sassoon*, Suicide in the Trenches
- *John Donne*, The Flea

Dissertation

1	**The process and expectations**	**241**
1.1	What is the dissertation?	242
1.2	The process	242
1.3	Learning points	248
2	**Comparing texts and developing an argument**	**249**
2.1	Comparative literary study: Opening	250
2.2	Developing an argument	253
2.3	Making links and comparing texts	255
2.4	Comparative literary study: Conclusion	256
2.5	Learning points	258
3	**Annotated exemplars**	**259**
3.1	Annotated exemplars	260
3.2	Dissertation: 'Poppy Shakespeare' and 'One Flew Over The Cuckoo's Nest'	260
3.3	Dissertation: T.S. Eliot	274
3.4	Learning points	289
4	**Acknowledgements**	**291**

Unit 4 Topic 1

The process and expectations

Contents
1.1 What is the dissertation? 242
1.2 The process 242
    1.2.1 Choosing texts 242
    1.2.2 The proposal 243
    1.2.3 Secondary sources 244
    1.2.4 Making notes 245
    1.2.5 Structure 245
    1.2.6 Referencing and bibliography 246
    1.2.7 Drafting 247
1.3 Learning points 248

Learning objective

By the end of this topic you will:

- understand the requirements of the dissertation;
- be able to select appropriate texts for study;
- be able to plan a proposal: what your dissertation will be about;
- be aware of how to plan and structure the writing;
- understand how to research your texts and use secondary sources, making notes as you go;
- be aware of how to use footnotes correctly and compile a bibliography;
- be aware of the importance of drafting and redrafting.

1.1 What is the dissertation?

The Advanced Higher English dissertation is an extended piece of writing which examines, in depth, one or more complex and sophisticated texts that you have read independently. It should be between 2500 and 3500 words in length and is worth 30 marks (30% of your final Advanced Higher English grade). It assesses:

- knowledge of literary forms and genres;
- the ability to apply in-depth knowledge and understanding to complex and sophisticated literary texts;
- the ability to plan, research and present the findings of an independent dissertation on an aspect of literature.

Your writing will show a detailed and mature understanding of and reaction to the text(s) you have read, as well as showing an ability to read and utilise the work of others to support your writing. You will also have to consider carefully an appropriate structure for your writing.

1.2 The process

Since this is probably the largest piece of work you have undertaken so far at school, you are likely to be most successful if you follow a process to plan and write it. The advice below will help you to do this.

1.2.1 Choosing texts

You can choose from a variety of literature including prose, poetry and drama for your dissertation: which do you enjoy reading the most? The SQA have provided a fairly comprehensive list of writers whose work is sufficiently challenging to meet the requirements of study for dissertation. You can find it in the SQA support notes on the Advanced Higher English page (http://bit.ly/1UedS5n).

This list is not exhaustive: you may have an interest in writers or texts that do not feature here. You may still be able to focus on them but check with your teacher to ensure that you are being sufficiently challenged. The preparation for all elements of the dissertation should be discussed in class: as always, sharing ideas is the best way to gain inspiration and explore new concepts. Additionally, you cannot use the same texts or texts by the same writer as those used in the Literary Study Paper of the exam.

You can write about:

- two or three texts by the same dramatist;
- texts written by two or more dramatists;
- a wide range (perhaps seven or more) of poems by one poet;
- a narrow range (six or fewer) of poems by one poet;
- texts written by two or more poets;
- a single text by a dramatist or novelist;

TOPIC 1. THE PROCESS AND EXPECTATIONS

- an epic poem;
- two or three texts by the same novelist;
- texts written by two or more novelists;
- short stories;
- graphic novels;
- literary non-fiction.

If you choose to write about just one text, make sure you are prepared to analyse it in eye-watering detail and depth! You might find it easier, however, to compare and contrast texts: just be careful that you are mindful of the word limit here, though, and resist the temptation to skim through everything in them. Focus your dissertation on the specific aspects contained in the proposal.

The best way to choose texts is, of course, to read and read! Explore different texts and think about what you might focus on in a dissertation: the more you have to select from, the better. Advice from the SQA is to avoid mixing genres, e.g. short stories and a novel or poetry and drama, even if the thematic links are very clear. It is extremely difficult to write well in this case: give yourself the best chance to do well.

1.2.2 The proposal

This is where you can set out the focus of your dissertation. Which text(s) will you examine? Which aspects will you write about? Think about the elements of your text(s) which stand out, or are similar e.g. setting, theme, use of language, characterisation.

The guidance and marking instructions provided by the SQA (http://bit.ly/1poWeBn) can help to focus your thinking. Read through the document, considering the texts you are hoping to study.

Your proposal ought to contain the following:

- the names of the text(s) and writer(s) to be studied;
- the main focus, e.g. feminist representations, racial stereotypes, flawed protagonists;
- the literary aims of the dissertations: the techniques you will examine, e.g. narrative style, setting(s), characterisation.

Advice from the SQA is to examine two or three literary techniques and/or features of language in depth, rather than look at each technique used by writers: this will help to ensure that your dissertation stays within the word limit and is sufficiently detailed for this level.

Below are two examples to give you an idea of how you might word your proposal.

© HERIOT-WATT UNIVERSITY

Example one

A detailed examination of the effects of colonisation on female identity[1] as conveyed through narrative voice and setting[2] in 'Nervous Conditions' by Tsitsi Dangarembga and 'The Joys of Motherhood' by Buchi Emecheta[3].

Notes:

[1] The main focus.
[2] The literary aims.
[3] The names of the texts and authors.

Example two

A comparative study of how Tennessee Williams[1] uses the dramatic techniques of characterisation and stagecraft[2] to convey the theme of illusion versus reality[3] in 'A Streetcar Named Desire' and 'Sweet Bird of Youth'[4].

Notes:

[1] The name of the author.
[2] The main focus.
[3] The literary aims.
[4] The names of the texts.

The proposal

Read over the following proposals and discuss with a classmate how to improve them in order that they meet the criteria above:

1. A study of madness in 'The Bell Jar' by Sylvia Plath and 'One Flew Over the Cuckoo's Nest' by Ken Kesey.

2. How characterisation is used in 'Emma' and 'Pride and Prejudice' by Jane Austen.

3. The flawed hero as presented by William Shakespeare in two plays.

1.2.3 Secondary sources

You will spend some time reading what have others have said about your texts and you should use what you read to inform your writing. You can source this type of text in a variety of places: your local library may have some useful books or maybe able to obtain some for you; your teacher or school library may also have some useful materials; the internet is a good place to look, too. Google Scholar (https://scholar.google.co.uk/) has a wide variety of articles and writing on thousands of literary texts.

Also, some universities have an external membership scheme that Advanced Higher pupils can take advantage of: ask your school or teacher to check this out for you.

Secondary sources can be used to add to your argument or you may dispute what others have said: however you use these, ensure that you acknowledge the ideas and words of others properly to avoid the risk of plagiarism. You can find out how to do this in the referencing / bibliography topic in this section.

1.2.4 Making notes

Once you have read your primary texts for the first time, you are ready to begin making notes. How you do this is up to you and there are a number of ways that you can consider:

- highlight and make notes on your text (make sure it is yours if you choose this method!). Do not depend on this entirely, however: you will need to write, too!;
- make notes in a separate document, electronic or hand-written, keeping a note of the page numbers when you are identifying potential quotations;
- a series of mind maps on each element that you are planning to tackle in the dissertation;
- with secondary sources paraphrase as much as possible: this is your dissertation and the majority of what you write needs to be your words and ideas. If a writer has used memorable word choice or has expressed something particularly well and it will work well as a quotation, then you can copy it (just remember to acknowledge this clearly in your writing!);
- leave some space in your notes for later comments, questions, reactions or second thoughts during the re-reading stage.

You will probably find that you use a combination of these and other methods. Again, keep careful track of which ideas and notes are yours, and which are from the primary and secondary texts.

It is important to be aware that you will make many, many more notes than you are likely to use in your dissertation. This is fine: you need to have an in-depth knowledge and understanding of all aspects of the text(s) in order to write well, although you will not focus on all of them as you plan and write the dissertation, just those outlined in your proposal.

1.2.5 Structure

This is probably the longest piece of work you have attempted as part of your study and, as such, you must spend time considering how you will structure the dissertation.

As with the majority of the writing you will have done for English so far, your dissertation will include:

1. an opening;
2. a main body; and
3. a conclusion.

Opening

This is described as an opening, rather than an introduction, because it will be more in-depth and lengthier than the introductions you are used to writing for critical essays at Higher. It will introduce the literary concerns and main ideas of the dissertation, beginning to demonstrate to the reader in which direction the writing will go: what your argument will be concerned with.

Depending upon the text(s) you have selected and the focus of your proposal, your opening may contain:

- some biographical detail about the author, if it is just one, to demonstrate your full understanding of the context in which they were created;
- an explanation of the significance of the theme you are focussing on;
- some discussion of the literary techniques to be examined in the dissertation.

Look carefully at the examples provided in the other topics in this section - 'Developing an argument and comparing texts' and 'Annotated Exemplars' - to see what a carefully constructed opening looks like.

Main Body

This is, of course, the bulk of your dissertation: where you examine in detail the text(s) you have chosen, addressing the proposal throughout. There are two ways to tackle this section: horizontal and vertical.

A horizontal dissertation is one which examines more than one text at a time. If your focus is on how an idea is examined in more than one text through a series of literary techniques, e.g. characterisation, setting and narrative voice, you would discuss each technique and how it is explored in both texts before moving on to the next technique. Although it can seem rather mechanical, like working through a checklist, good writing and skilled use of linking make this a highly successful method.

A vertical dissertation, on the other hand, is one where each text is examined separately. There is a real danger here, though, of simply writing separate critical essays and missing out a crucial element of many excellent examples of dissertation writing: the comparison of texts.

Comparing and contrasting texts is a skill that is developed throughout the Advanced Higher course. You will use it in the Literary Study and the skills you learn there stand you in good stead when it comes to the dissertation. Have a closer look at the 'Comparison of texts' topic in this section for more information and activities on this skill.

Conclusion

This is where you will come to the end of your argument. Make sure it is clear here what your stance is. Look at the other topics in this section - 'Developing an argument and comparing texts' and 'Annotated Exemplars' - for detailed annotations of what a good conclusion looks like.

1.2.6 Referencing and bibliography

A dissertation is a sophisticated piece of work which uses information from a variety of sources. It is vitally important that you are clear about exactly where the quotations and ideas you are using have come from: the SQA is extremely firm when it comes to plagiarism and, to this end, there are clear guidelines on how to reference properly.

Footnotes

Each time you quote from a text, you should include a footnote. This will appear at the bottom of the relevant page. The first time you quote from a text you must write out the details in full but each time after that you can shorten it.

Footnotes should be set out as follows:

- First mention: Welsh, Irvine 2013. Trainspotting, London: Vintage, p3.
- Subsequent mentions: Welsh, Irvine 2013, p25.

Bibliography

You are likely to consult a variety of texts while you research your dissertation and these must be listed at the end in a bibliography. There are a few ways to do this but one of the most common is the Harvard referencing system, used by many universities and colleges. This Harvard referencing system website - http://bit.ly/2gv4hw7 - gives useful advice on how to do this and can help to do it for you!

You can also check with your teacher to make sure you are using footnotes and referencing appropriately. You can go to the SQA support notes on the Advanced Higher English page (http://bit.ly/1UedS5n) to see exactly what the SQA advice is.

1.2.7 Drafting

This is an extremely important part of the process: being able to critically reflect on the work you have done and make changes to improve it is a valuable skill.

When you have written a first draft, or a section of it, you will look over it and think about the following questions:

1. Does it make sense? Sometimes we become so caught up in our work that it is difficult for others to understand the line of thought clearly. Imagine you are someone who has read the text(s) but not the secondary reading. Have you explained your argument clearly enough?

2. Is it addressing the concerns of the proposal throughout? Make sure that your argument is clear and everything you have written is relevant.

3. Are the secondary sources you have used enhancing your argument?

4. Have you selected the most appropriate quotations from primary and secondary sources?

5. Thinking about the dissertation as a whole, have you set out your argument clearly? Is there a section which is weaker than the rest? What can you do to remedy this?

You should recognise that you will redraft some, if not all, of the dissertation more than once. Think about these questions each time you stop to reread it.

1.3 Learning points

> **Summary**
>
> You should now feel more confident about tackling the dissertation and have a clear understanding of the following:
>
> - the requirements of the dissertation;
> - selecting appropriate texts for study;
> - planning a proposal: what your dissertation will be about;
> - how to plan and structure the writing;
> - how to research your texts and use secondary sources, making notes as you go;
> - the importance of drafting and redrafting.

Unit 4 Topic 2

Comparing texts and developing an argument

Contents

2.1 Comparative literary study: Opening 250
2.2 Developing an argument 253
2.3 Making links and comparing texts 255
2.4 Comparative literary study: Conclusion 256
2.5 Learning points 258

Learning objective

By the end of this topic you will:

- understand what makes an effective opening;
- understand what makes an effective conclusion;
- understand how to develop an argument;
- understand how to compare texts effectively in order to further your argument;
- understand how to make explicit links between the texts.

250 UNIT 4. DISSERTATION

2.1 Comparative literary study: Opening

Read through these proposals and openings on your own or with peers. Thinking about the advice provided in this section, how good is it? How well does it prepare the reader for what is to come? Is there anything lacking? Is there anything that shouldn't be there? Make notes and compare them with others, then click on the highlighted text to see the annotations.

Comparative literary study opening: 'Trainspotting' and 'A Clockwork Orange'

In general, the following comparative literary study opening functions well. It introduces the texts, provides a brief summary of the main ideas of each one and relates throughout to the ideas contained in the proposal.

This opening would be better if the candidate had made some reference to the techniques that will be examined in the main body of the dissertation.

There is a heavy focus on setting, in spite of stating that this is not one of the similarities shared by the novels. This opening is slightly long: some of the detail regarding setting could have been contained in the main body if absolutely necessary. Remember, you only have 3500 words!

A comparative literary study of the portrayal of choice in Irvine Welsh's 'Trainspotting' and Anthony Burgess' 'A Clockwork Orange'.[1]

The act of choosing, and the right we have to choose has been fuelling literature for as long as there have been choices to make[2]. Some of the most notable works of the modern age have become an examination of our world through the eyes of a character not only exploring the rules that we as a society bind ourselves to, but challenging the norm, pushing past the roles that people fall into - and promoting choice. Arguably, two of the most notable works in this line of literature are Irvine Welsh's 'Trainspotting', and Anthony Burgess' novel, 'A Clockwork Orange'[3]. 'A Clockwork Orange' takes place in an entirely new dystopian future, one that's controlled by a repressive totalitarian government. We witness Alex, a fourteen year old boy who leaps from one unthinkingly cruel crime to another, accompanied by his 'droogs' - Dim, Pete and Georgie. Soon incarcerated, he becomes the first to trial a new radical treatment, a type of shock conditioning therapy designed to take away the choice between good and evil, leaving only blind, unwavering good[4]. 'Trainspotting' follows Renton and his similar band of friends through the more familiar setting of Leith, Edinburgh. Brought up in an estate and successful in getting into University, 'Trainspotting' captures his subsequent derailment, and slide into heroin addiction[5]. These texts, despite the huge difference in setting, do just that - dissect our ability to choose, to stray from the mainstream - and even challenge the integrity of such choices[6]. Although the worlds the authors immerse their characters in are polar opposites, they both achieve the same end, and with some striking similarities irrespective of the setting[7]. 'Trainspotting' is established in a familiar scene - the notorious 1980s, where rebellion was in the minds of the younger generation. It was a time when Edinburgh became known for the huge influx of drugs due to the local manufacture of diamorphine - the issues that ensued reminiscent of 'A Clockwork Orange' and the violence that seemed to encapsulate the younger generation. Whereas the comment made on society in 'Trainspotting' is down to the microcosm created by Renton's questionable group of friends, 'A Clockwork Orange' is set in an entire new world - each aspect of the governmental structure, the society and its expectations crafted to make every choice by Alex meaningful and symbolic.

Notes:

[1] This proposal would be improved if there was reference to the literary aims of the dissertation.
[2] Introduces the main idea of the dissertation immediately with a general statement, ready to lead into discussing specific texts.
[3] Introduces the texts under discussion.
[4] Summary of the main ideas in 'A Clockwork Orange' as they relate to the proposal.
[5] Summary of the main ideas of 'Trainspotting' as they relate to the proposal.
[6] Another referral to the main ideas of the dissertation.
[7] The candidate has begun to compare and contrast the texts here, identifying a specific area of difference but also explaining that there are important similarities that will be explored in the main body.

Comparative literary study opening: 'The Great Gatsby' and 'The Beautiful and Damned'

In general the following comparative literary study opening is a well-written opening: it contains each of the essential elements of an opening as well as the very appropriate quotation at the beginning which opens a window onto the world that Scott Fitzgerald is writing about. It is also an appropriate length: remember that you only have 3500 words!

A comparative study of two novels by F. Scott Fitzgerald, 'The Great Gatsby' and 'The Beautiful and Damned', that examines how the author's literary techniques contribute to the portrayal of the pursuit of happiness and his views on human nature.[1]

"Even when you were broke, you didn't worry about money because it was in such profusion around you". These words from F. Scott Fitzgerald in a letter in the 1930s[2], referring to the Roaring Twenties, are both applicable and contradictory to his novels 'The Great Gatsby' and 'The Beautiful and Damned'. Money is in great abundance for the central characters; it is one of the main motifs in both novels and it is vital in terms of the characters' pursuit of happiness[3]. Both novels are set[4] in what Fitzgerald himself dubbed "the Jazz Age" - a phrase he coined to describe the flamboyant, "anything goes", era that emerged in America after World War I. Both texts offer insight into the glittering world of the young, beautiful and rich in this period. While the pursuit of happiness is a central motif[5] in both texts, the main characters[6] have very different ideas about happiness and use different methods to achieve it. Gatsby uses illegal methods to "get rich quick", but not out of greed: his intentions are simply to win the heart of Daisy Buchanan. In contrast[7], Anthony, in 'The Beautiful and Damned' believes that the only way he will be happy is when he inherits his grandfather's vast fortune. Both have very different ideas on the pursuit of happiness. Fitzgerald uses this - and its eventual outcome - to comment on the nature of humankind[8].

Notes:

[1] This proposal contains the names of the texts and author and the main ideas of the dissertation are clear. Literary techniques are referred to but not explicitly.
[2] A striking beginning: words from the author providing the kind of biographical and contextual detail that is important when writing about just one author. The quote comes from Scribner's Magazine in 1931 (see http://bit.ly/29H2h03).
[3] Clear reference to the main idea set out in the proposal.
[4] Introduction of literary technique to be discussed.
[5] Literary technique.
[6] Literary technique.
[7] Beginning to compare and contrast texts.
[8] Ends the opening with a clear indicator of what the main discussion of the dissertation will be - the pursuit of happiness and the nature of humankind.

2.2 Developing an argument

In your opening, you will have introduced the texts and authors, the main focus of the dissertation and made reference to the techniques you intend to examine throughout this piece of work.

The next step is to ensure that the focus is cleverly argued throughout the main body of the dissertation by comparing how these techniques are used in each of your texts, from your reading of the texts and any secondary reading you might do.

Comparing texts and creating an argument are skills that you will already be developing through your work on the Literary Study section of the course. Look at the relevant sections in the Literary study section here on SCHOLAR for a reminder of the general principles involved in developing and using these skills.

Thinking about the proposal and introduction you read on 'A Clockwork Orange' and 'Trainspotting', you will see that the main focus of this dissertation is choice. The remainder of the dissertation works hard to ensure that this focus is at the forefront of what is written.

Read this section and look at the annotations:

Example one

Whilst speaking to the judge, Renton adopts an entirely different manner of speaking[1]. He speaks of philosophy and addiction as if he'd been studying them for years, apparently interested in Kierkegaard's 'concepts of subjectivity and truth... his ideas concerning choice...[2]' The moment in which his dialect changes, his transition from 'typical junkie' to an educated man who is down on his luck is portrayed also. 'Naw. Eh, no, your honour'. He manages to come across as being both impressive and boastful and, for the first time, the trustworthiness of Renton's character is thrown into question. His reliability as a frank, blunt narrator is disrupted and the reader is faced with the two discrete sides of Renton's character[3]. His integrity is questioned when he makes the choice to flit so easily between dual personalities - all for his own benefit[4].

Notes:

[1] This is the technique under discussion: narrative voice and its effect on characterisation.
[2] The main focus of the dissertation is on choice - the candidate is beginning to set out the argument in this section.
[3] This is a detailed comment on the effect of Renton's change in narrative style on the reader's perception of the character.
[4] This statement links clearly to the main focus: Renton has made a choice to speak in a particular way and it makes a real difference to how he is perceived, both as a character and as a narrator.

Later, the candidate writes about setting and its effect on the issue of choice. Read this section on your own first: can you see the argument developing? How does the candidate continue his or her discussion of choice?

© HERIOT-WATT UNIVERSITY

Look at the annotations to see if you agree with what is being said:

> **Example two**
>
> When it comes to setting in relation to the question of choice and control[1] that these characters have, both authors have used their world and setting to their advantage. In 'Trainspotting', neither the viewpoint nor the location of the characters is immediately clear. The setting or location of these characters is fluid - there are places in and around Edinburgh which symbolise something for these characters. It could be argued it doesn't matter where these characters are. Renton, it seems, has the ability to flourish anywhere, as he did in London - the city in which he chose to break away from his caustic group of 'friends' and the influences of the city around him. Whereas Renton's attempt to live in the south of England initially resulted in some degree of success[2], Simon's experience ended in the same deviancy and law-breaking that he'd achieved in Edinburgh[3]. Although the dialect and overbearing 'Scottishness' in this novel appears to be all that breaks through for the reader, it is really the characters' choices that convey who they are: not where they come from or where they choose to be. There are drug addicts wherever you go - this social affliction is not subject to time, or place, but to choice. If anything, the fluidity of Welsh's setting goes to strengthen the perception of the characters' instability, constantly flickering from place to person and lacking all control or power.[4]
>
> **Notes:**
>
> [1] We can see that the idea of choice will now be examined with focus on another literary technique: setting.
> [2] A comment on how the change of setting had a positive influence on Renton's behaviour, which goes on to explain that this was less due to setting than to the choices made by the character.
> [3] The discussion here of Simon's continued negative behaviour illustrates that it is not setting but the will of the individual, i.e. choice, that dictates behaviour.
> [4] A piece of analysis summarising the candidate's point.

You can see from these extracts that the candidate is analysing different techniques in order to further the argument that choice is within the characters' power.

Once you have read your texts, had a look at some secondary reading and decided on the main focus of your dissertation, you are likely to use the same type of structure for your dissertation.

2.3 Making links and comparing texts

In Advanced Higher English, as you know, one of the differentiating factors in the study of literature is the ability to analyse more than one text at a time. The paragraphs above discuss just one text, 'Trainspotting' by Irvine Welsh, but the candidate has, in fact, chosen to analyse two texts in the dissertation and also examines 'A Clockwork Orange' by Anthony Burgess.

You do not have to do this - you can write in depth about one text - but if you do, you need to be able to do so effectively, comparing how different writers or texts employ similar techniques and commenting in detail on their similarities and/or differences. The most effective way to compare texts is technique by technique or issue by issue (horizontally), examining how each text uses or conveys these to further the main argument of your dissertation.

It is important when writing the main body of your dissertation that you use language to link your ideas about the different texts: don't just fly straight from one into the next with no preamble.

For example,

> Alex is in control of his actions, choosing to manipulate his speech, and he is perfectly aware of what he is doing, what can benefit him and the image people in authority have of him. This awareness is a trait that Renton seems to share and it comes across in the courtroom scene.

The use of "aware" and "awareness" here show clearly that the candidate has discussed the use of dialect in one text and is going on to do the same for the next one: it is a fairly simplistic use of language but it effectively helps the writing to flow, continuing the argument without a clumsy break.

Making links and comparing texts

Think about your dissertation texts (or if you haven't made a final selection yet) texts you have studied at school, for example, your literary study texts, and follow these steps:

1. Identify the main ideas in the texts which are similar: it could be themes like racism, relationships, identity, conflict.

2. Make a list of the techniques used by the writer(s) to convey these ideas, e.g. setting, language, characterisation, contrast.

3. Compare each technique and make notes on how each separate text uses them to convey the theme.

4. Choose one technique and expand your notes into paragraphs - make sure to use language to create a clear link between the texts.

2.4 Comparative literary study: Conclusion

Read the following conclusions on your own or with peers and make notes on what you think has been done well and what could be improved, then click on the highlighted sections to read the annotations. Think about the following:

- Does it summarise arguments from the main body?
- Does it contain reference to the literary techniques discussed?
- Does it state a position on the main idea put forward in the proposal?

Comparative literary study conclusion: 'Trainspotting' and 'A Clockwork Orange'

A comparative literary study of the portrayal of choice in Irvine Welsh's 'Trainspotting' and Anthony Burgess' 'A Clockwork Orange'.

'Trainspotting[1]' and 'A Clockwork Orange' are works of literature, both classic and contemporary, that use the structure of a first-person narrative in order to create a system of oppression in which the ability to choose allows the characters to thrive. Both Irvine Welsh and Anthony Burgess use these books to highlight the importance of our own free will, and the right to choose our own fate and to be in control of our own choices[2]. Both novels use language[3] to identify their characters, to give them a group or a class, to define them as the 'dregs' of a society[4] that still orbits around the class system that it has outgrown. Through 'Trainspotting' we are shown a different world, a world that's far closer to home than some would like to believe. We follow stories set in the familiar backdrop of Edinburgh, with unique characters and choices - often at times surprisingly heart-warming. 'A Clockwork Orange' presents us with a far more macabre portrayal of the world we live in, and the subsequent choices we make. The closing lines of 'A Clockwork Orange' detail Alex's ponderings about his future children, his own son - to be exact. These novels have a cyclical feeling - that despite the character's choices and experiences, the world around them doesn't change, and does not stretch to accommodate them. Regardless, the protagonists[5] - as well as the surrounding characters' actions - take the reader on a journey constructed by their choices, and the importance that lies in making sure that the choice you make is one of your own[6].

Notes:

[1] This conclusion contains reference to the literary techniques discussed in the dissertation, beginning with first-person narration.
[2] The main idea is set out again very clearly.
[3] Literary technique - use of language.
[4] Literary technique - setting.
[5] Literary technique - characterisation
[6] Conclusion ends by restating the importance of the main idea: choice.

Comparative literary study conclusion: 'The Great Gatsby' and 'The Beautiful and Damned'

Overall, this comparative literary study conclusion provides a summary of the dissertation: it restates and expands on the main idea of the pursuit of happiness through money and beauty. There is reference to techniques examined in the dissertation and the writer's position on happiness and the American Dream is stated clearly.

> A comparative study of two novels by F. Scott Fitzgerald, 'The Great Gatsby' and 'The Beautiful and Damned', that examines how the author's literary techniques contribute to the portrayal of the pursuit of happiness and his views on human nature.
>
> Through both novels F. Scott Fitzgerald portrays the pursuit of happiness[1] and the language[2] in both texts suggest the idea of illusion. Gatsby himself, his love for Daisy, Daisy and Gloria's beauty, all the money - all are portrayed as illusions. The author could be suggesting that the pursuit of happiness is an illusion - especially if you pursue it through money and beautiful women. We have seen that, while the characters' lives appear to be full of excitement and enjoyment, their dream is not real. Fitzgerald uses Anthony and Tom to represent the rich men of the time[3]. However, Gatsby is unique - a symbol of the American Dream, shown through his innocence and hope for life, and his death. Fitzgerald could be suggesting that pure and honest happiness can no longer be achieved and he successfully comments on the fact that happiness has become corrupt, that the purity of the American Dream no longer exists. The people who survive are the ones who look after themselves - not the ones who pursue honesty and innocence in happiness.
>
> **Notes:**
>
> [1] The main idea of the dissertation is restated here.
> [2] Literary technique - language.
> [3] Literary technique - symbolism.

2.5 Learning points

Summary

You will now:

- understand what makes an effective opening;
- understand what makes an effective conclusion;
- understand how to develop an argument;
- understand how to compare texts effectively in order to further your argument;
- understand how to make explicit links between the texts.

Unit 4 Topic 3

Annotated exemplars

Contents

- 3.1 Annotated exemplars 260
- 3.2 Dissertation: 'Poppy Shakespeare' and 'One Flew Over The Cuckoo's Nest' 260
  - 3.2.1 Annotated dissertation section one: Opening 266
  - 3.2.2 Annotated dissertation section two: Narration in 'Poppy Shakespeare' 267
  - 3.2.3 Annotated dissertation section three: Narration in 'One Flew Over the Cuckoo's Nest' 268
  - 3.2.4 Annotated dissertation section four: Minor characters in 'Poppy Shakespeare' 270
  - 3.2.5 Annotated dissertation section five: Minor characters in 'One Flew Over the Cuckoo's Nest' 271
  - 3.2.6 Annotated dissertation section six: Conclusion 272
  - 3.2.7 Annotated dissertation: Further comments 272
- 3.3 Dissertation: T.S. Eliot 274
  - 3.3.1 Annotated dissertation section one: Opening 280
  - 3.3.2 Annotated dissertation section two: Landscapes and surroundings 281
  - 3.3.3 Annotated dissertation section three: Futility 283
  - 3.3.4 Annotated dissertation section four: Time 285
  - 3.3.5 Annotated dissertation section five: Death 287
  - 3.3.6 Annotated dissertation section six: Conclusion 289
- 3.4 Learning points 289

> **Learning objective**
>
> By the end of this topic you will:
>
> - recognise a well-written dissertation;
> - identify where a dissertation is comparing more than one text;
> - identify where a dissertation is making explicit links between texts.

3.1 Annotated exemplars

By reading the following dissertations and the comments which accompany them, you will see good practice in dissertation writing as well as in referencing texts and creating bibliographies.

It is important to remember that, while these are good dissertations, they are not perfect and you can identify areas where you think they could be improved.

It is also vital to note, again, that there is a word limit in this task: your dissertation should be between 2500 and 3500 words. A penalty will be applied if you exceed 10% over this upper limit.

3.2 Dissertation: 'Poppy Shakespeare' and 'One Flew Over The Cuckoo's Nest'

Section one: Opening *(There is no requirement to include headings in your dissertation: these are here to help you follow and analyse these particular dissertations.)*

An exploration of how characterisation and narrative style in the novels 'Poppy Shakespeare' by Clare Allan and 'One Flew Over The Cuckoo's Nest' by Ken Kesey invite debate about what madness is.

The concept of insanity has been apparent in human nature for as long as we have lived. Mental health disorders can isolate victims from society and reality, but at what point does one go from being classed as mentally ill to insane? The idea of curing and preventing such problems naturally has trailed behind this, alongside the mental health system, which has evolved into the one we know today. However, despite many important discoveries in this field, have we managed to determine exactly what madness really is? 'Poppy Shakespeare', a shockingly brilliant debut novel by Clare Allan, and 'One Flew over the Cuckoo's Nest', by Ken Kesey, "One of the most important American novels of the post-war period"[1], are based on and inspired by the experiences and encounters the authors have had with the mental health system, and institutions connected to it. The key trait I find the novels share is how well they attempt to explore and invite debate over the concept of madness through characterisation . Although fictional, these books portray a seemingly real image of patients admitted both voluntarily and unwillingly into the mental health system, and the experiences and characters they discover within this quirky, confusing and at times, unpredictable world.

Both novels are inspired by the experiences the writers have had within the mental health system, and follow a similar plot and general idea. Clare Allan, author of 'Poppy Shakespeare' spent time inside hospitals as a patient, while Ken Kesey worked in earlier hospitals as staff, and is known to have experimented with a drug widely known for its mind altering effects, LSD. The plots within the texts both follow the life of an initially "sane" character sucked into the mental health system, and are narrated through the eyes of mental patients currently residing within the hospitals, who watch their lives turn upside down. In both cases, the narrators exchange positions with the people they are observing, and by the end of each tale the initially mad are cured of insanity, whilst the sane patients are plagued with it. This appears to suggest that the human mind can be persuaded into believing that it is either functional or dysfunctional; exactly the kind of inverted concept that is present throughout each book, and very apparent in characterisation.

Section two: Narration in 'Poppy Shakespeare'

Much like the characters that are changed by the mental health systems within these books, there is likeness between the narrators of the stories themselves. Both characters possess a certain way of narrating, connected to their own speech patterns and symptoms of insanity, making the texts individually entertaining. They also both happen to be greatly affected and, in the end made sane by, the protagonists of the books. The narrators, then, are at the heart of the question invited by the texts. "N", the narrator of 'Poppy Shakespeare', has been cursed with mental problems throughout her life, or, as she claims, "I been dribbling before I was even born." The word "Dribblers" is used to describe, in particular, patents who attend the day hospital alongside N. This brings to mind the somewhat comatose state a human would have to be in to be physically dribbling, suggesting the common use of drugs within the hospital. The character N, although she classes herself as a "dribbler", is in fact very intelligent. Although her language is often grammatically incorrect and occasionally unintelligible, it adds to the charm of the book. She uses some apt imagery, such as describing a grin as a "flicker of a smile, like a lighter low on fluid."[2] , painting an accurate picture of a smile that creeps onto the face to remain there for only an instant, fading in and out much like the flame would do on such a lighter. N also manages to tell the story in an incredibly humorous style, with some of her hallucinations and exaggerations causing the reader to laugh out loud:

> "Carmel's complaint been building for fifteen years. No one knew what it was sparked it off, not even Carmel no more. Carmel's complaint was a great-grandma at least. It been married, had kids and the kids had had kids and half of them was divorced remarried or living together or living alone and all the stepchildren, half-brothers and sisters, and foster kids too; her complaint had great nieces and their nephews had cousins and their cousins had more cousins four-times removed, and to find the complaint what started it all, do you know what I'm saying, was like trying to find Eve at the top of a family tree."[3]

This small section is merely an example of the way in which N uses humour and exaggeration to portray her thoughts. She often uses this technique - to compare whatever she happens to be describing to something completely different, using that different factor as an extended metaphor. N's pattern of thinking, this constant mixing of different situations in the name of description, helps gain the sense of a mixed and disorganised mind . At one point in 'Poppy Shakespeare', Astrid, nicknamed "Astrid Arsewipe" receives a letter, and, when printed within the novel, the letter itself is addressed to her full nickname. This obviously would not happen in "real life", and causes the reader to do a double - take - to question how much we are told is actually real, and how much a result of N's vast imagination, but also adds a nice touch of humour to the seemingly bleak letter. N's style of speech can also be relatively shocking - she describes the view of St Paul's from the fictional London based mental institution as the "size of a teenager's tit"[4], demonstrating how boldly she places exactly what enters her head onto paper and into speech. Furthering the charm of 'Poppy Shakespeare' is the way the chapters are introduced by N. They are labelled with whatever N happens to call them, usually beginning with the word "How", for instance - "How it all begun"[5], "How Brian the Butcher was late for his break and how he broke us the news about Pollyanna"[6], or "How Poppy eaten a piece of humble pie"[7]. Other chapters include "A bit about my childhood, you can skip if you ain't interested"[8], or "Why I like fireworks and stuff like that you can skip if you can't be arsed"[9]. The use of these informal and repetitive phrases increases the conversational tone of the book: N is unique, but does this mean she is mad? We are all shaped by how we grow up, and it is obvious that N's upbringing has led to her current personality - both her mother, and grandmother were classed as "mad" and their lives both ended in suicide. She also stumbled upon her closest friend's suicidal corpse when a child, and this left an obvious mental scar.

Section three: Narration in 'One Flew Over the Cuckoo's Nest'

Chief Bromden, the narrator in 'Cuckoo's Nest', has similarities to N when it comes to narration, such as the inclusion of personal voice and humour occasionally, and opinions/memories that tie his life in with the story. But the plot told by Chief Bromden is much darker than that being told by N. However sad the story of 'Poppy Shakespeare' is, the narration of N lightens the mood. Perhaps the tale of 'Cuckoo's Nest' is one so terrifying that it can only be told in a sombre way, and for that I find the quiet and reclusive character of Chief Bromden very appropriate. At 6 feet 8 inches, he is a giant of a man, yet he feels small. He looks back on his past with the thought "I was a whole lot bigger in those days"[10], but this is only a sense of his shrunken emotional strength. He is, of course, the same size, if not bigger, than he was, and admires McMurphy, the protagonist and initially "sane" character whose story he tells. He observes that McMurphy's current state of mind is much stronger than his own, and has not yet been destroyed by "The Combine". Within the introduction of the 'Cuckoo's Nest', Bromden says that the story he is about to tell may seem "too awful to be the truth", "But it's the truth even if it didn't happen."[11] This is very unusual and could have numerous meanings. It could signify that, although the (sometimes extreme) hallucinations that occur throughout 'Cuckoo's Nest' making it appear unreal are common, the story is still true, as he is merely telling us what he saw with all honesty. It could also mean that, as this is fiction, the story itself will not be true, but functions as a metaphor for the injustice apparent in mental health institutions. Bromden has several hallucinations that gradually clear through the novel, but these hallucinations, although perhaps having initially no more purpose than to create a sense of madness, have their own significance. He sees society as a machine - a colossal oppressive mass which he calls the "Combine", and this forever haunts his mind. He believes the hospital is a factory for "fixing up mistakes made in the neighbourhoods and in the schools and in the churches"[12] and that the chronics inside the hospital (of which he is a member) are merely "machines with flaws inside that can't be repaired."[13] After scrutinising these statements, they make perfect sense and are really an extended metaphor throughout the book. Society today is indeed somewhat similar to the machine it is being compared to - you must conform if you want to survive and live what is considered a normal life. Mental institutions are places that people, who for some reason or another could be considered "flawed" within modern day society, and cannot conform to or cope with it, end up. But are they really the crazy ones? Perhaps they could be considered sane and human, and this virtually alien environment turns them insane. In one incident Chief Bromden fails to take his evening medication and has a rather disturbing nightmare. Within this nightmare, an old member of the hospital is hung on a meat hook and slaughtered, but upon being disembowelled, rust and ash pour from his wound. When Bromden wakes up, Old Blastic is dead. This signifies that in Chief Bromden's opinion, the hospital is not a place promoting health, but a mechanized slaughter house - a weapon of the "combine" - in which not only humans, but humanity itself, is ruthlessly slaughtered. A further example of this machinery is the way he depicts Nurse Ratched's skin as "flesh coloured enamel"[14] and her chosen colour of lipstick and nail polish reflect that of polished steel. This demonstrates her doll-like appearance, her artificial nature and her reluctance to expose her humanity. The colour of her lips/fingertips could be related to metal, creating an illustration of Nurse Ratched as more of a mechanised object than a person, her metal insides exposed in these areas, repeating Chief's use of metaphor of machinery. An additional hallucination is referred to several times by Chief Bromden - that of fog. An imaginary fog covers him at the beginning of the novel, cutting off his surroundings. This reveals his state of mind at the time - he is either overly medicated or simply too frightened to face the reality beyond this fog. The fog machine also represents the powerlessness of the patients within the hospital, encouraged to stay hidden and isolated underneath their own "fogs". Bromden begins to notice that fog covers the rest of the patients after McMurphy has arrived at the hospital, which, ironically, is evidence for his own fog beginning to lift, due to the fact that he is beginning to take notice of his surroundings. By the end of the 'Cuckoo's Nest', the fog has completely lifted, and Chief Bromden can see clearly -

© HERIOT-WATT UNIVERSITY

a new man. Much like N, with the help and input of someone who did not belong in the hospital environment in the first place, his "chronic" mental illnesses were all but cured, yet again repeating the need for questioning the concept of madness, and challenging the traditional idea.

Section four: Minor characters in 'Poppy Shakespeare'

The usage of minor characters to highlight the questions raised is also clear in both texts, and, as the stories both happen to be situated in mental asylums, there is a large potential for plenty of minor character creation. Clare Allan takes advantage of this in 'Poppy Shakespeare', and she has managed some ingenious creation of minor "dribblers" the reader is introduced to throughout N's telling of the bizarre happenings in her everyday life. The minor characters are extremely two-dimensional, and serve the purpose of backing up the sense of madness within the hospital. Named from A to Z (Astrid to Zubin), they seem to each portray a form or symptom of mental illness. For instance, Dawn, an elderly member of the day hospital, has few lines within 'Poppy Shakespeare', and seems to exist specifically as an example of cruel and inappropriate treatment within the hospital, along with her (resulting) amnesia. An accidental incident which occurred years before in the hospital, which N describes for us, involving Dawn "wired up on the bed"[15], and "all of these students round, who was sposed to be learning how to do it"[16], ended in Dawn receiving a "massive electric shock"[17]:

> "It was so fucking massive it blown every fuse in the abaddon, and all the lights gone out and all the tellies gone off... and it blown all the memory out of Dawn's brain as well."[18]

Clare Allan describes this event early within the novel, leading the reader to an almost instant sense of dislike of the hospital for such seemingly inappropriate treatment . She goes on to turn Dawn's character into an example of amnesia, describing the after effects of the event:

> "But every cloud got a silver lining, 'cause Dawn was brilliant at making tables. The Dorothy Fish got this wood workshop. No one gone in there except for Dawn but Dawn gone in there pretty much all the time. She made that many tables you couldn't give them away but she never got bored 'cause she couldn't remember she'd ever made one before."[19]

Dawn also says that she has odd urges to make tables at random points throughout the book adding dark humour and irony to a rather miserable situation. Dawn's lines within 'Poppy Shakespeare' are limited but these few lines are all that is needed to serve as an example of this particular form of mental illness . There is virtually no end to the minor characters within this novel, the list as long as mental health disorders and symptoms alike. Yet, combined, these two dimensional characters give the text a great deal more of a third dimensional view into the world of the mentally unwell. They remain forever in the background of 'Poppy Shakespeare', there to stimulate notions of madness, and to help create the peculiar situations N finds herself in, which in turn cause us to truly think hard about the concept of what insanity involves.

© HERIOT-WATT UNIVERSITY

Section five: Minor characters in 'One Flew Over the Cuckoo's Nest'

The minor characters in 'Cuckoo's Nest' also appear to be there to provide examples of madness, but are more involved with the story, as opposed to the minor characters of 'Poppy Shakespeare', who exist mainly to exaggerate and prompt the variety of insane happenings. One such case of this is the timid character of Billy Bibbit . Although Billy does provide demonstration of a mentally ill patient, he also boasts a greater part to play in 'Cuckoo's Nest' than merely an illustration. Billy longs to be similar to McMurphy, who represents freedom. However, his extreme lack of self confidence prevents him from doing so. He cannot face the world on his own, as he believes he is not ready to do so, which he admits to McMurphy as he is too easily manipulated by Nurse Ratched - the opposing force to McMurphy in the novel. He entangles his legs and arms when Nurse Ratched speaks to him, reminding him of previous suicide attempts, representing how she manages to tie him into knots with her words alone. He is crippled by an overpowering sense of shyness and fear which is why he is immediately fascinated by the bold and strong character of McMurphy. McMurphy is saddened by Billy's state, and attempts to encourage him to embrace youth and overcome fear. With McMurphy's help, Billy gradually becomes more confident, until he confesses his attraction to Candy, a prostitute of McMurphy's acquaintance, who, naturally, encourages the healthy sexual craving on Billy's part, and persuades the two to sleep together. The following morning, Billy speaks for the first time without a stutter, and is applauded by others for his confidence. However, Nurse Ratched, who discovers the news, instantly makes Billy cower with shame.

> "She got the response she was after. Billy flinched and put his hand to his cheek like he'd been burned with acid."[20]

Nurse Ratched uses his mother as a tool against Billy, threatening to tell her the night's events.

> "We watched Billy folding into the floor, head going back, knees coming forward. He rubbed his hand up and down that green pant leg. He was shaking his head in panic like a kid that's been promised a whipping."[21]

We see the power of Ratched's manipulation and hatred twist Billy into a wreck here, and he chooses suicide over living under her repression any further, making an independent decision. Nurse Ratched does not flinch at this, in fact it seems almost like she is pleased by it; revenge, in a way, for McMurphy's tampering. This acts as a catalyst for the final clash between Ratched and McMurphy, the major forces of good and evil within the book. McMurphy, although sane, remains a patient, whilst Ratched, who we see must be virtually insane, continues to be a member of staff. It is perhaps this final repetition of injustice which causes me to question the definition of insanity once more, and whether or not society can correctly label its victims. And so Billy, although a minor character, is still complex enough to have a greater input to the story, and actually causes events within the novel to link one another, as opposed to simply re-enforcing the idea of insanity. We see madness, but also question the curable nature of this madness, unlike the minor characters in 'Poppy Shakespeare', in which we simply accept it.

Section six: Conclusion

Characterisation is the main tool within these novels used to raise the question and need for debate on madness, since madness itself is a solely human trait, and it is therefore most necessary to portray this aspect of humanity through characterisation as opposed to other literary techniques. We see madness through many different characters, and are communicated this in different ways, some subtler than others. I feel that, through this, the books manage to twist and warp situations, surrounding the reader with enough examples of inside out ideas to make them think twice about what true insanity actually is. Since, in every character within these books, including the so-called "sane" (through showing extreme forms of hate and injustice) there seems to be some form of mental corruption, it almost seems to invite a debate to which there is no conclusion or answer. Mental health is a definite issue and people do need help, but the corruptions within the so-called helping systems are successfully addressed. Insanity seems to be present throughout every single character in differing ways, which makes me look beyond the fiction and into fact - making madness apparent throughout human nature, and on both sides of locked ward doors.

Footnotes

[1] Huffman, B, 'Ken Kesey', The Literary Encyclopedia, 17 May 2002
[2] Allan, C, 'Poppy Shakespeare', Bloomsbury, 2007: 1
[3] 'Poppy Shakespeare': 129
[4] 'Poppy Shakespeare': 7
[5] 'Poppy Shakespeare': 1
[6] 'Poppy Shakespeare': 9
[7] 'Poppy Shakespeare': 97
[8] 'Poppy Shakespeare': 10
[9] 'Poppy Shakespeare': 264
[10] Kesey, K, 'One Flew Over The Cuckoo's Nest', Picador, 1973: 36
[11] 'One Flew Over The Cuckoo's Nest': 8
[12] 'One Flew Over The Cuckoo's Nest': 37
[13] 'One Flew Over The Cuckoo's Nest': 14
[14] 'One Flew Over The Cuckoo's Nest': 5
[15] 'Poppy Shakespeare': 13
[16] 'Poppy Shakespeare': 13
[17] 'Poppy Shakespeare': 13
[18] 'Poppy Shakespeare': 13
[19] 'Poppy Shakespeare': 13
[20] 'One Flew Over The Cuckoo's Nest': 299
[21] 'One Flew Over The Cuckoo's Nest': 300

Bibliography

Kesey, K, One Flew Over The Cuckoo's Nest, Picador, 1973

Allan, C, Poppy Shakespeare, Bloomsbury, 2007

Huffman, B, "Ken Kesey", The Literary Encyclopedia, 17 May 2002

3.2.1 Annotated dissertation section one: Opening

> **An exploration of how characterisation and narrative style[1] in the novels 'Poppy Shakespeare' by Clare Allan and 'One Flew Over The Cuckoo's Nest' by Ken Kesey [2] invite debate about what madness is[3].**
>
> The concept of insanity has been apparent in human nature for as long as we have lived. Mental health disorders can isolate victims from society and reality, but at what point does one go from being classed as mentally ill to insane? The idea of curing and preventing such problems naturally has trailed behind this, alongside the mental health system, which has evolved into the one we know today[4]. However, despite many important discoveries in this field, have we managed to determine exactly what madness really is? 'Poppy Shakespeare', a shockingly brilliant debut novel by Clare Allan, and 'One Flew Over The Cuckoo's Nest', by Ken Kesey, "One of the most important American novels of the post-war period"[5], are based on and inspired by the experiences and encounters the authors have had with the mental health system, and institutions connected to it[6]. The key trait I find the novels share is how well they attempt to explore and invite debate over the concept of madness through characterisation[7]. Although fictional, these books portray a seemingly real image of patients admitted both voluntarily and unwillingly into the mental health system, and the experiences and characters they discover within this quirky, confusing and at times, unpredictable world.
>
> Both novels are inspired by the experiences the writers have had within the mental health system, and follow a similar plot and general idea. Clare Allan, author of 'Poppy Shakespeare' spent time inside hospitals as a patient, while Ken Kesey worked in earlier hospitals as staff, and is known to have experimented with a drug widely known for its mind altering effects, LSD. The plots within the texts both follow the life of an initially "sane" character sucked into the mental health system, and are narrated through the eyes of mental patients currently residing within the hospitals, who watch their lives turn upside down[8]. In both cases, the narrators exchange positions with the people they are observing, and by the end of each tale the initially mad are cured of insanity, whilst the sane patients are plagued with it. This appears to suggest that the human mind can be persuaded into believing that it is either functional or dysfunctional; exactly the kind of inverted concept that is present throughout each book, and very apparent in characterisation.
>
> **Notes:**
>
> [1] Literary techniques to be discussed.
> [2] Texts and authors.
> [3] Introduces the main argument of the dissertation.
> [4] Beginning the opening with this detailed comment about madness allows the reader to see the candidate's stance immediately and sets out clearly what the main thrust of the dissertation will be.
> [5] Quote from Huffman, B, "Ken Kesey", The Literary Encyclopedia, 17 May 2002.
> [6] Some biographical detail, demonstrating secondary reading and an understanding of the contexts in which the novels were written.
> [7] One of the techniques which will be examined.
> [8] From this point until the end of the paragraph the candidate demonstrates an understanding of similarities between the texts as well as providing a brief overview

of the content of each novel.

3.2.2 Annotated dissertation section two: Narration in 'Poppy Shakespeare'

Much like the characters that are changed by the mental health systems within these books, there is likeness between the narrators of the stories[1]. Both characters possess a certain way of narrating, connected to their own speech patterns and symptoms of insanity, making the texts individually entertaining. They also both happen to be greatly affected and, in the end made sane by, the protagonists of the books. The narrators, then, are at the heart of the question invited by the texts. "N", the narrator of 'Poppy Shakespeare', has been cursed with mental problems throughout her life, or, as she claims, "I been dribbling before I was even born." The word "Dribblers" is used to describe, in particular, those patients who attend the day hospital alongside N. This brings to mind the somewhat comatose state a human would have to be in to be physically dribbling, suggesting the common use of drugs within the hospital. The character N, although she classes herself as a "dribbler", is in fact very intelligent. Although her language[2] is often grammatically incorrect and occasionally unintelligible, it adds to the charm factor of the book. She uses some apt imagery, such as describing a grin as a "flicker of a smile, like a lighter low on fluid.", painting an accurate picture of a smile that creeps onto the face to remain there for only an instant, fading in and out much like the flame would do on such a lighter. N also manages to tell the story in an incredibly humorous style, with some of her hallucinations and exaggerations causing the reader to laugh out loud:

> "Carmel's complaint been building for fifteen years. No one knew what it was sparked it off, not even Carmel no more. Carmel's complaint was a great-grandma at least. It been married, had kids and the kids had had kids and half of them was divorced remarried or living together or living alone and all the stepchildren, half-brothers and sisters, and foster kids too; her complaint had great nieces and their nephews had cousins and their cousins had more cousins four-times removed, and to find the complaint what started it all, do you know what I'm saying, was like trying to find Eve at the top of a family tree."

This small section is merely an example of the way in which N uses humour and exaggeration to portray her thoughts. She often uses this technique - to compare whatever she happens to be describing to something completely different, using that different factor as an extended metaphor. N's pattern of thinking, this constant mixing of different situations in the name of description, helps gain the sense of a mixed and disorganised mind[3]. At one point in 'Poppy Shakespeare', Astrid, nicknamed "Astrid Arsewipe" receives a letter, and, when printed within the novel, the letter itself is addressed to her full nickname. This obviously would not happen in "real life", and causes the reader to do a double - take - to question how much we are told is actually real, and how much a result of N's vast imagination[4], but also adds a nice touch of humour to the seemingly bleak letter. N's style of speech can also be relatively shocking - she describes the view of St Paul's from the fictional London based mental institution as the "size of a teenager's tit", demonstrating how boldly she places exactly what enters her head onto paper and into speech. Furthering the charm of 'Poppy Shakespeare' is the way the chapters are introduced by N. They are labelled with whatever N happens to call them, usually beginning with the word "How", for instance - "How it all begun", "How Brian the Butcher was late for his break and how he broke us the news about Pollyanna", or "How Poppy eaten a piece of humble pie". Other chapters include "A bit about my childhood, you can skip if you ain't interested", or "Why I like fireworks and stuff like that you can skip if you can't be arsed". The use of these informal and repetitive phrases increases the conversational tone of the book: N is unique, but does this mean she is mad? We are all shaped by how we grow up, and it is obvious that N's upbringing has led to her current personality - both her mother, and grandmother were classed as "mad" and their lives both ended in suicide. She also stumbled upon her closest friend's suicidal corpse when a child, and this left an obvious mental scar.

Notes:

[1] This sentence provides a link between the previous paragraph and this one, moving from the similarities between the characters' experiences to the similarities in narrative style.
[2] While the use of language is not specified in the opening as a technique which will be analysed, its inclusion improves the dissertation and is a good example of how to provide depth of analysis. Discussing the language N uses is an effective method by which the candidate examines not only the character, but also the setting.
[3] The analysis of language helps to tackle the main idea of the dissertation: it is being used to comment on N's state of mind.
[4] This is a comment on how the novel's narrative style affects our understanding of madness and reality.

3.2.3 Annotated dissertation section three: Narration in 'One Flew Over the Cuckoo's Nest'

Chief Bromden, the narrator in 'Cuckoo's Nest', holds similarities to N when it comes to narration[1], such as the inclusion of personal voice and humour occasionally, and opinions/memories that tie his life in with the story. But the plot told by Chief Bromden is much darker than that being told by N. However sad the story of 'Poppy Shakespeare' is, the narration of N lightens the mood. Perhaps the tale of 'Cuckoo's Nest' is one so terrifying that it can only be told in a sombre way, and for that I find the quiet and reclusive character of Chief Bromden very appropriate[2]. At 6 feet 8 inches, he is a giant of a man, yet he feels small. He looks back on his past with the thought "I was a whole lot bigger in those days", but this is only a sense of his shrunken emotional strength[3]. He is, of course, the same size, if not bigger, than he was, and admires McMurphy, the protagonist and initially "sane" character whose story he tells. He observes that McMurphy's current state of mind is much stronger than his own, and has not yet been destroyed by "The Combine". Within the introduction of the 'Cuckoo's Nest', Bromden says that the story he is about to tell may seem "too awful to be the truth", "But it's the truth even if it didn't happen." This is very unusual and could have numerous meanings. It could signify that, although the (sometimes extreme) hallucinations that occur throughout 'Cuckoo's Nest', making it appear unreal are common, the story is still true, as he is merely telling us what he saw with all honesty. It could also mean that, as this is fiction, the story itself will not be true, but functions as a metaphor for the injustice apparent in mental health institutions. Bromden has several hallucinations that gradually clear through the novel, but these hallucinations, although perhaps having initially no more purpose than to create a sense of madness, have their own significance[4]. He sees society as a machine - a colossal oppressive mass which he calls the "Combine", and this forever haunts his mind. He believes the hospital is a factory for "fixing up mistakes made in the neighbourhoods and in the schools and in the churches" and that the chronics inside the hospital (of which he is a member) are merely "machines with flaws inside that can't be repaired." After scrutinising these statements, they make perfect sense and are really an extended metaphor throughout the book. Society today is indeed somewhat similar to the machine it is being compared to - you must conform if you want to survive and live what is considered a normal life. Mental institutions are places that people, who for some reason or another could be considered "flawed" within modern day society, and cannot conform to or cope with it, end up. But are they really the crazy ones? Perhaps they could be considered sane and human, and this virtually alien environment turns them insane[5]. In one incident Chief Bromden fails to take his evening medication and has a rather disturbing nightmare. Within this nightmare, an old member of the hospital is hung on a meat hook and slaughtered, but upon being disembowelled, rust and ash pour from his wound. When Bromden wakes up, Old Blastic is dead. This signifies that in Chief Bromden's opinion, the hospital is not a place promoting health, but a mechanized slaughter house - a weapon of the "combine" - in which not only humans, but humanity itself, is ruthlessly slaughtered[6]. A further example of this machinery is the way he depicts Nurse Ratched's skin as "flesh coloured enamel" and her chosen colour of lipstick and nail polish reflect that of polished steel. This demonstrates her doll-like appearance, her artificial nature and her reluctance to expose her humanity. The colour of her lips/fingertips could be related to metal, creating an illustration of Nurse Ratched as more of a mechanised object than a person, her metal insides exposed in these areas, repeating Chief's theme of machinery. An additional hallucination is referred to several times by Chief Bromden - that of fog[7]. An imaginary fog covers him at the beginning of the novel, cutting off his surroundings. This reveals his state of mind at the time - he is either overly medicated or simply too frightened to face the reality beyond this fog. The fog machine also represents the powerlessness of the patients within the hospital, encouraged to stay hidden and isolated underneath their own "fogs". Bromden begins to notice that fog covers the rest of the patients after McMurphy has arrived at the hospital, which, ironically, is evidence for his own fog beginning to lift, due to the fact that he is beginning to take notice of his surroundings. By the end of the 'Cuckoo's Nest', the fog has completely lifted, and Chief Bromden can see clearly - a new man. Much like N, with the help and input of someone who did not belong in the hospital environment in the first place, his "chronic" mental illnesses were all but cured, yet again repeating the need for questioning the concept of madness, and challenging the traditional idea[8].

Notes:

[1] This is the first real point of comparison between the two novels: narrative style. Using this horizontal structure is effective as it allows for immediate comparison between the texts in a way that a vertical structure (discussing the texts separately) does not.
[2] Identification of a contrast between the novels: the narrators' personalities and their content.
[3] This shows insight into the character and is expressed well.
[4] This introduces an insightful examination of the Chief's hallucinations and how they invite debate about the nature of insanity.
[5] This comment reminds us of the purpose of the dissertation: to question the nature

and treatment of madness in society.
[6] An insightful comment on the nature of mental institutions like one in this novel.
[7] The following discussion of the 'fog' metaphor allows the candidate to examine language, characterisation and the nature of madness.
[8] Another textual comparison, leading to a comment on the main idea of the dissertation.

3.2.4 Annotated dissertation section four: Minor characters in 'Poppy Shakespeare'

The usage of minor characters[1] to highlight the questions raised is also clear in both texts, and, as the stories both happen to be situated in mental asylums, there is a large potential for plenty of minor character creation. Clare Allan takes advantage of this in 'Poppy Shakespeare', and she has managed some ingenious creation of minor "dribblers" the reader is introduced to throughout N's telling of the bizarre happenings in her everyday life. The minor characters are extremely two-dimensional, and serve the purpose of backing up the sense of madness within the hospital. Named from A to Z (Astrid to Zubin), they seem to each portray a form or symptom of mental illness. For instance, Dawn, an elderly member of the day hospital, has few lines within 'Poppy Shakespeare', and seems to exist specifically as an example of cruel and inappropriate treatment within the hospital, along with her (resulting) amnesia. An accidental incident which occurred years before in the hospital, which N describes for us, involving Dawn "wired up on the bed" , and "all of these students round, who was sposed to be learning how to do it" , ended in Dawn receiving a "massive electric shock":

"It was so fucking massive it blown every fuse in the abaddon, and all the lights gone out and all the tellies gone off... and it blown all the memory out of Dawn's brain as well."

Clare Allan describes this event early within the novel, leading the reader to an almost instant sense of dislike of the hospital for such seemingly inappropriate treatment[2]. She goes on to turn Dawn's character into an example of amnesia, describing the after effects of the event:

"But every cloud got a silver lining, 'cause Dawn was brilliant at making tables. The Dorothy Fish got this wood workshop. No one gone in there except for Dawn but Dawn gone in there pretty much all the time. She made that many tables you couldn't give them away but she never got bored 'cause she couldn't remember she'd ever made one before."

Dawn also says that she has odd urges to make tables at random points throughout the book adding dark humour and irony to a rather miserable situation. Dawn's lines within 'Poppy Shakespeare' are limited but these few lines are all that is needed to serve as an example of this particular form of mental illness[3]. There is virtually no end to the minor characters within this novel, the list as long as mental health disorders and symptoms alike. Yet, combined, these two dimensional characters give the text a great deal more of a third dimensional view into the world of the mentally unwell. They remain forever in the background of 'Poppy Shakespeare', there to stimulate notions of madness, and to help create the peculiar situations N finds herself in, which in turn cause us to truly think hard about the concept of what insanity involves.

Notes:

[1] Another technique.
[2] This shows awareness of the candidate's viewpoint on mental health treatment.
[3] A comment on the purpose and effect of Allan's use of characterisation.

3.2.5 Annotated dissertation section five: Minor characters in 'One Flew Over the Cuckoo's Nest'

The minor characters in 'Cuckoo's Nest' also appear to be there to provide examples of madness, but are more involved with the story, as opposed to the minor characters of 'Poppy Shakespeare', who exist mainly to exaggerate and prompt the variety of insane happenings[1]. One such case of this is the timid character of Billy Bibbit[2]. Although Billy does provide demonstration of a mentally ill patient, he also boasts a greater part to play in 'Cuckoo's Nest' than merely an illustration. Billy longs to be similar to McMurphy, who represents freedom. However, his extreme lack of self confidence prevents him from doing so. He cannot face the world on his own, as he believes he is not ready to do so, which he admits to McMurphy as he is too easily manipulated by Nurse Ratched - the opposing force to McMurphy in the novel. He entangles his legs and arms when Nurse Ratched speaks to him, reminding him of previous suicide attempts, representing how she manages to tie him into knots with her words alone. He is crippled by an overpowering sense of shyness and fear which is why he is immediately fascinated by the bold and strong character of McMurphy. McMurphy is saddened by Billy's state, and attempts to encourage him to embrace youth and overcome fear. With McMurphy's help, Billy gradually becomes more confident, until he confesses his attraction to Candy, a prostitute of McMurphy's acquaintance, who, naturally, encourages the healthy sexual craving on Billy's part, and persuades the two to sleep together. The following morning, Billy speaks for the first time without a stutter, and is applauded by others for his confidence. However, Nurse Ratched, who discovers the news, instantly makes Billy cower with shame.

"She got the response she was after. Billy flinched and put his hand to his cheek like he'd been burned with acid."

Nurse Ratched uses his mother as a tool against Billy, threatening to tell her the night's events.

"We watched Billy folding into the floor, head going back, knees coming forward. He rubbed his hand up and down that green pant leg. He was shaking his head in panic like a kid that's been promised a whipping."

We see the power of Ratched's manipulation and hatred twist Billy into a wreck here, and he chooses suicide over living under her repression any further, making an independent decision. Nurse Ratched does not flinch at this, in fact it seems almost like she is pleased by it; revenge, in a way, for McMurphy's tampering. This acts as a catalyst for the final clash between Ratched and McMurphy, the major forces of good and evil within the book. McMurphy, although sane, remains a patient, whilst Ratched, who we see must be virtually insane, continues to be a member of staff. It is perhaps this final repetition of injustice which causes me to question the definition of insanity once more, and whether or not society can correctly label its victims. And so Billy, although a minor character, is still complex enough to have a greater input to the story, and actually causes events within the novel to link one another, as opposed to simply re-enforcing the idea of insanity[3]. We see madness, but also question the curable nature of this madness, unlike the minor characters in 'Poppy Shakespeare', in which we simply accept it.

Notes:

[1] This comment compares the use of characterisation in the novels as well as showing awareness of their differences.
[2] This goes on to show a detailed understanding of the character of Billy and his relationships with the characters of McMurphy and Nurse Ratched.
[3] This comment discusses the importance of the minor character to the novel as a whole.

3.2.6 Annotated dissertation section six: Conclusion

Characterisation is the main tool within these novels used to raise the question and need for debate on madness, since madness itself is a solely human trait, and it is therefore most necessary to portray this aspect of humanity through characterisation as opposed to other literary techniques[1]. We see madness through many different characters, and are communicated this in different ways, some subtler than others. I feel that, through this, the books manage to twist and warp situations, surrounding the reader with enough examples of inside out ideas to make them think twice about what true insanity actually is. Since, in every character within these books, including the so-called "sane" (through showing extreme forms of hate and injustice) there seems to be some form of mental corruption, it almost seems to invite a debate to which there is no conclusion or answer. Mental health is a definite issue and people do need help, but the corruptions within the so-called helping systems are successfully addressed. Insanity seems to be present throughout every single character in differing ways[2], which makes me look beyond the fiction and into fact - making madness apparent throughout human nature, and on both sides of locked ward doors[3].

Notes:

[1] A clear introductory statement which allows the candidate to go on and summarise his/her argument about madness in these two novels.
[2] A summary of some of the ideas discussed in the dissertation.
[3] A statement summarising the candidate's stance on the issue of what madness is.

3.2.7 Annotated dissertation: Further comments

- Overall, this dissertation is well-structured and well-thought out. The proposal makes clear the issue to be examined, the texts involved and the literary techniques which will be analysed.
- The opening sets out clearly the candidate's stance and provides some biographical detail. It also discusses one of the techniques which will be examined, characterisation.
- The candidate has an understanding of the texts as a whole but manages to analyse in depth

the techniques of characterisation and narrative style.

- The task contained in the proposal is considered throughout.
- There is a wide variety of well-chosen textual evidence.
- The dissertation's structure is effective, making clear both the comparisons and contrasts between the novels with regard to the techniques under discussion.
- There is a little evidence of secondary reading in the opening but even more would be an improvement.

3.3 Dissertation: T.S. Eliot

Section one: Opening

An examination of the poetical techniques employed by T.S. Eliot to explore the theme of dissatisfaction with the modern world

Thomas Stearns Eliot, born in St. Louis, Missouri in 1888, is considered by many to be one of the greatest poets of the 20th Century and one of the world's leading "modernist" poets. He was famed for his depictions of real life on the streets of London, his intriguing and intricate writing style and his extensive body of critical work. Described by many as being a creative genius, he was awarded the Order of Merit and the Nobel Prize for Literature in 1948.

Much of Eliot's poetical work expresses a sense of unhappiness at the world in which he lives and this central idea is conveyed through his use of sterile landscapes, weak personas who live "unlived" lives and, at times, a yearning for death. In 'The Lovesong of J. Alfred Prufrock' (1917), 'Rhapsody on a Windy Night' (1917), 'The Wasteland' (1922), and 'Four Quartets' (1943), we see the main theme of dissatisfaction with the modern world explored but also developed as several major events in his own life, such as his conversion to Anglicanism in 1927, changed his views about the world.

Section two: Landscapes and surroundings

A common theme in much of Eliot's early poetry is the effect of the physical landscapes depicted in the poems on the psyche of the personas. They are sterile, empty and devoid of beauty, filled with the rubbish of the modern age and afflicted with a stifling sense of monotony. In 'Prufrock' the streets "follow like a tedious argument" suggesting that the dull streets just go on and on with no end in sight: every street is exactly the same as the last. The streets are tedious in their own monotony. A similar idea is also expressed in the poem 'Preludes':

> "One thinks of all the hands
> That are raising dingy shades
> In a thousand furnished rooms." (Lines 21-23)

Eliot appears to be suggesting that when confronted with such an uninspiring and unfulfilling environment, humans also become monotonous and almost mechanical in the ways in which they live their lives, repeating the same set of dull actions day after day.

One of Eliot's most famous metaphors is his description of the London smog in 'Prufrock':

> "The yellow fog that rubs its back upon the window panes
> The yellow smoke that rubs its muzzle on the window panes
> Licked its tongue into the corners of the evening
> Lingered upon the pools that stand in drains,
> Let fall upon its back the soot that falls from chimneys,
> Slipped by the terrace, made a sudden leap,
> And seeing that it was a soft October night,
> Curled once about the house, and fell asleep." (Lines 15-22)

This extended metaphor likens the smog, which was a typical feature of London at the time, to a domestic cat. Cats were a favourite topic of study for Eliot; he wrote a book of children's poetry based entirely on cats, and their presence in the image immediately conjures a feeling of familiarity, but it is a suffocating familiarity. The smog's stifling presence is an everyday part of modern life settling around our homes like a comforting blanket but one which suffocates all forms of life, leaving behind the empty "Unreal City" described in The Wasteland as being "Under the brown fog of a winter dawn,". The fog defiles the landscape, stripping away any sense of beauty which it might have once held. This could be seen as a yearning for the past, before humans polluted the London air with industry creating a dull mechanical landscape devoid of beauty and colour save the yellow/brown smog which strangles all life.

The poem 'Rhapsody on a Windy Night' relates the persona's walk home to his lodgings. The sights that he sees on his journey serve as a metaphor for the decaying, filthy and sordid world that we live in, such as a prostitute whose eye "Twists like a crooked pin,"; a twisted branch resembling a skeleton; rancid gutters and the smell of cheap cigarettes and alcohol, all of which suggests a world which is overrun with vice and immorality, a world where people have to turn to mind numbing substances in order to find the will just to survive. The persona's return to his home is described thus:

"The bed is open; the tooth brush hangs on the wall,
Put your shoes at the door, sleep, prepare for life.
The last twist of the knife." (Lines 77-79)

Throughout the poem home has represented an escape from the twisted outside world but instead the persona is confronted by a cruel irony. The normality of life represented by the bedroom is just as meaningless, irrelevant and pointless as the gutter life witnessed on his journey home. By separating the last line from the rest of the poem, Eliot adds emphasis to the cruelty of the persona's realisation that his home, which he had thought a refuge from the world, is just as dead as the outside environment. The rhyme between the last two lines emphasises the word "knife" suggesting that this realisation has destroyed the persona's ideals surrounding his home and that this bitter knowledge twists in his heart like a knife.

Section three: Futility

The literary critic Kristian Smidt presented a very interesting theory as to how Eliot came to have such a pessimistic view of modern life. He believes that, as an American, Eliot had a much-idealised vision of London being rich with tradition and culture. Upon arriving in the city he instead found "A drab London of swarming, aimless existences and joyless activities."[1] Another popular theory is that the devastation of the First World War led to Eliot's bleak outlook on life. Although he did not take part in the actual fighting, Eliot was undoubtedly affected by the War. His first volume of published poetry 'Prufrock and Other Observations' (1917) is dedicated to a young man who died on the battlefields in France. This bleakness is particularly evident in 'The Wasteland' and in particular the first section of the poem 'The Burial of the Dead' which speaks of the war which had "undone so many".

One of the most confusing aspects about 'The Wasteland' is its disjointed structure with several conflicting personas, storylines and equally desolate landscapes all jostling for space in the narrative. This does not seem to make much sense to the logical mind but the critic Michael Herbert suggests that Eliot is in fact actually presenting "a fragmented vision of the fragmented modern world."[2] The disjointed nature of the poem vividly expresses this fragmentation and the bleak landscapes within could be taken as a symbol of the modern world and its lack of unity and beauty. 'The Wasteland' is heavy with disillusionment; at one point Eliot pronounces:

I can connect
Nothing with nothing. (Lines 301-302)

The modern world is so fragmented that it has become something of an insolvable jigsaw puzzle. The pieces instead whirl around us in a chaotic cacophony outside the reach of our understanding. 'The Wasteland' also returns to the disgusting physical landscapes seen in 'Rhapsody'. The River

Thames is described as sweating "oil and tar" and a rat drags "its slimy belly on the bank". Again, this desolate landscape bleaches all meaning and happiness from life.

A common feature in much of Eliot's poetry is that many of his personas live futile lives lacking satisfaction. The persona of Prufrock, for example, is a truly pathetic figure. He is extremely self-conscious, constantly mocking himself and the futility of his dull life. A common technique used by Eliot is to juxtapose his personas and their empty lives with great figures of myth and literature as seen in 'Prufrock':

> "No! I am not Prince Hamlet, nor was meant to be:
> Am an attendant lord, one that will do
> To swell a progress, start a scene or two,
> Advise the prince; no doubt, an easy tool,
> Deferential, glad to be of use,
> Politic, cautious and meticulous;
> Full of high sentence, but a bit obtuse;
> At times, indeed, almost ridiculous -
> Almost at times, the Fool." (Lines 115-123)

Compared to Hamlet, Prufrock is fit for nothing save giving simple advice and acting the clown. There is nothing of importance in his life. His life is a life of "what ifs" and simple worries such as "Do I dare to eat a peach?" He has achieved nothing and all that lies ahead of him are the inevitable processes of aging and death. The images used at the start of the poem which liken the evening to a patient under anaesthetic and the fog to a sleeping cat give us a glimpse of the inertia of Prufrock's life. As the streets follow their "tedious argument" so does his life: never changing and never deviating. In a desperate move to escape the confines of his unsatisfying life, he turns to a fantasy life of living with mermaids but this only lasts

> "Till human voices wake us, and we drown." (Line 135)

He is pulled back cruelly to the stifling reality of his life and pushed back into the social settings in which he flounders miserably.

Similarly despairing personas are seen in several other poems. The realisation of the emptiness and pointlessness of life at the end of 'Rhapsody on a Windy Night' leaves the persona yearning for an escape and presents the idea that perhaps death is the better option compared to living in the modern world. This weariness with life is also expressed in 'Gerontion' where the persona describes himself as,

> "A dull head among windy spaces." (Line 16)

The world is empty and there is nothing about life that is worth remembering. All we can do is wait for death to liberate us from the confines of life, which is mechanical and dull. In 'The Wasteland' Eliot describes the normal activity of going home from work:

> "At the violet hour, when the eyes and back Turn upward from the desk, when the human engine waits Like a taxi throbbing waiting," (Lines 215-217)

People live their lives as though they were machines, performing the same repetitive actions day after day. We can gain nothing from such a lifestyle and so we achieve nothing in life.

Section four: Time

The idea of time is a theme which underwent enormous development during Eliot's career, with a radical shift in attitude attributed to Eliot's acceptance into the Anglican Church in 1927. His early poetry tends to focus on the present and wallows in the state of our modern lives whilst his later (more religious) poetry expresses the idea of waiting for better; that we must look to the future and to death in order to escape the confines of the modern world.

In 'Prufrock', time is seen as just another thing which conspires against the persona:

"I have measured out my life with coffee spoons;" (Line 51)

The pathetic means by which time is measured out further heightens the complete inertia of Prufrock's life. His life goes nowhere and he finds himself performing the same basic scenes time and time again. As time continues to pass he realises that there is no time left for him to achieve anything of importance leaving him with the bitter knowledge that his life has been comprised of nothing.

In order to understand the change in Eliot's views on time, we must understand the change in his religious views. Much of Eliot's early work is quite anti-religious and some poems, such as the very satirical pieces 'The Hippopotamus' and 'Mr Eliot's Sunday Morning Service' (both 1920), are openly critical of the Christian Church. Many critics believe that 'The Hollow Men' (1925) written two years before conversion marks the turning point in his view.

As a post-conversion piece, 'Four Quartets' is full of typical Eliot ideas and themes, such as the futility of life, but Eliot twists them in order to put across his Christian views. The theme of time is one which shows a drastic change from how it was portrayed in earlier works. In 'Four Quartets', time takes on a whole new meaning from the one seen in 'Prufrock'. In this later poem, time is the only way through which we gain experience and see the true meaning in our actions as we are incapable of seeing it at the time:

"But only in time can the moment in the rose-garden,
The moment in the arbour where the rain beat,
The moment in the draughty church at smokefall
Be remembered; involved with past and future.
Only through time time is conquered." ('Burnt Norton' lines 99-102)

In 'Prufrock' time was an entity which ate away at the persona showing him the insignificance of his life. 'Four Quartets' expresses the idea that only by waiting can we see the true significance of our lives. The only thing which can blow aside the corrosive effects of time's passage is time itself.

'Prufrock' and other early poems look at time and the future as bringing further unhappiness into the world. Eliot's later work such as 'Four Quartets' spouts the Christian belief of patience and waiting for better and so seems to offer a glimmer of hope. We only have to wait for time to reveal the truth of our lives to us in order for us to find happiness:

"We had the experience but missed the meaning,
And approach to the meaning restores the experience
In a different form, beyond any meaning
We can assign to happiness..." ('The Dry Salvages' lines 99-102)

Time will reveal to us all the insignificant moments and their true importance. We are also warned that we can never attempt to derive knowledge from experience as we will never know the true meaning of an experience until time has passed. Time will show us that our lives, which we thought were empty and desolate, are actually full of hidden meanings and pleasures which we cannot truly appreciate until we are near our journey's end.

Section five: Death

Death is a theme which is found frequently in all of Eliot's poetry and like many of his other prevalent themes and ideas, appears to have undergone a radical change in perception between the pre- and post-conversion poetry. Eliot's early poetry shows a profound fear of death.

Eliot demonstrates this fear through his use of macabre death imagery. This is particularly evident in 'The Wasteland' where Eliot creates a sinister "dead" landscape filled with many morbid images:

> "White bodies naked on the low damp ground
> And bones cast in a little low dry garret,
> Rattled by the rat's foot only, year to year." (Lines 193-195)

Eliot's use of imagery creates a forbidding and fearful atmosphere populated by traditional symbols of death: corpses, bones and rats. This image of death is a hideous one and it is something to be feared. 'The Wasteland' also contains an image which describes the ghosts of those who died in war travelling through the streets of London:

> "A crowd flowed over London Bridge, so many,
> I had not thought death had undone so many.
> Sighs, short and infrequent, were exhaled,
> And each man fixed his eyes before his feet." (Lines 62-65)

The dead are weary; in many ways death is just as empty and meaningless as the lives that they have left behind.

However, Eliot's later poetry shows a complete reversal of this opinion. 'Four Quartets' shows an acceptance of death rather than a fear of it:

> "Only in time; but that which is only living
> Can only die..." ('Burnt Norton' lines 145-146)

The personas of these later poems accept death as being part of the natural order and, in a possible religious connection, perhaps believe that it is a part of the next life. At the end of the second 'Quartet (East Coker)' Eliot writes "In my end is my beginning.", suggesting that rather than death being the end of everything, it is merely a stepping stone to a new and better life beyond the dreary modern world that we know. The theme of death has been developed into the theme of rebirth.

This is taken to its extreme in the final 'Quartet: Little Gidding'. In this poem, Eliot describes the three "stages" of death:

> "First, the cold friction of expiring sense
> Without enchantment, offering no promise
> But bitter tastelessness of shadow fruit
> As body and soul begin to fall asunder." (Lines 134-137)

The separation of body and soul is a painful and confusing process and it would seem that death can only offer us a pale imitation of our former lives hence why it is described as being "bitter". These bitter feelings lead directly on to the second stage:

> "Second, the conscious impotence of rage" (Line 138)

The dead feel anger at those who still live whilst they are stuck with their pale and bitter shadow life but they cannot direct their anger at anything or anyone. The third stage is probably the most painful and the most distressing of all three:

> "And last, the rending pain of re-enactment
> Of all that you have done, and been; the shame
> Of motives late revealed, and the awareness
> Of things ill done and done to others' harm" (Lines 141-144)

A dead soul is forced to relive all the most painful moments of their lives: all of the things that they have done wrong and all of the people whom they have hurt. This version of death sounds no better than the emptiness described in the early poems but there is a crucial difference here: death ultimately leads to something better:

> "From wrong to wrong the exasperated spirit
> Proceeds, unless restored by that refining fire" (Lines 147-148)

In keeping with the poem's Christian theme, this is an allusion to a spirit's journey through Purgatory before being reborn in Heaven. As a soul suffers in Purgatory, so they also suffer in Eliot's three stages of death until they are redeemed by the purifying power of the fire which washes away the sins of the modern world before they are finally able to enter the Kingdom of Heaven. Eliot's spiritual message is that we all must suffer greatly before we can achieve happiness. Our lives in the modern world are empty and futile but we will be rewarded with the bliss of Heaven.

Section six: Conclusion

Dissatisfaction with the modern world is a theme which is expressed in much of T.S. Eliot's poetry. Despite major changes in his personal life and views between his early poems and later works, a sense of unhappiness with the world is always present in some form. This dissatisfaction is shown through several means in the poems such as the physical landscapes, the emptiness of modern lives and through Eliot's use of grim imagery. Throughout his career it would seem that Eliot was always searching for a way to escape the confines of the ugly modern world in which he found himself to be trapped. He had an ever present need for a means, either literal or fantastical, through which he could escape the suffocating presence of the drab and dull world which plagued him, whether this be with the fantastical mermaids of 'Prufrock' or the next life in 'Four Quartets'.

Footnotes

[1] Smidt, K. (1949). 'Poetry and Belief in the Work of T.S. Eliot'. Oslo: I kommisjon hos J. Dybwad p.134

[2] Herbert, M. (2000). 'York Notes Advanced - Selected Poems of T.S. Eliot'. London: York Press p.33

Bibliography

Herbert, Michael. (2000). 'York Notes Advanced' - Selected Poems of T.S. Eliot. London: York Press

Smidt, Kristian. (1949). 'Poetry and Belief in the Work of T.S. Eliot'. Oslo: I kommisjon hos J. Dybwad

Williamson, George. (1955). 'A Reader's Guide to T.S. Eliot: A Poem by Poem Analysis'. London: Thames and Hudson.

All poetical extracts taken from: Eliot, T.S. (1974). 'Collected Poems 1909-1962'. London: Faber and Faber Ltd.

3.3.1 Annotated dissertation section one: Opening

An examination of the poetical techniques[1] employed by T.S. Eliot[2] to explore the theme of dissatisfaction with the modern world[3]

Thomas Stearns Eliot, born in St. Louis, Missouri in 1888, is considered by many to be one of the greatest poets of the 20th Century and one of the world's leading "modernist" poets. He was famed for his depictions of real life on the streets of London, his intriguing and intricate writing style and his extensive body of critical work. Described by many as being a creative genius, he was awarded the Order of Merit and the Nobel Prize for Literature in 1948.[4]

Much of Eliot's poetical work expresses a sense of unhappiness at the world in which he lives[5] and this central idea is conveyed through his use of sterile landscapes, weak personas who live "unlived" lives and, at times, a yearning for death[6]. In 'The Lovesong of J. Alfred Prufrock' (1917), 'Rhapsody on a Windy Night' (1917), 'The Wasteland' (1922), and 'Four Quartets' (1943)[7], we see the main theme of dissatisfaction with the modern world explored but also developed as several major events in his own life, such as his conversion to Anglicanism in 1927, changed his views about the world[8].

Notes:

[1] These are the techniques the candidate will use to explore the main idea.
[2] Name of poet: it is already clear that his poetry is under discussion.
[3] The main idea of the dissertation.
[4] Biographical detail which demonstrates secondary reading.
[5] Reference to the dissertation's main idea.
[6] This sets outs clearly which aspects of his poetry the candidate will be examining.
[7] Identification of the specific poems to be examined.
[8] More biographical detail, this time linking to how this affects the dissertation topic.

3.3.2 Annotated dissertation section two: Landscapes and surroundings

A common theme in much of Eliot's early poetry is the effect of the physical landscapes depicted in the poems on the psyche of the personas[1]. They are sterile, empty and devoid of beauty, filled with the rubbish of the modern age and afflicted with a stifling sense of monotony[2]. In 'Prufrock' the streets "follow like a tedious argument" suggesting that the dull streets just go on and on with no end in sight: every street is exactly the same as the last. The streets are tedious in their own monotony. A similar idea is also expressed in the poem 'Preludes'[3]:

> "One thinks of all the hands
> That are raising dingy shades
> In a thousand furnished rooms." (Lines 21-23)

Eliot appears to be suggesting that when confronted with such an uninspiring and unfulfilling environment, humans also become monotonous[4] and almost mechanical in the ways in which they live their lives, repeating the same set of dull actions day after day.

One of Eliot's most famous metaphors is his description of the London smog in 'Prufrock':

> "The yellow fog that rubs its back upon the window panes
> The yellow smoke that rubs its muzzle on the window panes
> Licked its tongue into the corners of the evening
> Lingered upon the pools that stand in drains,
> Let fall upon its back the soot that falls from chimneys,
> Slipped by the terrace, made a sudden leap,
> And seeing that it was a soft October night,
> Curled once about the house, and fell asleep." (Lines 15-22)

This extended metaphor[5] likens the smog, which was a typical feature of London at the time, to a domestic cat. Cats were a favourite topic of study for Eliot; he wrote a book of children's poetry based entirely on cats, and their presence in the image immediately conjures a feeling of familiarity, but it is a suffocating familiarity. The smog's stifling presence is an everyday part of modern life settling around our homes like a comforting blanket but one which suffocates all forms of life, leaving behind the empty "Unreal City" described in The Wasteland as being "Under the brown fog of a winter dawn,". The fog defiles the landscape, stripping away any sense of beauty which it might have once held. This could be seen as a yearning for the past, before humans polluted the London air with industry creating a dull mechanical landscape devoid of beauty and colour save the yellow/brown smog which strangles all life.

The poem 'Rhapsody on a Windy Night'[6] relates the persona's walk home to his lodgings. The sights that he sees on his journey serve as a metaphor for the decaying, filthy and sordid world that we live in[7], such as a prostitute whose eye "Twists like a crooked pin,"; a twisted branch resembling a skeleton; rancid gutters and the smell of cheap cigarettes and alcohol, all of which suggests a world which is overrun with vice and immorality, a world where people have to turn to mind numbing substances in order to find the will just to survive. The persona's return to his home is described thus:

> "The bed is open; the tooth brush hangs on the wall,
> Put your shoes at the door, sleep, prepare for life.
> The last twist of the knife." (Lines 77-79)

Throughout the poem home has represented an escape from the twisted outside world but instead the persona is confronted by a cruel irony. The normality of life represented by the bedroom is just as meaningless, irrelevant and pointless as the gutter life witnessed on his journey home. By separating the last line from the rest of the poem, Eliot adds emphasis to the cruelty of the persona's realisation that his home, which he had thought a refuge from the world, is just as dead as the outside environment. The rhyme between the last two lines emphasises the word "knife" suggesting that this realisation has destroyed the persona's ideals surrounding his home and that this bitter knowledge twists in his heart like a knife.

Notes:

[1] An introductory sentence which lets the reader know which element of Eliot's writing will be examined in this section.
[2] This clearly describes Eliot's landscapes, in readiness to analyse examples from the poetry.
[3] This is a clear link between the poems.
[4] Another link: the candidate has used monotony in analysis of the previous poem.
[5] This paragraph is a detailed analysis of the metaphor and its effect, tackling the task well.
[6] The candidate continues to analyse a variety of poems, adding strength to the persuasiveness of the argument.
[7] More analysis of language and ideas, demonstrating an understanding of how this is used to make comment on his dissatisfaction with the modern world.

3.3.3 Annotated dissertation section three: Futility

The literary critic Kristian Smidt presented a very interesting theory as to how Eliot came to have such a pessimistic view of modern life. He believes that, as an American, Eliot had a much-idealised vision of London being rich with tradition and culture. Upon arriving in the city he instead found "A drab London of swarming, aimless existences and joyless activities." Another popular theory is that the devastation of the First World War led to Eliot's bleak outlook on life. Although he did not take part in the actual fighting, Eliot was undoubtedly affected by the War. His first volume of published poetry 'Prufrock and Other Observations' (1917) is dedicated to a young man who died on the battlefields in France[1]. This bleakness is particularly evident in 'The Wasteland' and in particular the first section of the poem 'The Burial of the Dead' which speaks of the war which had "undone so many".

One of the most confusing aspects about 'The Wasteland' is its disjointed structure[2] with several conflicting personas, storylines and equally desolate landscapes all jostling for space in the narrative. This does not seem to make much sense to the logical mind but the critic Michael Herbert suggests that Eliot is in fact actually presenting "a fragmented vision of the fragmented modern world." The disjointed nature of the poem vividly expresses this fragmentation and the bleak landscapes within could be taken as a symbol of the modern world and its lack of unity and beauty. 'The Wasteland' is heavy with disillusionment; at one point Eliot pronounces:

> I can connect
> Nothing with nothing. (Lines 301-302)

The modern world is so fragmented that it has become something of an insolvable jigsaw puzzle[3]. The pieces instead whirl around us in a chaotic cacophony outside the reach of our understanding. 'The Wasteland' also returns to the disgusting physical landscapes seen in 'Rhapsody'. The River Thames is described as sweating "oil and tar" and a rat drags "its slimy belly on the bank". Again, this desolate landscape bleaches all meaning and happiness from life.

A common feature in much of Eliot's poetry is that many of his personas live futile lives lacking satisfaction[4]. The persona of Prufrock, for example, is a truly pathetic figure. He is extremely self-conscious, constantly mocking himself and the futility of his dull life. A common technique used by Eliot is to juxtapose his personas and their empty lives with great figures of myth and literature as seen in 'Prufrock':

> "No! I am not Prince Hamlet, nor was meant to be:
> Am an attendant lord, one that will do
> To swell a progress, start a scene or two,
> Advise the prince; no doubt, an easy tool,
> Deferential, glad to be of use,
> Politic, cautious and meticulous;
> Full of high sentence, but a bit obtuse;
> At times, indeed, almost ridiculous -
> Almost at times, the Fool." (Lines 115-123)

Compared to Hamlet, Prufrock is fit for nothing save giving simple advice and acting the clown. There is nothing of importance in his life. His life is a life of "what ifs" and simple worries such as "Do I dare to eat a peach?" He has achieved nothing and all that lies ahead of him are the inevitable processes of aging and death. The images used at the start of the poem which liken the evening to a patient under anaesthetic and the fog to a sleeping cat give us a glimpse of the inertia of Prufrock's life. As the streets follow their "tedious argument" so does his life: never changing and never deviating. In a desperate move to escape the confines of his unsatisfying life, he turns to a fantasy life of living with mermaids but this only lasts

> "Till human voices wake us, and we drown." (Line 135)

He is pulled back cruelly to the stifling reality of his life and pushed back into the social settings in which he flounders miserably.

Similarly despairing personas are seen in several other poems[5]. The realisation of the emptiness and pointlessness of life at the end of 'Rhapsody on a Windy Night' leaves the persona yearning for an escape and presents the idea that perhaps death is the better option compared to living in the modern world. This weariness with life is also expressed in 'Gerontion' where the persona describes himself as,

> "A dull head among windy spaces." (Line 16)

The world is empty and there is nothing about life that is worth remembering. All we can do is wait for death to liberate us from the confines of life, which is mechanical and dull. In 'The Wasteland' Eliot describes the normal activity of going home from work:

> "At the violet hour, when the eyes and back Turn upward from the desk, when the human engine waits Like a taxi throbbing waiting," (Lines 215-217)

People live their lives as though they were machines, performing the same repetitive actions day after day. We can gain nothing from such a lifestyle and so we achieve nothing in life.

Notes:

[1] Helpful and insightful comments on Eliot's life: further evidence of secondary reading.
[2] Introducing a further poetic technique and its contribution to how Eliot conveys his view of society.
[3] Good use of imagery to explain further the disjointed nature of the poetry.
[4] Topic sentence detailing the next area for analysis: the personas of the poems.
[5] A clear link to the other poems that will be discussed in this section.

3.3.4 Annotated dissertation section four: Time

The idea of time is a theme[1] which underwent enormous development during Eliot's career, with a radical shift in attitude attributed to Eliot's acceptance into the Anglican Church in 1927. His early poetry tends to focus on the present and wallows in the state of our modern lives whilst his later (more religious) poetry expresses the idea of waiting for better; that we must look to the future and to death in order to escape the confines of the modern world.

In 'Prufrock', time is seen as just another thing which conspires against the persona:

"I have measured out my life with coffee spoons;" (Line 51)

The pathetic means by which time is measured out further heightens the complete inertia of Prufrock's life. His life goes nowhere and he finds himself performing the same basic scenes time and time again. As time continues to pass he realises that there is no time left for him to achieve anything of importance leaving him with the bitter knowledge that his life has been comprised of nothing.

In order to understand the change in Eliot's views on time, we must understand the change in his religious views. Much of Eliot's early work is quite anti-religious and some poems, such as the very satirical pieces 'The Hippopotamus' and 'Mr Eliot's Sunday Morning Service' (both 1920), are openly critical of the Christian Church. Many critics believe that 'The Hollow Men' (1925) written two years before conversion marks the turning point in his view.

As a post-conversion piece, 'Four Quartets' is full of typical Eliot ideas and themes, such as the futility of life, but Eliot twists them in order to put across his Christian views. The theme of time is one which shows a drastic change from how it was portrayed in earlier works. In 'Four Quartets', time takes on a whole new meaning from the one seen in 'Prufrock'. In this later poem, time is the only way through which we gain experience and see the true meaning in our actions as we are incapable of seeing it at the time:

"But only in time can the moment in the rose-garden,
The moment in the arbour where the rain beat,
The moment in the draughty church at smokefall
Be remembered; involved with past and future.
Only through time time is conquered." ('Burnt Norton' lines 99-102)

In 'Prufrock' time was an entity which ate away at the persona showing him the insignificance of his life. 'Four Quartets' expresses the idea that only by waiting can we see the true significance of our lives. The only thing which can blow aside the corrosive effects of time's passage is time itself.[2]

'Prufrock' and other early poems look at time and the future as bringing further unhappiness into the world. Eliot's later work[3] such as 'Four Quartets' spouts the Christian belief of patience and waiting for better and so seems to offer a glimmer of hope. We only have to wait for time to reveal the truth of our lives to us in order for us to find happiness:

"We had the experience but missed the meaning,
And approach to the meaning restores the experience
In a different form, beyond any meaning
We can assign to happiness..." ('The Dry Salvages' lines 99-102)

Time will reveal to us all the insignificant moments and their true importance. We are also warned that we can never attempt to derive knowledge from experience as we will never know the true meaning of an experience until time has passed. Time will show us that our lives, which we thought were empty and desolate, are actually full of hidden meanings and pleasures which we cannot truly appreciate until we are near our journey's end. [4]

Notes:

[1] The next area for analysis: time.
[2] Clear and insightful comparison of Eliot's treatment of the passing of time in these poems.
[3] Links forward to the poetry which will now be analysed.
[4] A clear conclusion to this section.

3.3.5 Annotated dissertation section five: Death

Death is a theme which is found frequently in all of Eliot's poetry[1] and like many of his other prevalent themes and ideas[2], appears to have undergone a radical change in perception between the pre- and post-conversion poetry. Eliot's early poetry shows a profound fear of death.

Eliot[3] demonstrates this fear through his use of macabre death imagery. This is particularly evident in 'The Wasteland' where Eliot creates a sinister "dead" landscape filled with many morbid images:

"White bodies naked on the low damp ground
And bones cast in a little low dry garret,
Rattled by the rat's foot only, year to year." (Lines 193-195)

Eliot's use of imagery creates a forbidding and fearful atmosphere populated by traditional symbols of death: corpses, bones and rats. This image of death is a hideous one and it is something to be feared. 'The Wasteland' also contains an image which describes the ghosts of those who died in war travelling through the streets of London:

"A crowd flowed over London Bridge, so many,
I had not thought death had undone so many.
Sighs, short and infrequent, were exhaled,
And each man fixed his eyes before his feet." (Lines 62-65)

The dead are weary; in many ways death is just as empty and meaningless as the lives that they have left behind.

However, Eliot's later poetry shows a complete reversal of this opinion[4]. 'Four Quartets[5]' shows an acceptance of death rather than a fear of it:

"Only in time; but that which is only living
Can only die..." ('Burnt Norton' lines 145-146)

The personas of these later poems accept death as being part of the natural order and, in a possible religious connection, perhaps believe that it is a part of the next life. At the end of the second 'Quartet (East Coker)' Eliot writes "In my end is my beginning.", suggesting that rather than death being the end of everything, it is merely a stepping stone to a new and better life beyond the dreary modern world that we know. The theme of death has been developed into the theme of rebirth.

This is taken to its extreme in the final 'Quartet: Little Gidding'. In this poem, Eliot describes the three "stages" of death:

"First, the cold friction of expiring sense
Without enchantment, offering no promise
But bitter tastelessness of shadow fruit
As body and soul begin to fall asunder." (Lines 134-137)

The separation of body and soul is a painful and confusing process and it would seem that death can only offer us a pale imitation of our former lives hence why it is described as being "bitter". These bitter feelings lead directly on to the second stage:

"Second, the conscious impotence of rage" (Line 138)

The dead feel anger at those who still live whilst they are stuck with their pale and bitter shadow life but they cannot direct their anger at anything or anyone. The third stage is probably the most painful and the most distressing of all three:

> "And last, the rending pain of re-enactment
> Of all that you have done, and been; the shame
> Of motives late revealed, and the awareness
> Of things ill done and done to others' harm" (Lines 141-144)

A dead soul is forced to relive all the most painful moments of their lives: all of the things that they have done wrong and all of the people whom they have hurt. This version of death sounds no better than the emptiness described in the early poems but there is a crucial difference here: death ultimately leads to something better:

> "From wrong to wrong the exasperated spirit
> Proceeds, unless restored by that refining fire" (Lines 147-148)

In keeping with the poem's Christian theme, this is an allusion to a spirit's journey through Purgatory before being reborn in Heaven. As a soul suffers in Purgatory, so they also suffer in Eliot's three stages of death until they are redeemed by the purifying power of the fire which washes away the sins of the modern world before they are finally able to enter the Kingdom of Heaven. Eliot's spiritual message is that we all must suffer greatly before we can achieve happiness. Our lives in the modern world are empty and futile but we will be rewarded with the bliss of Heaven.

Notes:

[1] The next area for analysis: death.
[2] A link to what has already been discussed.
[3] The next two paragraphs continue discussing Eliot's treatment of death in his earlier poetry.
[4] The candidate successfully demonstrates the contrast in the treatment of death between the earlier and 'post-conversion' poetry.
[5] The analysis of this poem which follows is detailed and insightful.

3.3.6 Annotated dissertation section six: Conclusion

Dissatisfaction with the modern world[1] is a theme which is expressed in much of T.S. Eliot's poetry. Despite major changes in his personal life and views between his early poems and later works, a sense of unhappiness with the world is always present in some form. This dissatisfaction is shown through several means in the poems such as the physical landscapes, the emptiness of modern lives and through Eliot's use of grim imagery[2]. Throughout his career it would seem that Eliot was always searching for a way to escape the confines of the ugly modern world in which he found himself to be trapped. He had an ever present need for a means, either literal or fantastical, through which he could escape the suffocating presence of the drab and dull world which plagued him, whether this be with the fantastical mermaids of 'Prufrock' or the next life in 'Four Quartets'[3].

Notes:

[1] The candidate reiterates the main idea of the dissertation at the beginning of the conclusion.
[2] Summarising the areas of Eliot's poetry that have been examined in the dissertation.
[3] A detailed final comment on the main idea: how Eliot explored his dissatisfaction with the world in which he lived through his poetry. The candidate's stance is clear: he sought escape from this in a variety of ways, made clear by the content of the poems discussed.

3.4 Learning points

Summary

You will now:

- recognise a well-written dissertation;
- identify where a dissertation is comparing more than one text;
- identify where a dissertation is making explicit links between texts.

Unit 4 Topic 4

Acknowledgements

- *Irvine Welsh*, Trainspotting
- *Anthony Burgess*, A Clockwork Orange
- *F Scott Fitzgerald*, The Great Gatsby
- *F Scott Fitzgerald*, The Beautiful and Damned
- *Clare Allan*, Poppy Shakespeare
- *Ken Kesey*, One Flew Over the Cuckoo's Nest

Answers to questions and activities for Literary study: The critical essay

Topic 2: The question

Annotating questions (page 16)

Q1:

> With close analysis[1] of at least three poems[2], discuss how the poet(s) reflect on aspects of change[3].
>
> **Notes:**
>
> [1] You must consider the effect of various poetic techniques (form, structure, imagery, word choice...) in conveying "aspects of change".
> [2] You must always discuss three or more poems in an essay on poetry. You may refer to more than one poet.
> [3] The focus of the discussion is therefore how the poet's techniques convey the theme of change. What *ideas* about change are explored in the poems? You may deal with more than one poet.

Q2:

> Analyse the use[1] of one or more poetic form(s)[2] such as: the dramatic monologue; the sonnet; the address; the elegy.
>
> In your answer you should refer to at least three poems[3].
>
> **Notes:**
>
> [1] You must discuss the *effect* of the poetic form, as well as other poetic techniques such as imagery and word choice. You must consider the theme(s) conveyed and how the specific poetic form adds to your understanding of theme(s).
> [2] You should think in terms of comparing *one poetic form* in at least three poems, *or* comparing the treatment of *one theme* across one or more poetic forms. You must choose poems which are written in a specific poetic form but the form need not be one of those listed.
> [3] You must always discuss three or more poems in a critical essay on poetry. You may refer to more than one poet.

Q3:

"The short story form is more than a vehicle for stylistic devices[1] (a collection of miniatures, a vignette, a fragment, a twist in the tale...) and can achieve the presentation of a significant theme[2]."

Discuss how far you agree[3] with this quotation with reference to at least three short stories[4].

Notes:

[1] Which "stylistic devices" do your short stories make use of? What is their effect?
[2] You must identify the theme and consider how it is presented: through characterisation; setting; symbolism; key events; narrative voice...
[3] To what extent do your chosen short stories deploy "stylistic devices" but also present a "significant theme"?
[4] You must always deal with at least three texts when answering questions on short stories.

Q4:

Discuss the thematic significance[1] of the presentation[2] of a flawed hero or heroine[3] in any two novels[4].

Notes:

[1] What theme(s) are conveyed by the flawed character and what happens to him/her?
[2] How are the writer's ideas about the hero/heroine conveyed? Through characterisation (relationships, conflicts...); setting; decisions the character makes; key events; symbolism; narrative voice...
[3] In what way is your character flawed? The discussion must focus on the nature of the character's flaws and the theme(s) which is/are developed through the character's situation.
[4] Advanced Higher essay questions always demand a comparison of an aspect of at least two texts.

Q5:

"It is in the ability to combine the particular[1] with the universal[2] that a writer displays their craft to the fullest extent."

Discuss how successful at least two non-fiction texts are in combining "the particular with the universal"[3].

Notes:

[1] This means the situation **specific** to the people or setting of the text.
[2] This means how the specific situation of the people/setting of the text carries a **theme** of significance to all of us.
[3] You must discuss how your chosen texts deal with **both** situations specific to the people and/or setting of the text *as well as* conveying a theme which is universal: of relevance to *all* our lives.

Q6:

Discuss how[1] at least two non-fiction texts present political, social or moral issues[2] in similar or different ways[3].

Notes:

[1] You must argue *how* the issue is presented: through the people; the setting; situations; symbolism....
[2] You must choose *one* of these issues, although there may well be overlap between what might be considered a moral issue and what might be considered a social issue.
[3] You must compare or contrast how the issue is presented in each text.

Q7:

With reference to two plays[1] discuss the effectiveness of the opening scenes[2] in establishing the tone[3] of the action which follows[4]

Notes:

[1] Advanced Higher essay questions always demand a comparison of an aspect of at least two texts.
[2] This means there must be an **evaluation** of the opening scenes' effectiveness. The focus is the opening scenes of two plays. "Opening scenes" cannot be exactly quantified; you must use your judgement about the point in the play when characters, key ideas and setting have all been **established** by the playwright(s).
[3] This means the expectations the audience will have about the ways the play might develop.
[4] This means that you must go on to discuss how aspects of the opening scenes (character, key ideas, setting, themes...) are **developed** as the play progresses. Your discussion must therefore include detailed consideration of aspects of the play **beyond** the opening scenes.

Q8:

With reference to two plays[1], discuss the contribution setting makes[2] to the development of significant theme(s)[3].

Notes:

[1] You must discuss two plays, and you must **compare** aspects of your texts' settings.
[2] This means an analytical discussion of aspects of each play's setting: the location; the time in which the action takes place; the values of this place/time and the characters associated with it; use of symbolism; dramatic properties...
[3] You must identify an appropriate theme and discuss how aspects of setting convey the writer's theme(s).

Topic 4: Writing an effective introduction and conclusion

Introductions to essays (page 31)

Q1:

> In many of her poems, Sylvia Plath explores the relationship that exists between man and nature.[1] In 'Sleep in the Mojave Desert', we read of the persona and her companion travelling in the bleak wilderness of the Californian desert. 'Two Campers in Cloud Country' again depicts the couple, this time at Rock Lake, whilst in the poems 'Blackberrying' and 'Wuthering Heights', the persona experiences nature alone.[2] These poems, like much of Plath's work, are characterised by their expression of powerful emotions. However, the expression of the persona's feelings is tightly controlled by Plath's precise use of imagery, in particular, as well as other poetic techniques.[3] In all of these poems, Plath suggests that nature is a hostile force and that essentially man is insignificant or impotent, even, in the face of that force.[4]
>
> **Notes:**
>
> [1] States the name of the author.
> [2] States the name of the texts and makes the statement outlining what each text is about.
> [3] Refers to the key words of the question.
> [4] Makes a statement about the key themes of the texts.

Q2:

> The novels 'The Great Gatsby' and 'Tender is the Night' by F. Scott Fitzgerald explore the corruption of the so-called jazz-age of America, a time of unprecedented prosperity and corresponding excess.[1] In both novels, the 1920s are portrayed as a time when social and moral values were increasingly tarnished by the relentless **pursuit of wealth**.[2] The characters' lives are filled with empty pleasures: opulent parties, illicit affairs and indolent days. Gatsby, Daisy and the Divers, Nicole and Dick, illustrate this all-consuming obsession with **money and status**[3], and they all illustrate the damage wrought when moral values and basic decency take second place to material acquisition[4].
>
> **Notes:**
>
> [1] States the name of the texts and the author.
> [2] Makes the statement outlining what each text is about. The phrase **'pursuit of wealth'** refers to the key words of the question.
> [3] Makes the statement outlining what each text is about. The phrase **'money and status'** refers to the key words of the question.
> [4] Makes a statement about the key themes of the texts.

Q3:

> In Tennessee Willliams' plays, 'A Streetcar Named Desire' and 'Sweet Bird of Youth'[1], he writes about characters whose lives have spiraled out of control because they have fundamental flaws in their personalities which they are ultimately unable to overcome. The main characters, Blanche Dubois and Chance Wayne, struggle to live in the real world, and they seek refuge from reality in alcohol, drugs and sex.[2] In both plays, Williams makes significant use of dramatic techniques which go beyond the effective use of dialogue. His use of "plastic theatre" - musical underscoring, costumes, props and other aspects of staging - combines with dialogue to enhance the audience's understanding of characters[3] and his theme of the corruption of "goodness" in the face of a brutal world which threatens to crush us if we are unable to adapt to it.[4]
>
> **Notes:**
>
> [1] States the name of the texts and the author.
> [2] Makes the statement outlining what each text is about.
> [3] Refers to the key words of the question.
> [4] Makes a statement about the key themes of the texts.

Conclusions to essays (page 34)

Q4:

> In Sylvia Plath's poems about nature, she undoubtedly conveys **powerful feelings** about humankind's insignificance in the face of nature's overwhelming grandeur. This grandeur, perhaps contrary to our expectations, is often expressed as something hostile and even malevolent: something which can do great damage to us.[1] Plath's **poetic technique, however, is very tightly controlled, and rather than feeling particularly spontaneous** her poems give the impression of being very precise pieces of art.[2] Through these poems, Plath explores the nature of the human condition and our place in the natural world.[3].
>
> **Notes:**
>
> [1] Returns to the main focus of the question. The part in bold 'powerful feelings' uses the key words of the question.
> [2] Returns to the main focus of the question. The part in bold 'poetic technique, however, is very tightly controlled, and rather than feeling particularly spontaneous' uses the key words of the question.
> [3] States for the final time how the writer's themes are conveyed through the aspect identified in the question.

Q5:

In F. Scott Fitzgerald's novels, 'The Great Gatsby' and 'Tender is the Night', he explores the connected ideas of **money and power** through his morally degenerate characters and their empty lives[1]. Through their experiences, Fitzgerald comments on the nature of 1920s America, and the loss of more noble aspirations as a result of the greedy, self-obsessed search for material possessions and social status[2].

Notes:

[1] Returns to the main focus of the question. The part in bold 'money and power' uses the key words of the question.
[2] States for the final time how the writer's themes are conveyed through the aspect identified in the question.

Q6:

In Tennessee Williams' plays, 'A Streetcar Named Desire' and 'Sweet Bird of Youth', **plastic theatre, characterisation and dialogue** are all used effectively[1] to comment on the nature of human experience, revealing how individuals who fail to adapt to the truth of their situations will struggle to survive and will, ultimately, be destroyed by the brutal nature of the real world[2].

Notes:

[1] Returns to the main focus of the question. The part in bold 'plastic theatre, characterisation and dialogue' uses the key words of the question.
[2] States for the final time how the writer's themes are conveyed through the aspect identified in the question.

© HERIOT-WATT UNIVERSITY

Topic 7: Exemplar literary essays

Sylvia Plath essay (page 57)

Q1:

> *Sylvia Plath essay*
>
> In the poems, 'Sleep in the Mojave Desert', 'Two Campers in Cloud Country' and 'Blackberrying', Sylvia Plath makes use of the natural world to convey her ideas about the overwhelming stature of nature, the hostility of the natural environment and the persona's feelings of loss of self-worth and identity.[1]
>
> The idea of the over-whelming stature of the natural world[2] is one which is developed throughout 'Two Campers in Cloud Country'. Plath's main concern in this poem is the insignificance of man, compared with the grandeur of the natural world. Although this theme is explored in all three poems, it is of particular significance in 'Two Campers'[3]. We see this from the opening line of the poem, when Plath writes,
> "In this country there is neither measure nor balance."
> The 'measure' and 'balance' referred to here are presumably those qualities we associate with humans; they are based on human terms and human ways of interpreting the world. If the ways by which humans understand the world - all their 'measure' and 'balance' - have no meaning in the wider context of our natural environment, then humans are, in reality, nothing but a dot on a much vaster landscape. Plath also introduces an important idea developed in many of her poems about nature: the natural world's indifference to man's ways, which man has always assumed are superior.
>
> This theme of the superiority of nature over man is developed when Plath writes about the clouds in Rock Lake, describing them as 'man-shaming'. The sense of superiority which humankind feels about itself is purely self-created and hints at arrogance, but when set against the stature of clouds, mankind's superiority is rendered meaningless. More than this, we are seen to be very much inferior and completely insignificant in comparison to nature. Man would assume that he is superior to a mere cloud in the sky, but Plath shows us that the truth is the reverse: **man is nothing compared to the grandeur of nature, whether living or inanimate**. We see this again when Plath writes of the clouds:
> "No gesture of yours or mine could catch their attention,
> No word make them..."
> Here we see the basis of human understanding turned on its head. Our 'gestures' and 'words' mean nothing to nature and so we ourselves, and our place in the world, therefore mean nothing too. The combination of this idea and the idea that the "Pilgrims and Indians might not have happened" creates an overall suggestion of the sheer extent of the gap between man and nature. The idea of ineffectual 'gestures' and 'words' combined with the idea of the 'Pilgrims and the Indians' reinforces that nature is very much superior to us. This is because through the reference to the Pilgrims and Indians, Plath shows that generations of whole civilisations have lived in this landscape and left no impression on it. The natural environment is so large and incomparably vaster than humankind that we simply cannot compete with the scale and grandeur of it. It shrugs off our presence and does not pay its respects to us: we

mean nothing.[4]

We also see the theme of the overwhelming power of nature in "Sleep in the Mojave Desert"[5]. Here Plath uses personification to suggest the power that the natural environment has to distort and control insignificant humankind. We see this when she writes about the 'mad straight road'. In the desert, Plath sees a line of trees along her path, a path which is never ending and which she feels is taunting her. In the same way she used the idea of the pilgrims and Indians in 'Two Campers' to express man's inability to shape or tame nature, in 'Sleep in the Mojave Desert', Plath writes that the landscape gives very little away about its past. She says that, "One can remember men and houses...", suggesting that there is no trace of previous inhabitants. More disturbingly, and different from 'Two Campers', Plath introduces the harshness of the natural world. Plath suggests that the reason for her being only able to 'remember' this civilisation is because it could not be sustained in the harsh environment of the desert. Once again, despite his best efforts, man has been unable to tame nature and claim it for his own.

This idea of nature's hostility towards man[6] is developed in "Blackberrying". In this poem, Plath expresses the idea of the threat of nature, and one of its threats is its overwhelming power over man. We see this conveyed as the persona walks towards the sea, describing the blackberry bushes as 'hooks', as if she is being pulled against her will, hooked into facing a terrible ordeal.

The end of the poem acts to show the threat and danger of the natural world because of its uncontrollable, overwhelming superiority and power over our lives. Here, Plath reaches what she has been anticipating with dread throughout the poem: the sea. She describes the noise of the sea as:

"... a din like silversmiths
Beating and beating at an intractable metal."

The repetition of 'beating' suggests the sea's threatening nature, and the persona's hopelessness of ever being in a position to make a connection with nature. Not only is nature superior to human life, it is also incompatible with it. Nature has no place for humankind and the likening of it to an 'intractable metal' suggests that no amount of human effort can ever change this reality. Nature is simply too powerful, and does not need man's intervention in any way[7].

We see this idea of the hostility of nature[8] described in all three poems. It is prominent in "Sleep in the Mojave Desert" and 'Blackberrying'. In the first of the two, we get the impression of this idea from the very beginning of the poem. The opening line, "Out here there are no hearthstones", suggests the coldness and lack of comfort towards man. Hearthstones have connotations of warmth and homeliness. The absence of these representative things shows nature's unwillingness to accommodate man and the threat that could result from this. Plath goes on to write,

"It is dry, dry/And the air dangerous".

To suggest that the very air presents danger shows the sheer extent of nature's harshness. The air is, of course, all around, so if it is dangerous then there is no escaping the hostility of nature. It is all around and unavoidable. This idea is echoed[9] in 'Blackberrying' when the persona describes the 'slap' of the wind as she makes her way along the sea path.

We again see the hostility when she writes,
"And the crickets come creeping into our hair
To fiddle the short night away."

The use of the word 'fiddle' here could be interpreted as symbolic of hell and the fiddling duel a person must have with the devil in order to save his or her soul. This suggests a strong conflict between the natural environment and man, comparable to the battle between good and evil or man and the devil. The devil presents a danger and threat to man, and so having nature representative of this figure of the greatest threat draws the same comparison. Just as with the devil, nature is something to be feared and highly wary of, not something that can live harmoniously alongside man.

In a similar way[10], "Blackberrying" shows a progressive fear of nature and the threat it presents. The word 'blackberries' is repeated in each of the first four lines, which suggests an oppressive, claustrophobic atmosphere in which the persona is stifled. Her path is surrounded by them. She cannot escape them. It is almost as if they are closing in on her. She describes the sea as being, "Somewhere at the end of it". The fact that she cannot see an end emphasises the fear of the situation heightening her claustrophobia and feeling of being trapped.

As well as being caught by the blackberries' hooks, the persona observes that the blackberries insinuate themselves upon her:

"...blue-red juices. These squander on my fingers.
I had not asked for such a blood sisterhood;"

The idea of her blood mixing with the blood-like juice of the berries suggests that the persona feels as if a connection between her and nature has been imposed upon her; a connection which perhaps nature uses to mock her insignificance. The connection is false, allowing nature to show that it does not need her and that she is not welcome. This idea links with the persona's perceived lack of self-worth[11]. Knowing she is insignificant in terms of her stature in the natural world and her inability to tame its wild nature, she feels unworthy of the berries' attention. That she is an outsider in an unfriendly world is reinforced by the symbolic choughs, which caw repeatedly as she makes her way to the sea:

"Theirs is the only voice, protesting, protesting."

Choughs, as a member of the crow family, are traditionally representative of death. They are often used as a metaphor to describe the journey from the physical to the spiritual world, carrying the souls from one to the other. And, for those souls who cannot make it to the spiritual world, the crows cry out. So here it could be said that as the choughs cry out for those who are caught between two worlds, they cry for the persona who is caught between the worlds of nature and humanity, belonging to neither.

We also see a suggestion towards the persona's feeling of self-worthlessness at the end of "Two Campers", but in this poem the suggestion is much less threatening. The persona describes the "old simplicities" as "Lethe", a river in Greek mythology which provokes forgetfulness of the past. It seems that the persona is content to forget the past and live in a world where she is of no significance, and there are no expectations of her. Acceptance of her second-best place in the world brings a liberation and ease.[12]

The natural world in many of Plath's poems is conveyed in a negative light. In these three particular poems, she explores our insignificance in the face of nature's overwhelming grandeur as well as nature's capacity to embody hostility and threat. Her poems about the natural world lead us to contemplate, as the persona does, our place in the world.[13]

Notes:

[1] A straightforward introduction which uses the question's words and identifies three significant themes conveyed by the poet's use of the natural world. Remember, in Topic 3 we discussed that it is helpful to plan poetry essays in terms of the main ideas explored in the texts.

[2] Section 1 in the candidate's argument: the overwhelming stature of the natural world.

[3] The candidate identifies that she will deal with the poem 'Two Campers' first, but acknowledges that the idea is relevant to all three of her chosen poems.

[4] A detailed discussion of 'Two Campers', firmly connected to the idea of the overwhelming stature of nature. Includes the clear identification of one of Plath's themes (highlighted in bold).

[5] The candidate discusses the same idea of the overwhelming stature of nature but this time with reference to 'Sleep in the Mojave Desert'. Note the use of comparative phrases - 'In the same way' and 'More disturbingly, and different from...' - to draw comparisons between 'Two Campers' and 'Mojave'.

[6] Section 2 in the candidate's argument: the hostility of nature towards mankind.

[7] A detailed discussion of 'Blackberrying'.

[8] A continued discussion of the idea of nature's hostility in 'Blackberrying' and 'Mojave'.

[9] A comparative point between the two poems being discussed in this section of the essay.

[10] Linking phrase used to introduce a further point of comparison.

[11] Introduction of section 3 of the argument: the persona's feelings of lack of self-worth in the face of nature's power.

[12] Discussion of the persona's lack of self-worth in 'Blackberrying' and 'Two Campers'.

[13] A straightforward conclusion summing up Plath's main idea about nature, and outlining the three key themes discussed in the essay.

Topic 8: Literary study test

Literary study test (page 60)

Q1: A plan for an essay on the 'role and function' of two central characters in the Robin Jenkins novels, "The Changeling" and "Just Duffy" might look like this:

1. Introduction
2. Section 1: character. Comparative discussion of aspects of Tom and Duffy's character: their situations; the ways they cope with their realities; their relationships with other key characters. Link to the themes Jenkins explores through these central characters and their experiences.
3. Section 2: key incidents. Comparative discussion of two key incidents in each novel, focusing on what is revealed about the central characters, and the thematic significance of each incident.
4. Section 3: the significance of each novel's ending.
5. Conclusion

Q2: A plan for an essay on the 'female voice and women's experiences' represented in three poems ("Lady Lazarus", "Ariel" and "Daddy") by Sylvia Plath might look like this:

1. Introduction
2. Section 1: comparative discussion of the persona's experience of oppression by male figures in her life, referring to "Daddy" and "Lady Lazarus".
3. Section 2: comparative discussion of the persona's feelings of lack of self-worth, referring to "Daddy" and "Lady Lazarus".
4. Section 3: comparative discussion of the persona's ultimate triumph of being 'reborn' as a strong, confident woman, referring in detail to "Ariel" and "Lady Lazarus".
5. Conclusion

Q3: A plan for an essay on 'internal and external conflict' in two plays by Tennessee Williams might look like this:

1. Introduction
2. Section 1: character. Comparative discussion of aspects of Blanche and Chance's characters, focusing on their internal conflicts: their pasts; their lives now; the ways they escape their realities. Link to the themes Williams explores through these characters and the internal conflicts they experience.
3. Section 2: key scenes revealing external conflicts. Comparative discussion of the conflict arising between Blanche and Stanley, and Chance and Boss Finlay. Link to thematic significance of these conflicts. Reference to Williams' dramatic techniques (music, lighting, backdrops).
4. Section 3: the significance of each play's ending in resolving internal/external conflicts.
5. Conclusion

Answers to questions and activities for Textual analysis

Topic 2: Poetry

Notions of change and permanence (page 72)

Q1:

> Let me not to the marriage of true minds
> Admit impediments. Love is not love
> Which alters when it alteration finds,
> Or bends with the remover to remove:
> O no! it is an ever-fixed mark,[1]
> That looks on tempests, and is never shaken[2];
> It is the star to every wandering bark,
> Whose worth's unknown, although his height be taken.
> Love's not Time's fool, though rosy lips and cheeks
> Within his bending sickle's compass come;
> Love alters not[3] with his brief hours and weeks,
> But bears it out[4] even to the edge of doom.
> If this be error and upon me proved,
> I never writ[5], nor no man ever loved.
>
> **Notes:**
>
> [1] Terms associated with the notions of change and permanence.
> [2] Term associated with the notion of permanence.
> [3] Term associated with the notion of permanence.
> [4] Term associated with the notion of permanence.
> [5] It is common in the sonnet to have an explicit reference to art or writing or the creative process - a self-conscious element on the part of the poet given that the sonnet was intended to immortalize a person or an idea.

Change the word order (page 72)

Q2: Let me not admit impediments to the marriage of true minds. Love is not love
Which alters when it finds alteration,
Or bends to remove with the remover:

John Keats 'When I have fears' (page 73)

Q3: Terms and images that support this statement:

- Before my pen has glean'd my teeming brain, Before high piled books, in charact'ry
- symbols
- trace
- magic hand of chance
- Fame

Q4: Points to include:

- **Repetition**:
  - each quatrain begins with "When I", marking each very clearly but also highlighting the aspect of time (passing or being anticipated or feared);
  - the repetition of 'when' adds to the coherence of the sonnet at the start of these lines, rather like the rhyme scheme does for the ends of lines;
  - further repetition of "before" gain highlights the notion of time while drawing attention to all the things he has yet to achieve;
  - Repetition of "never" three times (lines 7,10,11) - effect as above (fears about time) and the negative slant precede what appears to be a resolving of these fears in lines 12, 13 and 14.
- **Sound**:
  - alliteration of 'glean'd' 'garners' and 'grain' create coherence and it could be argued fairly harsh sounds, reflecting initial expression of fears of death;
  - assonance in 'fears', 'cease', 'glean'd' and 'teeming' in the first 2 lines give a very distinct sound, drawing the reader's attention - after all, his fears are universal;
  - 'softer' sounds from the second quatrain with 'behold', 'upon', 'symbols', 'romance' and 'shadows' makes it distinct from the first quatrain because the imagery has shifted to natural elements.
- **Line structure**: The unexpected breaking off of line 12 and the sudden beginning of the poet's decision or resolution to deal with his fears - with "then" giving a powerful echo to the previous 'never', 'when' and 'before'. These are, arguably, arresting elements and the reader can almost feel the strength of his resolve in that abrupt line 12 and in the moving image of "then on the shore of the wide world I stand alone. . . " "Think" and "sink" may be in a rhyming couplet but they juxtapose powerfully, the 'thinking' allowing him to put aside his fears, which then 'sink'.

Two sonnets (page 73)

Q5: Points to include:

- Shakespeare seems unconcerned about **_time's effect on love_**: "Love's not Time's fool" means love is not at the mercy of time (i.e. love is ever-lasting). Keats, however, is very afraid that love is short-lived because life itself is short-lived: "fair creature of an hour" explicitly underlines the mortality of whoever it is he's addressing while Shakespeare doesn't really bother with mortality in 116. Keats' third quatrain, the one about love, is abruptly broken off to make way for the early, concluding couplet - perhaps a reflection not only of Keats' views about love being short-lived but about the fears of early death at the centre of this poem.

- **Word choice**: Keats uses lots of words relating to time, many of which repeated, e.g. "when", "never", "before", "then". These are all literal, straightforward, terms, in contrast with Shakespeare's very flowery imagery: having personified Time in line 9, in line 10 he has a "bending sickle" suggesting the image of death (like the scythe used by the 'grim 'reaper') coming within reach of physical aspects of love ("rosy lips and cheeks"), i.e. time has an effect on our physical appearance, but not on love itself. More references to time: the "brief hours and weeks" - perhaps any amount of time - will not change love, again in stark contrast to Keats' vision and fears.
- Many of the points to include in the previous activity 'Body of work', relating to structural matters, should be included here, too, because they emphasise Keats' fears about the passing of time before coming to fruition as an artist.
- General point: students should be able to elaborate in detail on the stark contrast between these two poets' voices regarding the theme of time and its effect. Worth noting that sonnet 116 is not primarily concerned with time - not until line 9 does it become so - while Keats' sonnet is.

Robert Browning 'The Lost Leader' (page 74)

Q6: Points to include:

- **Tone:** must be identified as: angry, furious, indignant, scathing, disappointed - at perceived betrayal and abandonment - anything along these lines;
- **Structure**:
  - **Punctuation**: The most obvious contributors to the angry tone are the copious exclamation marks (five in the first stanza) leaving the reader in no doubt as to the poet's sense of loss and disappointment. Prominent, too, are the hyphens, inserted to pause and create emphasis for the contrast or exclusion that follows, as in " - not thro' his presence" and " - not from his lyre".
  - **Repetition**: "Just" at the very start of lines one and two bring into immediate focus the perceived futility and loss of Wordsworth as the 'leader' of the group of poets that included Browning as his admirers.
  - **Repetition** of "not...not..."; "one more...one more..." "he alone...he alone..." highlight the distance between Wordsworth and Browning and his allies, adding to the tone of disappointment at perceived rejection and perhaps even betrayal.
  - Each 16-line stanza is itself clearly divided into eight lines making separate points in Browning's arguments and giving it a highly crafted, deliberate form that leaves the reader in no doubt about Browning's feelings.

- *Sound*:
  - Lots of **alliteration** and **assonance** adding to sound and the quality of the sound: the quality of the alliteration occasionally has a 'spitting' effect, heightening the sense of anger portrayed: "prospering...presence...inspirit..."
  - "Menace...master"...contrasting in terms of word choice but heightened by alliteration, which only makes the contrast more hurtful in its effect.
  - "Mild...magnificent..." are glued together to highlight how Browning and others once felt about Wordsworth
  - End rhyme and exclamation marks at the ends of lines heighten the 'shouty' nature of the tone, presumably the effect Browning was aiming for given its subject and the reasons for writing it.
  - **Assonance**: "hesitation...pain...praise..." heighten the effect of the strong words used when Browning imagines Wordsworth returning to them, his previous allies.

Robert Browning 'My Last Duchess' (page 76)

Q7: General point: there should be a solid appreciation of the 'drama' aspect of the dramatic monologue: the creation of a character who is speaking to an imagined listener, during which the reader learns much about the speaker.

Structure:

- Because there are no separate stanzas and because enjambment and punctuation direct our reading and hold the structure together (despite the end-stop couplets) it could be noted this poem reads like continuous prose - appropriate, given it relays an extended, almost casual, speech from one man to another.
- Although the poem comprises 28 rhymed couplets they are not end stops such as those in The Lost Leader. In 'Duchess' we rely on enjambment and punctuation for meaning and understanding, the end-rhyme not being stressed but having a subtler function that the overtly 'noisy' end rhyme in 'The Lost Leader'.
- The central narrative - the story of the hapless Duchess as relayed by her murdering husband - is carefully positioned between lines 5 ("Will't please you sit...?") and 47 ("Will't please you rise?") The precision of this placement suggests a link with the calculated, planned murder of the Duchess. Note also that the beginning and ending of the narrative are positioned mid-verse in lines 13 and 47 respectively, creating the effect of a sudden, almost casual 'chat' rather than a monologue restrained by matters of line length.
- Repetition contributes to structure (as noted with "Will't please you...") but also increasing alarm in, for example, the repetition of "smile" in lines 43, 45 and 46 where the word is used more as a curse against the Duchess than regarded as a blessing.
- Alliteration and assonance throughout the poem contribute to structure and any student's response should offer ample examples of this.
- Punctuation and structure essential here: only when the reader pays close attention to punctuation and enjambment does the Duke's speech to what must be an increasingly pale and alarmed marriage agent come to its own.

Voice:

- On the surface, the voice is casual, conversational: "Will't please you stand and look at her?" "How shall I say it?"; "Will't please you rise?"; "Nay, we'll go together down, sir". These suggest a friendly, chatty character even as it dawns on the reader that a cold-blooded killer is speaking.
- The underlying chill in some of the following: "looking as if she were alive"; I chose never to stoop" and "I gave commands | Then all smiles stopped together" - make the reader wonder how many times he's done this and whether he will hesitate to do it again. He's boasting about having killed her, giving reasons why, emphasised with the repetition of "smile" three times in lines 43, 45 and 46.
- There is subtle humour in a speaker like this one in such an accomplished poem claiming he has no "skill in speech".

Other points:

- The meaning of "last" becomes clear only with the reading of the whole poem. Early in the poem we might think he's simply showing a painting of his late wife, until Browning peels away the veil and we learn the horror of her murder. "Last", then, could mean there were (dead) wives before this one (so: 'last' means 'most recent') or it could simply mean 'previous' - but not the more respectful 'late'.
- The "curtain" in line 10 behind which the painting is kept (which only the Duke is permitted to draw) can be taken on a metaphorical level to be the slowly-revealed truth of the Duchess' fate as it is narrated by the Duke.
- Part of the enjoyment for the reader comes from imagining the effect the Duke's story has on the person he's addressing - the same man tasked with brokering a new marriage for the Duke with his client, the Count. Further impact comes from the outrageous candour with which the Duke tells the story of how he came to murder his wife - and why - making us alarmed on behalf of any further prospective Duchess.

Poetry: Exam practice (page 78)

Q8: **Central concerns** of the poem include: celebrating the earth; the cycle of life; redemption and renewal; decay and re-birth; celebration of nature; notion of nature being greater than human existence; celebrating the gifts of life (food) that nature bestows on humans; incredulity at how little humans give nature in return; incredulity at how nature/earth can give clean and healthy food to humans who merely put waste products back into it; despair at the way humans appear to take earth for granted; (m)any similar suggestions.

Structure

- The poem comprises three distinct, numbered, **parts** that present different aspects of the concerns/arguments/points being made by the poet. Each part itself has a different structure, too: Part 1 has three stanzas of five lines; part 2 has two stanzas of 14 and 12 lines respectively; Part 3 is the shortest with only a sestet to finish.
- Part 3 is **linked** to the others in several ways: beginning with "Now", it suggests the poet has been on a journey - whether mentally, spiritually, emotionally or physically - and returns to the present with "Now" as well as the expression of fear we find in the opening lines of Part 1 - fear of nature, the Earth - or simply awe at the Earth's powers. This kind of **linking** gives a circular effect within the poem, perhaps echoing the cycle of life that is being celebrated here.

- Despite the three distinct parts and distinct stanzas it's not rhythm or rhyme that hold the poem together, but **repetition and lists** - particularly repetition of **questions and exclamations**, and lists of natural phenomena and verbs. As such it is a very busy, very noisy poem - entirely appropriate to the central themes and preoccupations it presents. Examples: Part 1, second stanza comprises only questions and there are several in stanza 3 ("Oh how... how... how..."; "where... where.."), all of which contribute to the sense of bewilderment expressed here; Part 2 has **repetition** and **exclamation/command** in "Behold....behold..." followed by countless items of nature's food products listed and celebrated ("grass... bean....onion... apple...") culminating, before the volta, with "The summer growth is innocent" juxtaposed with "sour dead" to emphasise the contrast; later in Part 2 the repetition of "That" at the start of nearly all the 12 lines after the volta to heighten the poet awe that Nature and its bounty are safe despite the "sour dead" humans deposit in her; Part 3 is marked by the list of verbs ("grows... turns.....distills....renews") further emphasising Nature's incredible powers.
- Further **repetition** of phrases such as "sour dead", "foul meat" and "disease" are scattered throughout the distinct Parts and stanzas (more about word choice, below).
- The effect of so much **repetition** is the poem can give the impression of a mantra, an incantation, song or prayer - all of which can be argued in connection with the poet's main preoccupation of the wonders of Nature and her powers of giving.
- **Alliteration** and **assonance** are important for structure here, offering cohesion within and between lines: from lines 1 and 2 ("Something startles....safest... still") to line 45 ("distills... exquisite winds...... infused fector") there are too many examples - suffice to say any response to the question about this poem should offer numerous examples and comment on how alliteration and assonance contribute to the poem's structure.

Sound As noted above, exclamation, alliteration and assonance all contribute to sound in this poem. Students might note that the exclamations contribute to the sense of awe, fear and/or bewilderment experienced by the poet and expressed here. A repeated exclamation such as: "Behold this compost! behold it well!...Yet behold!" serves as a command and a rallying cry to the audience to take note of what is going on between humans and nature, suggesting this is not a relationship of equals; "What chemistry!" is a further expression of awe or incredulity as Nature's powers; "Now I am terrified at the Earth!" shouts the poet towards the end of the journey: he appears to have moved from merely "startled" in line 1 to "terrified" in line 42, suggesting that the more he has 'unearthed', observed and answered his own questions, the less comfortable he is about the relationship between humans and Nature.

Other features

- **Word choice** and **juxtaposition** are prominent and effective contributors to the presentation of central concerns. Word choice is powerful in its presentation of death and decay: "sicken"; "corpses"; "sour dead"; "carcasses"; "foul liquid and meat"; "infectious"; "poison"; "disease"; "corruptions" and "fetor" - all these, Whitman observes, are what human kind contribute to Earth in exchange for clean, healthy "summer growth" that is "innocent" - the very opposite of rot and decay. Juxtaposition is particularly prominent in the final sestet: "sweet things" versus "corruptions" (line 43); "harmless" versus "diseased" (line 44); "gives" versus "leavings" (line 47) and there are many more examples students should comment on to further their argument.

Topic 3: Prose fiction

Extract one from 'Butcher's Broom' (page 95)

Q1: Students' answers should include quotations and/or specific (line) references to support the following points:

- long sentences punctuated by semi-colons and commas separating items in lists;
- entire paragraphs devoted to descriptions of plants' medicinal applications;
- extensive descriptions of the character and the setting (the natural world);
- said paragraphs acting as digressions from the immediate action being narrated, which is Mairi's recent healing visit to the sick man.

Q2: Students' answers should include quotations and/or specific (line) references to support the following points:

- use of positive/celebratory language to refer to nature, including: Analogy between childhood and "small bright waves on a beach"; "sea in a good mood"; "breathes its sweet fragrance"; exhilaration of autumn";
- the assumption that "a person can always tell what the weather is to be by smelling the sea";
- extensive knowledge of plants' properties: two whole paragraphs from "All of that sea … "healed the wound";
- Mairi's healing expertise shown in "they had sent for her"; "she had a reputation for healing";
- short sentences showing her efficiency in working on the sick man, from "The sick man … strong enough"."

Extract two from 'Butcher's Broom' (page 98)

Q3: Students' answers should include quotations and/or specific (line) references to support the following points:

- "to the amusement of some of his neighbours" and "made good fun" tells the reader there's mischief regarding the prospective yellow oats old Angus could accidentally have made;
- the initial rhyme about the canaries and Angus' quick reply, his "knowledge of the ancient poetry" and "everyone cheered the old man" when he replied, showing liking and respect for him from the community;
- "improvising was one of their great amusements"; "lucky vein"; "some of the girls were very good at it"; "instantly delighted"; "explosion of laughter" at Murdoch;
- "great game among the children" suggests the whole community is in on this fun, not just adults;
- "Iain my young calf" shows kindness towards a child asking a question and getting involved;
- Seonaid "misquotes" which, if done deliberately, show as much linguistic wit as quoting accurately;
- the "war of proverbs", "hurtling" and "combat" using the language of battle but by this time we know it's good sport and, if anything, these terms show us how seriously this is taken;
- "the company obviously delighted"; "Davie's excited voice"; Seonaid smiled" - all of these add to the convivial atmosphere in the room;

- Anna has "pleasant manners", was "smiling"; "yet delaying because of the gaiety"; "she liked this sound and fun in her home; she liked old Angus" - all strengthen the impression that Gunn has great sympathy and fondness for this community and their characters.

Q4: Students' answers should include quotations and/or specific (line) references to support the following points:

- "the ancient poetry"; "this improvising"; "a couple of lines were struck out"; "Murdoch's satire"; the girl changed the rhythm"; "game... riddles"; "the war of proverbs" - should be a comment about the **range** of terms here to show understanding of the knowledge and sophistication involved in this tradition.

Q5: Students' answers should include quotations and/or specific (line) references to support the following points:

- the characters' improvised verses/stanzas that break up the continuous narration, and a short and quick to read, add to the speeding-up of the reading experience;
- "Angus answered the poet at once" indicates these are quick exchanges;
- further exclamations dotted throughout the continuous prose, such as "That's you on your back" and the dialogue, again laid out in continuous prose, contrast with the lengthy descriptions of extract one and make this a pacier read;
- short exchanges "what would you do to her" contribute to same;
- "Then the war..." moves the action on;
- in general, the amusing content is likely to make this an easier and more speedy reading experience - this is connected to what the author is trying to portray, which is the quick-wittedness and fun involved in such gatherings. The other reason for doing it is to create variety and amusement for the reader.

Topic 4: Prose non-fiction

Extract one from 'My Own Story' (page 113)

Q1: Theme of slavery and emancipation has been part of her life "from infancy" and its language is second nature to her - the reader may wonder in awe at how many five-year-olds know the meaning of these words.

She weaves together all the views and opinions from several layers: "the British government", "public opinion", "the propertied classes", "the circle of our family friends" and "my father" - five layers with different views on the themes of the text, the layers becoming less distant as the paragraph continues, ending in her own home with 'my father'.

'Uncle Tom's Cabin' - a major event in literary history as well as a vivid childhood recollection: "she used it continually... fascinated ears"; "stories" juxtaposed with "morning papers" equates fiction with fact. In other words, both played an equally important role in her young life.

Extract two from 'My Own Story' (page 114)

Q2: Note the *emotive language:*

- "appalling";
- "hordes";
- "literally starving to death";
- "wretched hovels";
- "at the very gates...";
- "misery";
- "social anarchy".

and make comment about how the language heightens the awfulness, amplifies the sense of poverty, emphasises the scale of the poverty, etc.

Size/scale of the workhouse emphasises the scale of poverty (see margin note); conditions exacerbated by poor administration:

- "very harshly administered";
- "the kind of men...";
- "not very astute guardians...";
- "a frightful waste of food".

Aspects of **effectiveness**: directly addressing readers from another country/culture "for the benefit of American readers", "You have, I believe..."; arguably also adding to effectiveness: Pankhurst's overt admiration for QE and her Poor Law policy:

- "one of the greatest reforms";
- "that wise and humane monarch";
- "great queen... great woman";
- "..responsibility rightfully rests..".

Techniques and features typically found in prose non-fiction - 'My Own Story' (page 115)

Q3:

Those men and women are fortunate who are born at a time when a great struggle for human freedom is in progress. It is an added good fortune to have parents who take a personal part in the great movements of their time. I am glad and thankful that this was my case[1].

One of my earliest recollections is of a great bazaar which was held in my native city of Manchester, the object of the bazaar being to raise money to relieve the poverty of the newly emancipated negro slaves in the United States. My mother took an active part in this effort, and I, as, a small child, was entrusted with a lucky bag by means of which I helped to collect money.[2]

Young as I was - I could not have been older than five years[3] - I knew perfectly well the meaning of the words slavery and emancipation. From infancy I had been accustomed to hear pro and con discussions of slavery and the American Civil War. Although the British government finally decided not to recognise the Confederacy , public opinion in England was sharply divided on the questions both of slavery and of secession. Broadly speaking, the propertied classes were pro-slavery, but there were many exceptions to the rule. Most of those who formed the circle of our family friends were opposed to slavery, and my father, Robert Goulden, was always a most ardent abolitionist[4]. He was prominent enough in the movement to be appointed on a committee to meet and welcome Henry-Ward Beecher when he arrived in England for a lecture tour[5]. Mrs Harriet Beecher Stowe's novel, 'Uncle Tom's Cabin' , was so great a favourite with my mother that she used it continually as a source of bedtime stories for our fascinated ears[6]. These stories, told almost fifty years ago, are as fresh in my mind[7] today as events detailed in the morning's papers. Indeed they are more vivid[8], because they made a much deeper impression[9] on my consciousness.

Notes:

[1] Personal feelings and opinion
[2] Personal memories
[3] Personal memories
[4] Explanation
[5] Historical events and people
[6] Personal feelings and opinion
[7] Personal feelings and opinion
[8] Personal feelings and opinion
[9] Personal feelings and opinion

ANSWERS: UNIT 2 TOPIC 4

Q4:

For the benefit of American readers I shall explain something of the operation of our English Poor Law. The duty of the law is to administer an act of Queen Elizabeth, one of the greatest reforms[1] effected by that wise and humane monarch[2]. When Elizabeth came to the throne she found England, the Merrie England of contemporary poets, in a state of appalling poverty. Hordes of people were literally starving to death, in wretched hovels, in the street, and at the very gates of the palace. The cause of all this misery was the religious reformation under Henry VIII, and the secession from Rome of the English Church. King Henry, it is known, seized all the Church lands, the abbeys and the convents, and gave them as rewards to those nobles and favourites who had supported his policies. But in taking over the Church property the Protestant nobles by no means assumed the Church's ancient responsibilities of lodging wayfarers, giving alms, nursing the sick, educating youths, and caring for the young and the superannuated. When the monks and the nuns were turned out of their convents these duties devolved on no one. The result, after the brief reign of Edward VI and the bloody one of Queen Mary, was the social anarchy inherited by Elizabeth[3].

This great queen and great woman[4], perceiving that the responsibility for the poor and the helpless rightfully[5] rests on the community, caused an act to be passed creating in the parishes public bodies to deal with local conditions of poverty. The Board of Poor Law Guardians disburses for the poor the money coming from the Poor Rates (taxes), and some additional moneys allowed by the local government board, the president of which is a cabinet minister. Mr John Burns is the present incumbent of the office. The Board of Guardians has control of the institution we call the workhouse[6]. You have, I believe, almshouses [sic], or poorhouses, but they are not quite so extensive as our workhouses, which are all kinds of institutions in one. We had, in my workhouse, a hospital with nine hundred beds, a school with several hundred children, a farm, and many workshops[7].

When I came into office I found that the law in our district, Chorlton, was being very harshly administered[8]. The old board had been made up of the kind of men who are known as rate savers. They were guardians, not of the poor but of the rates, and, as I soon discovered, not very astute guardians even of money. For instance, although the inmates were being very poorly fed, a frightful waste of food was apparent. Each inmate was given each day a certain weight of food, and bread formed so much of the ration that hardly anyone consumed all of his portion. In the farm department pigs were kept on purpose to consume this surplus of bread, and as pigs do not thrive on a solid diet of stale bread the animals fetched in the market a much lower price than properly fed farm pigs. I suggested that, instead of giving a solid weight of bread in one lump, the loaf be cut in slices and buttered with margarine, each person being allowed all that he cared to eat[9].

Notes:

[1] Personal feelings and opinion
[2] Personal feelings and opinion
[3] Explanation

© HERIOT-WATT UNIVERSITY

- [4] Personal feelings and opinion
- [5] Personal feelings and opinion
- [6] Historical events and people
- [7] Explanation
- [8] Personal feelings and opinion
- [9] Personal memories

Q5: There is no suggested answer. Highlight the various 'typical' non-fiction techniques while underlining where devices normally associated with the other genres are used.

Topic 5: Drama

Extract from 'Antigone' (page 130)

Q1: Antigone is "anxious and urgent" which immediately suggests a problem; she "follows" her sister, which tells the audience her sister is the person she needs to share this anxious problem with; she "closes the door carefully" tells the audience there is an element of secrecy or perhaps even danger about her urgent problem.

Q2: This line "And now is the time" shows Antigone challenging her sister to prove she 'deserves' to be royal - as if, only by joining her in defiance of the King, will she be deemed "worthy"; L48 "He has no right..." shows for the first time Antigone's open defiance of the King's order and another indication of hubris (pride, or arrogance); L84-86 the language gets even stronger when Antigone anticipates a glorious death following her defiance - a bit like a martyr - "if I die... what happiness!" and she'll be happy to be found guilty of this act of love, again, showing a type of arrogance in being convinced she's performing a great act; L97 "you need not fear for me" again suggests she'll be in safe hands after death, having done a great deed and L100-101 "Publish it to all the world!" again the exclamation mark gives the language more urgency while the words suggest she wants to be famous for her defiance. Finally: "There is no punishment..." L109-110 confirms Antigone's belief that punishment by death will make her "honourable" and great - confirming the pride before the fall.

Q3: The fact that Ismene goes "into the Palace" shows the audience clearly she is committed to sticking to the rules of the King and staying loyal and safe; Antigone, on the other hand, "leaves the stage by a side exit" not only shows her opposition to the Palace - she is moving away from the Palace - but also from her sister. The other interesting thing about this staging is the dramatist doesn't even indicate whether the "side exit" is left or right, almost as if it doesn't really matter because her fate is sealed regardless of which direction she moves in.

Q4: The words "hail", "brightest", "sun" and "golden" are very positive words of beauty and celebration that contrast sharply with the dark and doom of the sisters' speech and exit preceding the Chorus; this celebratory tone is enhanced by the numerous exclamation marks in these five short lines; repetition of "Hail" enhances this tone.

Q5: Repetition of "against us" three times here in addition to "around us" and "consume us" formalizes the language and gives the telling of the battle a lot of gravitas, which is important for the nation's sense of pride because Polynices was the enemy and was beaten in this battle; repetition of "blood" and "fled" for dramatic effect; lots of 'battle words' like "army", "angry", "ravening", "swooped", "blood", "swords", "jaws", "roar", "fire", "thunder" and "war" are all very harsh words that invite the audience to be in awe of the battle and victory because the enemy is described in such fearsome terms that to have beaten him becomes an even greater achievement; imagery enhances this: "like a ravening bird of prey"; "white wings flashing"; "his jaws were opened against us" - the Chorus makes the opposing army sound like a huge monster who was slain: "fled with the roar of the dragon behind him" to make their victory even more glorious.

Q6: Questioning: "What will be the end of us..." to get Antigone to think before she acts - because they've already lost their whole family; "We are women..." appealing to Antigone to 'know her place' and act appropriately to her gender ("It is not for us to fight against men"); "We must obey in this..." and "I can do... as I am commanded" using words that highlight duty and compliance, suggesting the opposite is "madness" (which is the opposite of reason); "At least be secret" again trying to be reasonable and measured in her actions; "You're bound to fail" warning of the consequences, and finally "folly" again the opposite of reason. The tragedy that unfolds is because this voice of reason has no effect on Antigone's hubris.

Characters' language (page 131)

Q7: Sisters' language

Ismene

Ismene functions (structurally) as the voice of reason, counter-balancing Antigone's fury and zeal, but also wants to spare her sister's life. Her language shows or suggests she is weaker than Antigone or simply more compliant in nature; perhaps more cautious and wiser; less of a firebrand; less of a rebel:

- "I am not strong enough";
- "I cannot act against the state";
- "I fear for you";
- "Creon has expressly forbidden it";
- "Do not breath a word";
- "It is not for us to fight against men";
- "You're bound to fail";
- "A hopeless task";
- "Your folly";
- repetition of "love" towards the end.

Antigone

In contrast with Ismene, Antigone is unafraid to challenge authority:

- "He has no right...";
- "I will bury my brother...";
- "Defy the holiest laws...";
- "You need not fear for me";
- "Publish it to all the world!";
- "There is no punishment can rob me of my honourable death".

Her zeal and determination show in:

- "Would you help me lift the body?";
- "I shall never desert him, never";
- "I will bury my brother" - the use of "my" and not "our" highlights their division - "I know my duty";
- "Leave me alone with my own madness".

Her fury and indignation are revealed in:

- "The noble Creon!" [sarcarsm];
- "If I die for it, what happiness!";
- repetition of "hate" three times towards the end of the dialogue.

Q8: Central conflict

- Antigone wants to act "against the order" of the king; she says she'd be happy to die - "what happiness!" - for this cause and is steadfastly convinced of her right to bury her brother;
- "Would you help me lift the body?" signals the start of her motivation/action at the centre of the conflict;
- "I shall never desert him, never" strong words & repetition underlining her determination;
- "He has no right to keep me from my own" - Antigone claims possession and responsibility and therefore the right to bury her bother;
- "I will bury my brother" apparently at any cost, because "I shall be content to lie beside a brother whom I love";
- "You need not fear for me" shows her bravery and the single-mindedness that conflicts directly with Creon's order;
- "I know my duty, where true duty lies" is directly opposed to Creon's perceived duty as protector of the country (see below), cementing the conflict.

Creon is her antagonist, as the audience quickly learns. The first important section of his speech ends with "Such is my policy for our common weal", summing up Creon's policy about protecting his kingdom from enemies - whether from within or from outside his country. Creon sounds entirely reasonable, and the use of pronouns "my" and "our" signal good leadership and togetherness; "my people" suggests he is a protective father figure; the country is referred to as "she", which personalises it, and "she rides safely" compares the country to a vessel, maybe a ship (which are always personified as female) that he keeps on course.

Up until this point Creon sounds like a wise, benevolent leader. This changes with: "...proclamation... as follows:" and what follows is a tirade against "the other" (199) with words like "burn", "destroy", "blood", "slaves" to refer to Polynices' crimes (lines 200-202) to justify his order of letting him rot without burial; refers to him as "evil" (208) and the "penalty" (222) for defiance is death.

Q9: Nature of the tragedy

The following quotes show the beginning of the tragedy because Antigone's speech and action show what will lead to her downfall:

- "Would you help me lift the body?";
- "He has no right...";
- "I will bury my brother";
- "Convicted of reverence...";
- "I will...heap a mound of earth over my brother";
- "Publish it to all the world!";
- "I know my duty";
- stage direction "Antigone leaves by a side exit".

It is confirmed that her planned action is punishable by death in the exchange between chorus and Creon: "Ay, that is the penalty" at the end of this extract. But it had been hinted at earlier by Antigone herself:

- "The punishment for disobedience is death by stoning";
- "And if I die for it..."

The chorus (page 131)

Q10:

- Celebratory language "Hail!", "Sun", "golden" to help audience understand context of the recently won war;
- lots of repetition of "us" to highlight that chorus is "the people" and on the side of the king;
- poetic structure, imagery and embellished diction (lines 120 - 127) to highlight their own importance and that of the victorious battle;
- lots of exclamation for added effect;
- language is presented in stanzas, as in a poem, to lend further gravitas to their words, especially as the four stanzas from "The Father of Heaven" continue to relay the events of the victorious battle in further colourful terms.

Then: function of chorus changes with "But see, the king comes", and, following Creon's speech, the chorus become a 'normal' character embedded within the action, conversing with the king and showing reverence to him: "what other duty remains"; "your will is law" again showing the chorus represents the audience, like it's speaking for the people - because that's how the people are expected to behave towards a king.

Topic 7: Textual analysis test

Textual analysis test (page 144)

Q1: **Central concerns** of the poem include:

- celebrating the earth;
- the cycle of life;
- redemption and renewal;
- decay and rebirth;
- celebration of nature;
- notion of nature being greater than human existence;
- celebrating the gifts of life (food) that nature bestows on humans;
- incredulity at how little humans give nature in return;
- incredulity at how nature/earth can give clean and healthy food to humans who merely put waste products back into it;
- despair at the way humans appear to take earth for granted;
- (m)any similar suggestions.

Structure:

- The poem comprises three distinct, numbered, **parts** that present different aspects of the concerns/arguments/points being made by the poet. Each part itself has a different structure, too: Part 1 has three stanzas of five lines; Part 2 has two stanzas of 14 and 12 lines respectively; Part 3 is the shortest with only a sestet to finish.
- Part 3 is **linked** to the others in several ways: beginning with "Now", it suggests the poet has been on a journey - whether mentally, spiritually, emotionally or physically - and returns to the present with "Now" as well as the expression of fear we find in the opening lines of Part 1 - fear of nature, the Earth - or simply awe at the Earth's powers. This kind of **linking** gives a circular effect within the poem, perhaps echoing the cycle of life that is being celebrated here.
- Despite the three distinct parts and distinct stanzas it's not rhythm or rhyme that hold the poem together, but **repetition and lists** - particularly repetition of **questions** and **exclamations**, and lists of natural phenomena and verbs. As such it is a very busy, very noisy poem - entirely appropriate to the central themes and preoccupations it presents. Examples: Part 1, second stanza comprises only questions and there are several in the third stanza ("Oh how... how... how..."; "where... where.."), all of which contribute to the sense of bewilderment expressed here; Part 2 has **repetition** and **exclamation/command** in "Behold... behold..." followed by countless items of nature's food products listed and celebrated ("grass... bean... onion... apple...") culminating, before the volta, with "The summer growth is innocent" juxtaposed with "sour dead" to emphasise the contrast; later in Part 2 the repetition of "That" at the start of nearly all the 12 lines after the volta to heighten the poet awe that Nature and its bounty are safe despite the "sour dead" humans deposit in her; Part 3 is marked by the list of verbs ("grows... turns... distills... renews") further emphasising Nature's incredible powers.
- Further **repetition** of phrases such as "sour dead", "foul meat" and "disease" are scattered throughout the distinct parts and stanzas (more about word choice, below).
- The effect of so much **repetition** is the poem can give the impression of a mantra, an incantation, song or prayer - all of which can be argued in connection with the poet's main preoccupation of the wonders of Nature and her powers of giving.

- **Alliteration** and **assonance** are important for structure here, offering cohesion within and between lines: from lines 1 and 2 ("Something startles... safest... still") to line 45 ("distills... exquisite winds... infused fector") there are too many examples - suffice to say any response to the question about this poem should offer numerous examples and comment on how alliteration and assonance contribute to the poem's structure.

Sound:

- As noted above, exclamation, alliteration and assonance all contribute to sound in this poem. Students might note that the exclamations contribute to the sense of awe, fear and/or bewilderment experienced by the poet and expressed here. A repeated exclamation such as: "Behold this compost! behold it well!... Yet behold!" serves as a command and a rallying cry to the audience to take note of what is going on between humans and nature, suggesting this is not a relationship of equals; "What chemistry!" is a further expression of awe or incredulity as Nature's powers; "Now I am terrified at the Earth!" shouts the poet towards the end of the journey: he appears to have moved from merely "startled" in line 1 to "terrified" in line 42, suggesting that the more he has 'unearthed', observed and answered his own questions, the less comfortable he is about the relationship between humans and Nature.

Other features:

- **Word choice** and **juxtaposition** are prominent and effective contributors to the presentation of central concerns. Word choice is powerful in its presentation of death and decay: "sicken"; "corpses"; "sour dead"; "carcasses"; "foul liquid and meat"; "infectious"; "poison"; "disease"; "corruptions" and "fetor". All these, Whitman observes, are what human kind contribute to Earth in exchange for clean, healthy "summer growth" that is "innocent" - the very opposite of rot and decay. Juxtaposition is particularly prominent in the final sestet: "sweet things" versus "corruptions" (line 43); "harmless" versus "diseased" (line 44); "gives" versus "leavings" (line 47) and there are many more examples students should comment on to further their argument.

Q2: Suggestions / recommendations for students' answers:
1. In the passage, the natural world is represented through frequent, and repeated, references to all of the following:
    - sea;
    - light/darkness;
    - plants and healing;
    - weather;
    - seasons;
    - smells.
2. Lots of positive words used in connection with the natural elements (above): paragraphs one, three, four:
    - "bright sea";
    - "sea... good mood";
    - "pleasant scent";
    - "fine weather";
    - "keen dry lifting tang of wind";
    - "sweet fragrance";
    - "exhilaration of autumn";
    - use of positive/celebratory language to refer to nature, including: Analogy between childhood and "small bright waves on a beach"; "sea in a good mood"; "breathes its sweet fragrance"; exhilaration of autumn";
    - the assumption that "a person can always tell what the weather is to be by smelling the sea";
    - extensive knowledge of plants' properties: two whole paragraphs from "All of that sea... healed the wound";
    - Mairi's healing expertise shown in "they had sent for her"; "she had a reputation for healing";
    - short sentences showing her efficiency in working on the sick man, from "The sick man... strong enough".
3. Healing plants are referred to as "gifts" that Mairi would never appear without; suggesting inextricable connection between plants and human knowledge, lives and well-being; connection so strong that their very lives depend on the proper application and usage of the plants.
4. The character's very name is connected to nature, partly due to the naming system of the Gaels but in Mairi's case also because of her deep knowledge of the sea and its "gifts" to humans. Furthermore, she is described in terms of nature: her expression compared to a "stone" and the statement that "she might have... leaving no sign" (paragraph seven) suggests there's little distinction between her and a mountain, as if they are 'one'.
5. In the passage, natural items are personified - suggesting humans and nature are 'as one', i.e. there is no distinction between them. Examples:
    - paragraph one: the valley gives "dark comfort";
    - paragraph two: sea-water "breaks on the shore of the mind";
    - paragraph three: the sea "had been in a good mood"; "the sea... breathes".
6. Further imagery: "the storm burst" used to refer to the sick man's fever breaking.
7. In more general terms: the total faith and confidence placed in the effectiveness of the remedy and the calm, matter-of-fact manner in which Mairi attends to the sick man - all add to the impression that natural and human life, in the world of this passage, are inextricably linked.

© HERIOT-WATT UNIVERSITY

Q3: Confident *tone* in first paragraph created by:
- "determined to answer...";
- "if... was all that was necessary...";
- "demanded";
- "we could undertake to satisfy...";
- "we knew";
- "we determined".

All these suggest the women will defy Gladstone's thinking about what can be expected of them.

Punctuation in second paragraph indicates the extent of the women's skills and organisational talent: the long sentence "We covered the hoardings... were also shown" shows how far-reaching their advertising was, well beyond London itself, to attract women into London for the demonstration; commas and semi-colons serve to separate the actions taken during the planning (maps, plans) while the *word choice* in this same long sentence - "great posters", "twenty platforms", "seven processions" - give us an idea of the scale and professionalism of this organisation, which highlights how serious they are about this - about being able to defy Gladstone.

Still in the second paragraph the *long sentence* "For weeks.... both Houses of Parliament" is another long sentence, this time with lots of *verbs* indicating busy activities and *punctuated* by lots of commas to give a cumulative effect: "chalking, distributing, canvassing, advertising.." all of which heighten the reader's sense of the "small army" covering a lot of ground and building up to something huge.

Use of *exclamation* "What a day!" at the start of third paragraph, in addition to *word choice* "radiant" and "golden sunshine" promise the reader something incredible and suggesting they reached their target to have a huge event, heightened by the *phrase* "As I advanced, leading..." which slows the reader down and creates a sense of anticipation and grandeur.

The scale is portrayed with:
- "the first of the seven processions";
- "... all London had turned out.";
- "a goodly part of London...";
- "the mighty throngs";
- "the endless crowds";
- "still pouring in... from all directions".

- showing how this demonstration defied Gladstone's presumption about women's capabilities. The *language* becomes more colourful as Pankhurst expresses her own awe and perhaps even amazement at their achievement:
- "gay and beautiful";
- "... awe-inspiring spectacle";
- "... a vast garden in full bloom".

The use of *newspaper quotes* to strengthen and support her own observations serve to emphasise for the reader the significance of this event and its success: the women actually made history, and it is particularly satisfying that it's a "Gladstone meeting" from years before that is used with which to measure the success of this one. The Times quote has *language* even more flowery than some of Pankhurst's, likening the numbers at this event to the vastness of the galaxy.

© HERIOT-WATT UNIVERSITY

Q4: Language

The language shows the conflict is strongly driven by differences in status, gender and age as much as by opposing principles regarding the burial. Antigone doesn't care that Creon is king:

- "I did not think your edicts strong enough... you being only a man";
- "I should have to die... with or without your order";
- "There is nothing you can say that I would wish to hear";
- "To speak and act just as he likes is a king's prerogative".

While Creon tries to remind her of her 'place' as a subject and as a (younger) woman:

- "Proud thoughts to not sit well upon subordinates";
- "This girl's proud spirit";
- "We'll have no woman's law here, while I live";
- "vile creature".

This is not just about the burial; it's about Antigone not honouring what Creon regards as his unshakable status as king. He can't control her as he does his other subjects, so he'll have to kill her.

The sisters' speech includes many questions - Antigone's questions amplify the challenges to Creon:

- "Does that seem foolish to you? Or is it that you are foolish to judge me so?";
- "Who knows?"

... while Ismene's questions are of a pleading nature, to her sister and to Creon:

- "How can I still help you?";
- "How could I... live without my sister?";
- "You could not... kill your own son's bride?";
- "Can your father spite you so?" - it is here we first learn that Antigone is engaged to Creon's son, Haemon, making his determination to kill her all the more brutal.

Creon's uses metaphor freely, contrasting with the sisters' straightforward, simple speech:

- "as the strongest iron will snap... brittleness";
- "A little halter... wildest horses";
- "You crawling viper!... suck my blood!";
- "Oh, there are other fields for him to plough".

Various comments on Creon's uses of imagery can be made: it could be to amplify his higher status - as a way of 'looking down' on his nieces - or the playwright chose this to highlight their differences in opinion and hence their conflict.

Dramatic function

The Chorus - true to form - performs its function in two ways in terms of showing the audience how the conflict develops:

1. it announces the arrival of Ismene in sobbing terms: "weeping... sorrow... darkened brow... flushed... flooding rain" to show that Antigone's problems do not end with Creon but that she has a loyal, loving sister to contend with as well;

2. it 'speaks for' the audience when it double-checks with Creon that he really intends to go through with this: "Sir, would you take her from your own son's arms?" before acquiescing: "Be it so".

Ismene's function could be seen as the 'voice of reason', pleading both with Antigone and with Creon to abandon their conflict. This only enhances the tragedy: Ismene pretends to be complicit in the burial in order to mitigate her sister's punishment, yet neither her sister nor Creon are moved to change by her efforts.